CHANGING CULTURES

The Nayars Today

CHANGING CULTURES
General Editor: Jack Goody

The aim of the series is to show how specific non-industrial societies have developed and changed in response to the conditions of the modern world. Each volume will present a comprehensive analysis, drawing on recent fieldwork, of the contemporary organisation of a particular society, but cast in a dynamic perspective that relates the present both to the past of the society and to the external forces that have impinged upon it. By concentrating on peoples that have been the subjects of earlier studies, some of these volumes will also reflect the developing interests and concerns of the social sciences.

Also in the series
The Skolt Lapps Today *by* Tim Ingold

The Nayars Today

C. J. FULLER
Lecturer, Department of Social Anthropology
University of Manchester

CAMBRIDGE UNIVERSITY PRESS
CAMBRIDGE
LONDON · NEW YORK · MELBOURNE

Published by the Syndics of the Cambridge University Press
The Pitt Building, Trumpington Street, Cambridge CB2 1RP
Bentley House, 200 Euston Road, London NW1 2DB
32 East 57th Street, New York, NY 10022, USA
296 Beaconsfield Parade, Middle Park, Melbourne 3206, Australia

© Cambridge University Press 1976

First published 1976

Printed in Great Britain at the
University Printing House, Cambridge
(Euan Phillips, University Printer)

Library of Congress Cataloguing in Publication Data
Fuller, Christopher J. 1949–
The Nayars Today.
(Changing cultures)
Based, in part, on the author's thesis, University of Manchester, 1974.
Includes bibliographical references and index.
1. Nairs – Social life and customs. 2. Kinship – India – Kerala (State) I. Title.
DS432·N324F84   301·45'19'48'05483   76-11078
ISBN 0 521 21301 0 hard covers
ISBN 0 521 29091 0 paperback

Contents

List of illustrations	vi
List of tables	vii
Preface	ix
1 'The Nobles of Malabar': foreign images of the Nayars	1
2 Introduction to the Nayars in Central Travancore	17
3 The Nayar Kinship System in Ramankara	51
4 The Nayar Marriage System in Ramankara	73
5 The 'Traditional' Nayar Marriage System	99
6 The Disintegration of the Matrilineal Joint-family System	123
Notes	151
Glossary	161
References	163
Index	172

Illustrations

1	A group of people in Ramankara	26
2	A typical lane in Ramankara	26
3	A traditional joint-family house in Central Kerala	52
4	The younger occupants of the joint-family house	52
5	A fairly wealthy Nayar farmer in Ramankara	81
6	A village goldsmith	81
7	The front view of the main Ramankara temple	136
8	A Communist party demonstration	136

Charts

1	Marriages of the *karanavans* of the 7 principal *taravads* and their siblings who made 'big four' marriages (generations 1 and 2 only)	96
2	Part of Vilangu clan	96
3	Part of Kizhakkil clan	97
4	Part of Kunnam sub-clan	97
5	Inter-marriages between the children of the wealthiest households in generation 2	98
6	Marriages of Raman Vilangu's daughters' children	98

Figure

1	A *taravad* at the point of partition	57

Map

Kerala. Also showing Travancore, Cochin and Malabar	xii

Tables

1	Average monthly rainfall in Kottayam District	23
2	Population growth in Kerala, Travancore, Kottayam District and India	24
3	Ramankara sample census: households by caste	29
4	Ramankara land revenue unit, 1908: landownership by caste	29
5	Ramankara sample census: landowning by caste, household table	30
6	Ramankara sample census: landowning by caste	30
7	Ramankara sample census: cumulative table of landownership	31
8	Caste populations (main castes only)	37
9	A list of Nayar subdivisions	40
10	Populations of Nayar subdivisions	41
11	Household types among Ramankara Nayars (after Kolenda)	64
12	'Maternal' and 'paternal' features of Nayar kinship system	71
13	Marriages of 'big four' clan members	83
14	Marriages of the *karanavans*' brothers and sisters	86
15	Areas of land owned by the seven wealthiest *taravads*, 1908	87
16	Genealogical data (cf. table 13): spouses' villages	91
17	Census data: extant marriages only. Classified by age of husband (excluding 13 marriages in which both H and W from outside Ramankara)	92
18	Census data: extant marriages only. Classified by landowning of household (excluding 13 marriages in which both H and W from outside Ramankara)	93
19	Household types in a Cochin village, 1949 and 1964	139
20	Residence of married men in a Cochin village, 1949 and 1964	139
21	Husbands' residence in two South Malabar villages	140
22	Household types in a South Malabar village	140
23	Household types in a North Malabar village	143
24	Residence of married couples in a North Malabar village	143

Preface

Kerala is sometimes referred to by the people of the adjoining district of Coorg as the 'land of ignorance', a wrongheaded prejudice which is attributed by Srinivas (1952: 232) to the prevalence of matriliny there. Of the various matrilineal communities in Kerala, the Nayars are the most prominent; if they have not always been accused of ignorance, they have certainly been almost universally regarded as extraordinary and exotic by those who have visited them. The Nayars have been a perennial source of fascination, too, for Indian and foreign anthropologists who have, though, been able to show that they are certainly not the benighted and bizarre Orientals that they have so often been taken for.

The number of Nayars must now exceed three million. No-one, I trust, would presume that the culture of such a large community could be uniform. During the last few years, I have had many conversations with people who have a deep knowledge about the Nayars in different parts of Kerala. In virtually all these conversations, one or other, but more usually both of us, have been surprised to discover that some feature of Nayar life which we had always assumed to be ubiquitous was in fact not so. Indeed, the more I have learnt about the Nayars, the more I have realised the dangers inherent in generalising about them.

This book, however, contains a good deal of generalisation about the Nayars. In fact, my main aim has been to present a comparative survey of the community, and more especially of the kinship system, which is wider than any presently existing in the literature. But I should, I think, indicate to the reader the necessary limits to generalisation and simultaneously explain something about the structure of this book. As the reader will see, the majority of travellers only visited the central area of Kerala. Here, too, most of the modern anthropological field-work has been conducted. Further, it is only in this region that Nayar society diverged so far from the mundane norm. Thus the Nayars living in the central part of Kerala are those for whom we have the most information, as well as those who pose the most interesting anthropological problems.

My own field-work was carried out in the southern half of Kerala, a region visited by few travellers in the past and in which there has been very little research. I hope the data I collected, pertaining mainly to kinship and marriage, and presented in chapters 2, 3 and 4, will not be found uninteresting. It is, though, the case that the Nayars in the area where I worked did not have a kinship system which could parallel in

Preface

exoticism that of the Nayars to their north. Thus they do not raise such complicated theoretical conundrums for an anthropologist and this, together with the relative paucity of information on them, means that in my discussion of the 'traditional' marriage system (chapter 5), the Nayars of the central area return to the forefront. However, in looking at the disintegration of the matrilineal-joint-family system (chapter 6), I have tried to focus attention on Nayars in both halves of Kerala, for it is my firm belief that previous discussion has paid insufficient attention to regional diversity within Kerala. I apologise to the reader who, in spite of this explanation, feels irritated by any discontinuity he detects between different sections of the book.

One of my principal aims throughout this book has been to set the material firmly within its historical context. The extent to which I have succeeded in this is, of course, for the reader to judge. To my mind, however, there can be no dispute about the desirability of this aim. 'Timeless India' was always a myth. But 'timeless Kerala' would be an arrant absurdity. The evidence for this should be clear enough in the pages below.

The reader is entitled to some information about how I gathered my data in the field. I did in fact study two villages in Kerala. One of these, which I have called Ramankara in this book, is dominated by Nayars; the other, contiguous with it, is dominated by Syrian Christians (whom I have discussed in more detail elsewhere). I lived in the latter from August 1971 until July 1972, spending almost all of that period in and around the two villages. I did, I think, get to know many of the people in Ramankara fairly well, but I did not, of course, see quite as much of them as I did of some of the people in the village where I lived. I revisited the villages again for a few days in October 1972, and I was able to pay another flying visit, lasting only five days, in December 1975. In the latter part of my field-work I was able to understand, more or less, spoken Malayalam, but I never gained fluency in it, and most of my investigations in the village were done with the aid of an interpreter. Chapters 3 and 4, and parts of chapter 2, were included in slightly different form in my unpublished Ph.D. dissertation (1974); the remainder of the book, based mostly on library research, has been written since I completed the dissertation.

The book contains an essential minimum of Indian words, most of them Malayalam. Names have been given their conventional English spellings; where alternative spellings exist, I have adopted the one which seemed to me most commonly used. All other Indian words have been transliterated accurately, but without diacritical marks, normally according to the spelling in Gundert's Malayalam dictionary. These words are all transliterated with diacritical marks in the glossary. With a few words such as *taravad,* which have virtually entered the anthropological vocabulary, I have however retained the conventional spelling, even though it is not an accurate transliteration. All Indian words have been pluralised by adding

Preface

's'. The word *nayar* is an honorific plural used as a singular. I have preferred Nayar over Nair, and also the forms Nambudiri and Izhava. Ramankara, like the names of families and individuals in the village, is a pseudonym.

Like all anthropologists, I have incurred many debts to many people. First and foremost, I must thank the people of Ramankara, and also the village in which I lived, for their kindness and hospitality, especially my landlord Mr P. S. Job, his wife Mariamma, and their children Scaria, Solly, Kurian, Ousephachen, Somey and Soji. I should also like to express my thanks to N. M. Joseph, my interpreter, assistant and all-round trouble-shooter; Professors Sir Edmund Leach and S. J. Tambiah, who supervised my doctoral research and gave me endless encouragement; Professor Joan Mencher, who gave me the benefit of her extensive knowledge of Kerala and, with Professor Frank Southworth, much hospitality in India as well; Professor Kathleen Gough, who willingly provided me with information and copies of her papers; Professors André Béteille, K. Raman Unni, T. N. Krishnan, C. Z. Scaria and Mr K. J. John, for much aid and hospitality in India; Christopher May, Jonathan Parry and Deborah Swallow, for their comments on various chapters of this book; my mother, Mrs Christine Fuller, who typed the manuscript; and my wife, Pauline.

Financial support for my doctoral research was provided by the Social Science Research Council, the Smuts Memorial Fund, the Esperanza Trust, the Henry Ling Roth Research Fund and Peterhouse, Cambridge. A grant from Manchester University enabled me to visit India in 1975. I would like to express my gratitude to all these bodies.

Manchester C. J. F.
February 1976

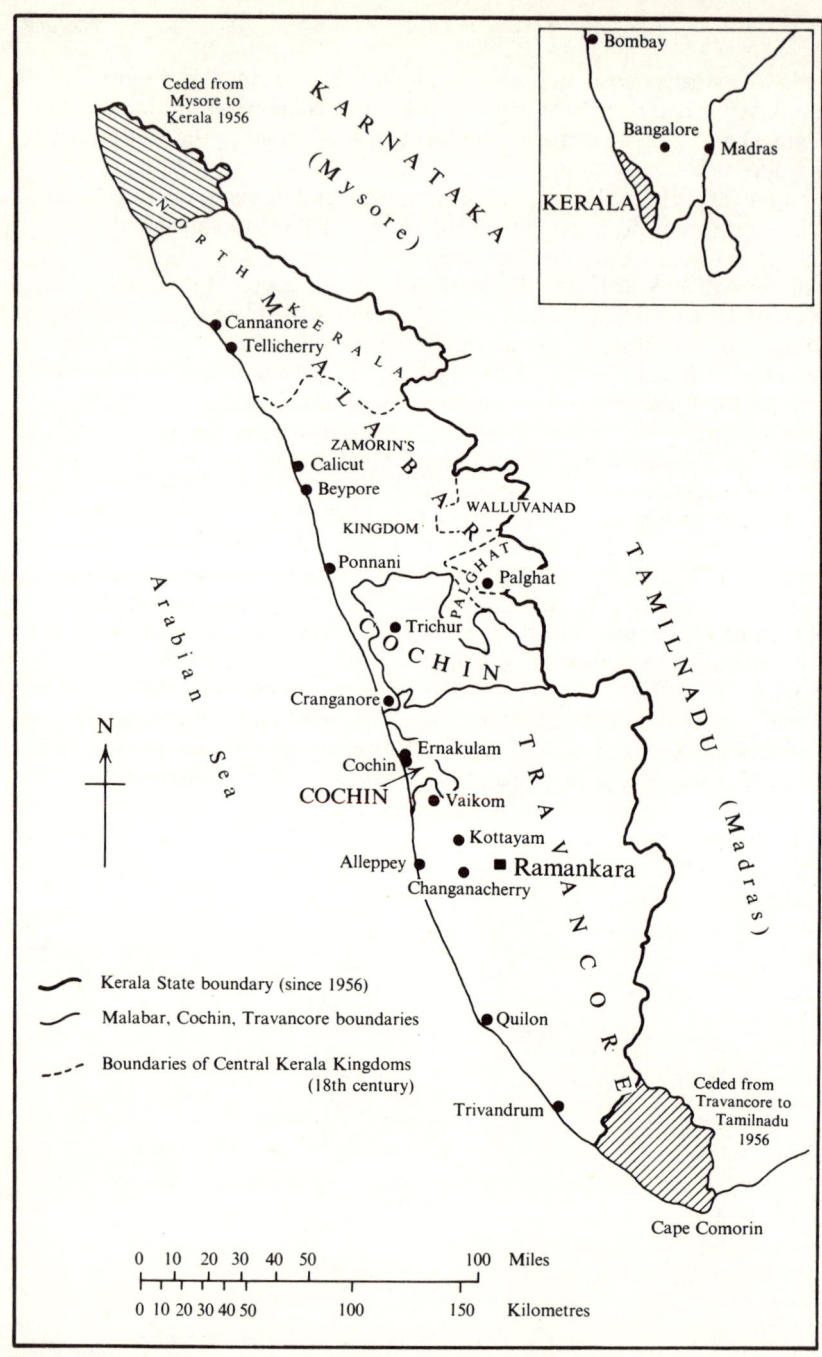

Kerala. Also showing Travancore, Cochin and Malabar

1 'The Nobles of Malabar': foreign images of the Nayars

Centuries before the birth of modern anthropology, the Nayars had provoked astonishment in a succession of visitors to Kerala, the land (also known as the Malabar Coast) which lies in the extreme south-west of India. In Western literature, Pliny is probably the first to mention them; in his *Natural History* (VI, xxiii, 74), written in A.D. 77, he refers to the 'Nareae, who are shut in by the Capitalis range, the highest of all the mountains in India'. Though we cannot be certain, it is probable that this refers to the Western Ghats, the range of mountains in western India cutting Kerala off from Karnataka (Mysore) and Tamilnadu, and that the 'Nareae' are indeed the Nayars. The first useful description dates from the fourteenth century; we owe it to Ibn Batuta, in India between 1325 and 1354, who although he spent most of his time in northern India did visit Kerala as well. The first really detailed accounts appeared in the sixteenth century, from the pens of travellers visiting Kerala in the wake of the Portuguese, who gained effective control of the Arabian Sea and the Kerala spice trade within a few years of Vasco da Gama's landfall at Calicut in 1498.[1]

The early visitors, like all those who were to follow them in later centuries, were struck by three particular aspects of Kerala society: the matrilineal, polyandrous kinship and marriage system of the Nayars and the kings; the martial prowess of the Nayars; and the extreme complexity and rigidity of the Kerala caste system. I propose to introduce the reader to the Nayars through the eyes of these foreign travellers, and I shall consider each of these three aspects in turn. That the accounts quoted below tell us not only about the Nayars but also about their authors should not, I trust, need underlining. It would be foolish to expect their comments to have been informed by all our current ideas and values.

It is important to note, as the reader will see later, that most of the travellers' accounts refer to Calicut and Cochin; there is little mention of northern Malabar or the region to the south of Cochin. The reason for this is simple enough: Calicut and Cochin were the two greatest trading ports on the Malabar Coast (Logan 1887: 73-80). According to Yule (1915: 87), the Malabar ports 'appear to have become the entrepôts for commercial exchange between China and the West', although the Chinese seem to have stopped coming there in the fifteenth century. Calicut probably rose to prominence in the eleventh or twelfth century and maintained its predominance until the arrival of the Portuguese who,

The Nayars Today

unable to extract from the Zamorin (king) of Calicut the concessions they demanded, undermined its power by destroying its Arab trade. The Portuguese, like the Dutch, the English and Independent India after them, favoured Cochin, which has been from the sixteenth century until the present day the principal port on the coast. Calicut and Cochin remained the two most important kingdoms until the mid-eighteenth century, when their power was destroyed by the rise of Travancore to their south and the Mysorean invaders from the north. The Mysoreans were eventually defeated by the British in 1792; Malabar was then annexed and later incorporated into the Madras Presidency. The kingdoms of Calicut and Cochin, together with the two smaller inland kingdoms of Walluvanad and Palghat, make up the area called by Kathleen Gough 'Central Kerala'. The region to the north of Calicut and the Kora river she terms 'North Kerala'; 'South Kerala' is equivalent to Travancore (Gough 1961: 305).[2]

Matriliny and polyandry

In the past, the Nayars lived in matrilineal joint families, known as *taravads*. The *taravad* comprised all the matrilineal descendants of a common ancestress and a child, of course, belonged to its mother's *taravad*. A *taravad* might have consisted of a set of sisters, their brothers, their children and their daughters' children, but many *taravads* contained a much wider span of relatives. For instance, it might have included the matrilineal descendants of several sets of sisters, each of these sets being linked through a common mother's mother, or more remote ancestress. A *taravad* might have had twenty, thirty or even more members, all living together in one large house. Each *taravad* was an independent economic unit; its members collectively owned property from which they derived their livelihood. The Nambudiri Brahmans, the highest-ranking caste in Kerala, also lived in joint families, called *illams*. *Illams* were very similar to *taravads,* except in one important respect: they were patrilineal and comprised all the patrilineal descendants of a common ancestor. The relation between the Nayars and the Nambudiris will be a constant theme of this book.

What fascinated Kerala's visitors was not joint families themselves so much, but rather the marriage system with which the family organisation was, of course, intimately linked. By far the most accurate and detailed of the accounts written by the earliest travellers is by Duarte Barbosa, a Portuguese who learnt Malayalam (the language of Kerala). He returned to Lisbon in about 1518 after spending several years on the Malabar Coast, mainly in the Calicut region. He wrote of the Nambudiris:

They marry only once in our manner, and only the eldest son marries, he is treated like the head of an entailed estate. The other brothers remain single all their lives. These Bramenes keep their wives well guarded, and greatly honoured, so that no other men may sleep with them... The brothers who remain bachelors sleep with the Nayre women, they hold it to be a great honour, and as they are Bramenes no women refuses herself to them, yet they may not sleep with any woman older than themselves. (1921: 34–5)

Barbosa refers here to all the principal features of the Nambudiri marriage system. In order to maintain their patrilineal joint families intact, only the eldest son was permitted to marry a Nambudiri woman. By this means, the number of legitimate heirs was restricted and pressure to partition the estate minimised. All younger sons derived their sexual pleasures from unions with women of the lower matrilineal castes – Nayars and the royal houses. Eldest sons were also allowed to form such liaisons, even though they had Brahman wives as well. Although eldest sons often took several women in marriage (pace Barbosa), it was of course the case that the majority of Nambudiri women died unmarried. They were kept in strict seclusion throughout their lives in order to prevent them entering any illegitimate liaisons which could endanger the purity of the caste.

Turning now to Nayar marriage, we learn from Barbosa that:

These men are not married, their nephews (sisters' sons) are their heirs. The Nayre women of good birth are very independent, and dispose of themselves as they please with Bramenes, and Nayres, but they do not sleep with men of caste lower than their own under pain of death. When they reach the age of twelve years their mothers hold a great ceremony. (ibid.: 40)

Once again Barbosa's account, albeit brief, outlines the main features of Nayar marriage. The 'great ceremony' referred to is the *tali*-tying ceremony, at which each Nayar girl had a *tali* fastened around her neck. The *tali* is an emblem which, among other South Indian communities, is a sign that a women is married. Whether this was really its significance among the Nayars will be discussed in chapter 5, but it does not matter for the present. What is important to note is that the *tali* was tied before a Nayar girl reached puberty; after puberty, she began to receive 'lovers' from her own and higher castes – but never from lower castes – in a relationship known as *sambandham*. A woman, as we shall see, could take several lovers and it is this feature – polyandry – which has been mainly responsible for the Nayars' fame.

Barbosa goes on to describe the arrangements whereby a Nayar woman takes her lovers; he says that she may have three or four but 'the more lovers she has the greater is her honour' (ibid.: 42). Almost all commentators have disagreed as to whether there was a limit to the number of a woman's lovers, or if so what this number was, and the matter remains in dispute. Buchanan, in Malabar in the early nineteenth century, agreed with Barbosa: 'It is no kind of reflection on a women's character to say, that she has formed the closest intimacy with many persons; on the contrary, the Nair women are proud of reckoning among their favoured lovers many Brahmans, Rajas, or other persons of high birth' (1807: 411). Others, however, like Hamilton, have indicated that the number was restricted; he gave it as twelve (1727: 310). We shall probably never know what was the case, but Gough's tentative conclusion appears acceptable: ' It seems possible ... that each women had a small number of regular husbands, but that a man might without difficulty gain access to a strange women when he was away from his village on military service' (1952a: 74). Barbosa, like several other writers, implies that the Nayar women received their companions in some sort of pre-arranged rota; others suggest that there were no fixed arrangements. Many accounts refer to a Nayar leaving his arms outside the woman's door when he was with her, thus indicating to others that she was presently unavailable.

That these liaisons could be formed and broken off again with ease is attested to by almost all reports; from Barbosa once more:

If any of them wishes to leave her, he leaves her, and takes another, and she also if she is weary of a man, she tells him to go, and he does so, or makes terms with her. Any children they may have stay with the mother who has to bring them up, for they hold them not to be the children of any man, even if they bear his likeness, and they do not consider them their children, nor are they heirs to their estates, for as I have already stated their heirs are their nephews, sons of their sisters (1921: 42)

The sexual freedom permitted not only to the men but to the women as well was, unsurprisingly, remarked upon by virtually every visitor to Kerala. The most frequent cause for comment was the apparent absence of jealousy amongst the men or of objections by the women. Shaikh Zain al-Din compared the polyandrous system with its polygynous converse amongst Muslims and went on to say that ' it is seldom that any hostility or disagreement takes place between the men, in consequence of this their possession in common of the same female ' (1833: 65). Two hundred years later, Forbes remarked: ' Their marriages are very extraordinary, and directly contrary to the usual system of polygamy adopted in Asia. ... These marriages are attended with fewer disputes, and disagreeable consequences than might be imagined ... ' (1813: 385).

Some were not only surprised but shocked as well; for instance, Sir Thomas Herbert said: 'they commonly exchange their Wives one for another, nor seeme the Women angry at it; Polygamy is sufferable; but in this they differ from other libidinous Lawgivers; as the men have many wives, so one woman may have many husbands ... ' (1638: 303). Francis Day also proclaimed his views clearly enough: ' Until a change in this system occurs, this portion of India can hardly be said to be advancing in civilization ' (1863: 318). And Tippu Sultan, the Muslim king of Mysore who continued his father Haider Ali's attempt to subjugate Malabar in the eighteenth century, backed his objections with a threat his soldiers were only too willing to execute. The following is part of a proclamation he is said to have addressed to the people of Malabar in 1789:

and since it is a practice with you for one woman to associate with ten men, and you leave your mother and sisters unconstrained in their obscene practices, and are thence all born in adultery, and are more shameless in your connexions than the beasts of the field: I hereby require you to forsake these sinful practices, and live like the rest of mankind. And if you are disobedient to these commands, I have made repeated vows to honor the whole of you with Islam. (qu. by Logan 1887: 455)

However, the majority opinion of Kerala's visitors appears to have been in agreement with the Portuguese poet, Luis de Camoens, who was in India and the East between 1556 and 1567; taking a dig at religious laws at the same time, he wrote:

They* kill no living thing, and highly blame
All flesh to eat, with wondrous abstinence:
   But other flesh their Law doth not forbid,
   Yet They as prone thereto as if it did.

Their Wives are common: but are so to none
Save those who of their Husbands'. Kindred† are.
(O blessed lot, blest Generation,
On whom fierce jealousie doth wage no war!)

(*Lusiad* 1940: canto VII, verses 40, 41; Richard Fanshawe's translation.
* i.e. the Nambudiri Brahmans; † caste.)

Many writers, of course, noted that succession and inheritance were matrilineal, but most of them explained this custom, somewhat tautologically, as a simple consequence of polyandry: for example, Buchanan, who wrote that: 'In consequence of this strange manner of propagating the species, no Nair knows his father; and every man looks upon his sisters' children as his heirs' (1807: 412). Barbosa, however, realised that there was more to it than mere ignorance of paternity: 'the kings of the Nayres instituted it [matriliny] in order that the Nayres should not be held back from their service by the burden and labour of rearing children' (1921: 42-5). Montesquieu, whose source was Pyrard de Laval, came to a similar conclusion about polyandry, though he found it necessary to invoke a certain amount of climatological determinism as well:

The origin of this custom [polyandry] is not I believe difficult to discover. The Naires ... are the soldiers of all those nations. In Europe, soldiers are forbidden to marry; in Malabar, where the climate requires greater indulgence, they are satisfied with rendering marriage as little burdensome to them as possible: they give one wife amongst many men, which consequently diminishes the attachment to a family, and the cares of housekeeping, and leaves them in the free possession of a military spirit. (*The Spirit of the Laws* 1952: bk. XVI, ch. 5)

In their conclusions, Barbosa and Montesquieu anticipated by several centuries the results of modern anthropological research, and the connection between the Nayars' military organisation and their matrilineal, polyandrous system will be discussed in greater detail in chapter 6.

The system of matriliny and polyandry, which I have tried to describe through the various travellers' writings, came under increasing attack during the nineteenth and early twentieth centuries. Today it has vanished.

The Nayars Today

Later, I shall discuss in more detail how and why the system changed. I should, perhaps, remark again that the system as described above was probably confined to Central Kerala; it never, apparently, had this form in North Kerala or southern Travancore, while in northern Travancore a somewhat less exotic version seems to have prevailed. As I shall argue at greater length in chapter 6, the traditional kinship systems of the various Nayar communities altered, not solely as a consequence of objective factors, but also because they were out of keeping with the spirit of the times around the turn of the century. That spirit is now changing rapidly and the position of women has become a central issue in our society. It cannot be argued that Nayar women were ever completely equal to Nayar men; they were not - the head of the joint family, for instance, was a man. But they were much less subjugated than was, or is, the case in the overwhelming majority of the world's communities. Fawcett was one observer who regarded the system highly:

Equality of the sexes in all sexual matters, the man and the woman being on terms of equality, having equal freedom, is certainly an uncommon merit in the [matrilineal] system. Either party may terminate the union - even after one night of hymeneal bliss; and those who are unsuited to each other sexually, or in the way of temperament, in fact in any way, may put an end to their union and turn towards other partners. (1901: 236-7)

And though some may not forgive what they will see as a faux pas in the following statement by the Cochin Census Commissioner in 1901, M. Sankara Menon (a Nayar), others may agree with his general thesis:

The condition of women under this complicated system requires to be specially noticed. The two sexes are nearly on a par as to inheritance of property. Again, conjugal freedom also being not all on one side, the relations of the sexes appear to be more rational than amongst most other communities, as man does not enjoy any exclusive privilege of asserting or abusing his natural superiority. Further, the women is free to enjoy the pleasures of social life, as it seldom falls to her lot to be worried with the miseries of domestic seclusion. (Census 1901, Cochin: 100)

The military role of the Nayars

Honour and gallantry! Love and battle! My sword and my mistress! These were their devices, and they were ticklish sticklers for the point of honour. (Unknown origin, qu. in Census 1901, Cochin: 150)

The traditional occupation of the Nayars was soldiering. This does not mean that all Nayars were soldiers, for they were not. There is evidence that only Nayars belonging to certain sections of the caste bore arms, and of course only fit males were recruited into the armies. Nonetheless, the great majority of Nayars probably spent some time under arms. The armies were raised by the kings and chiefs, and were mostly engaged in fighting each other, rather than external enemies, although naturally this had to change when foreign interlopers became more aggressive. Although there probably was a minority of non-Nayars in many of the armies, it has always been the Nayars who have been most closely identified with the military life, and few visitors to Kerala did not feel moved to comment on the Nayars' martial prowess.

In Giovanni Maffei's description of Calicut, there appears one of the fullest accounts of the Nayars' military training and performance (1588: 25-6).[3] From the age of seven or so, he says, Nayar boys began their physical training, taking part in many exercises and massaging their limbs with sesame oil – all under the guidance of 'highly skilled wrestling masters'. By virtue of this training, continues Maffei, they can twist and turn 'as if they had no bones'. They are expert wrestlers, but are still more proficient in the use of weapons.

At one time, their weapons were the spear, arrows, the sword [and] the shield; but after these inventions of men, modern devices and machines, had been introduced there, they understood so well the entire business of casting, burnishing and aiming, that they employ all cannons and firearms, large and small, with consummate skill; nowadays, the Indian muskets, whether of iron or bronze [?], and gunpowder far surpass those of the Portuguese. Naked, with only their private parts covered, do they go into battle, wearing neither breastplates nor helmets; hence in combat our soldiers [i.e. Europeans] are much steadier – their weight and that of their armour press harder on the enemy. Moreover, their [i.e. the Nayars'] greatest protection is in flight itself.

Maffei describes how the Nayar soldiers flee and then reappear in a flash and, somewhat implausibly, states that 'what is perhaps deadliest of all' is that 'they hurl their javelins scarcely less accurately backwards than forwards'. But, he continues, 'if either necessity compels or the occasion demands that they engage in hand to hand combat, they do most of the killing'.

Quite how skilled they were as soldiers is not entirely clear. Pyrard de Laval thought them 'the best soldiers in the world' (1887: 380) and exceptionally agile, while Baldaeus states that they were 'the best Wrestlers in the World' and that he had seen them 'give a Salvo with the same order and dexterity as our best disciplin'd troops in Europe' (1704: 644). But in most European eyes, their military discipline seems to have left something to be desired; according to Dellon: 'They go to war in disorder, that is to say they neither form ranks nor march in step ...' (1699: 149). Mahé de la Bourdonnais, who captured Mahé (near Tellicherry) for the French in 1725 and had some experience in the field against them, confirms Dellon's description but insists on their qualities: 'They have no calling but the military, and would be excellent soldiers were they disciplined: but their fighting is disorganised, they take flight as soon as they are subjected to the least pressure; nevertheless, if they are heavily pressed and believe themselves in danger, they return to the offensive and never surrender' (qu. in Logan 1887: 137). Sir Hector Munro, the only prominent British general to have fought the Nayars, in 1761 said this of them: 'One may as well look for a needle in a Bottle of Hay as any of them in the daytime, they being lurking behind sand-banks and bushes except when we are marching towards the Fort, and then they appear like bees out in the month of June. Besides which, they point their guns well and fire them well also'. (qu. in idem.). Logan's conclusion (idem.) that although they were excellent in 'skirmishing', they were too disorganised to defeat a well-disciplined army is probably correct. No doubt, they would have had more success had they fought as guerrillas.

Baldaeus asserts that they went into battle drugged with opium 'to intoxicate their Brains' (1704: 622) and Nieuhof makes a similar claim: 'When they are to Attack an Enemy, they take a good Quantity of it; which makes them fall on like enraged wild Beasts, and the Virtue of the Amfion [opium] being gone, they don't remember what has past, which shews that it is very obnoxious to the Memory' (1704: 271). Their opiated minds, according to Nieuhof, often led Malayalis to forget agreements; he recommended to them that they take wine instead. Quite how widespread the use of opium was is difficult to tell. However, a representative of the English East India Company, writing in 1666, was moved to complain about the way in which the Dutch had cornered the Kerala pepper market by supplying opium in exchange, 'for the natives of those parts [especially Cochin] not being able to live without ophium, which now they cannot have but from the Dutch, who have already brought it into such esteem among them, that they have all the pepper which is the growth of those parts in truck for it' (qu. in Foster 1925: 101). This suggests a considerable consumption of opium in Kerala at that time, although I have not found any certain evidence that soldiers were particularly partial to the drug.

Before the arrival of the Portuguese, war in Kerala was quite different from war in Europe. It was, albeit murderous, 'a game governed by an elaborate set of rules, the violation of any one of which involved dishonour worse than death'. War engaged only the actual participants; 'The labourer in the field could go on with his work unmolested while a fierce struggle was going on in his immediate neighbourhood' (Menon 1911: 56). Fighting took place only in daylight; in the morning, the opposing forces bathed together and chatted and joked, exchanging betel, until the battle was heralded by drums. The armies then formed up: a vanguard of swordsmen, a middle rank of archers and men armed with clubs, with lancers bringing up the rear. There was no cavalry. The armies advanced slowly, intermittently retreating. When ranks finally broke, a general bloody mêlée developed, inevitably resulting in many deaths and woundings. When sunset approached, the drums sounded the battle's end; it ceased at once. The antagonists again mingled together as they had done in the morning. Menon does not say what happened to the dead or wounded. A victorious army never annexed territory, although it might exact tribute or depose a defeated chief or king.

According to Baldaeus: 'The Power of the Kings of Malabar is generally esteemed by the number of Nairos under their Jurisdiction' (1704: 644). Barretto states that the Zamorin could field 160000 men and the Cochin raja 140000. He also provides a brief description of the politico-military organisation: 'The custom in Malabar is to divide the kingdom into several provinces, which are given to chiefs, responsible for raising a body of soldiers and holding them ready at all times; this is how these kings are able to call upon huge armies at short notice' (1646: 194). Barbosa describes how Nayars entered the king's service and says that they never lost their commissions, even when old (1921: 45-51). It would appear from his account that the Nayars were well treated by their rulers:

When the kings go to war they pay all the Nayres who serve therein, even though they be in the service of other Lords, their daily wages... The King is obliged to maintain the mother and the nephews of Nayres who fall in battle, and forthwith assigns them a pension. If they are wounded the King orders them to be well cured, as well as giving them their customary pay. (ibid.: 52-3)

The Nayars, so it appears, always bore their arms, usually a sword and a shield. Herbert remarks that: 'they goe no whither but are as well armed as if friends and enemies had no difference' (1638: 301); as a result of which, according to him, they are involved in endless violent altercations. Buchanan took rather the same view: 'Their chief delight is in parading up and down fully armed. Each man has a firelock, and at least one sword; but all those who wish to be thought men of extraordinary courage carry two sabres' (1807: 388). And, he says later: 'they are more inclined to use them for assassination, or surprise, than in the open field' (ibid.: 410). How just these comments are is impossible to tell. But many Nayars, even in peacetime, would be carrying weapons in the course of duty, for they acted as guards to travellers in Kerala – a custom commented on by many foreign visitors to the country who employed Nayars in this role. It was even reported in Diderot's *Encyclopédie* (XXII, 2: 152), that they are 'so loyal that they kill themselves, should he whom they are conducting be killed on the road'.

The Nayar armies were disbanded in the eighteenth and early nineteenth centuries (see chapters 2 and 6). Travancore and Cochin did maintain Nayar brigades until 1947, but they were, of course, modelled on modern European armies. Many later observers, no doubt with more romanticism than accuracy, seem to have felt that demobilisation had enfeebled and corrupted the Nayar caste. Logan (1887: 138) was one such, but his feeling was shared by Indians too; for instance, Anantakrishna Iyer (a Tamil Brahman) said: 'the Nayars have almost lost their warlike characteristics, through successive generations of peace and have now become attached to the land. Even writing in 1855 [?], Captain Drury [1858: 204] contrasts the Nayar's effeminate disposition with the martial valour of his forefathers ... He now prefers a quiet swing in the verandah or a lounge under a tree, chewing betel' (1912: 7).

The Nayars Today

The Kerala caste system

Many readers will have some knowledge of the Indian caste system, but for the rest a brief description may be desirable. An attempt to define 'caste' is, in my opinion, inevitably defeated by insuperable analytical difficulties. But this does not mean that a general outline of the caste system cannot be given, so long as the reader remains aware that such an outline cannot take account of theoretical problems and must necessarily be subject to innumerable qualifications. Every Indian belongs to one and only one caste. He or she is born into this one caste and dies in it; in other words, no mobility between castes is possible. In general – though the Nayars are an exception to this – castes are endogamous and thus legitimate children belong to the same caste as their parents. When husband and wife do not belong to the same caste, the husband's caste is invariably ranked higher than his wife's.

Each caste usually has a traditional occupational specialisation, although the significance of this is both problematic and easily exaggerated, and it is certainly true that many Indians are not engaged in their own caste-occupation. In theory, the castes in any one region can all be ranked with respect to each other to form a hierarchy, the principle on which they are ranked being that of relative purity. The concept of purity is central in Hindu society, but the criteria which define one caste as purer than another need not be discussed here. All that we need note here is that if one caste is purer than another, it is equivalent to saying that the first caste is ranked higher than the second. There may be thirty or more castes in any one Indian village, but in theory they can all be arranged in order of rank. I say 'in theory' because although the villagers will agree that it *ought* to be possible to construct such a hierarchy, they are very unlikely to agree about which castes rank above which others. The main exceptions to this are at the top and the bottom: Brahmans are always ranked highest and Harijans (or, as they used to be called, Untouchables) are always ranked lowest. Any Hindu's purity is at risk if he comes into too close contact with a member of a lower caste. In daily life, this is perhaps predominantly a question of food and water, and so high-caste members often refuse to eat with, or take food and water from, low-caste members. If they did so, they would suffer pollution, which they would then have to remove by an appropriate ritual act. The simplest of these, to remove mild pollution, is bathing; more severe pollution could demand more complicated rituals. Some acts, such as sexual relations with a lower-caste man, are so polluting to a woman that she would be outcasted – ejected from her caste and denied all contact with her former caste fellows. This paragraph is mainly descriptive of the 'traditional' caste system. In modern India, the system has 'weakened'; it no longer circumscribes behaviour with the force or rigidity it used to. But this is a problem too large to tackle here. This description of caste, albeit brief, will hopefully suffice for the present.

Virtually every foreign visitor to India, since Megasthenes in the fourth to third centuries B.C., has remarked on the caste system. Arguably, however, it is those who came to Kerala who were most astonished, for it was in this part of India that the caste system achieved its greatest elaboration and rigidity. The social distance between the Nambudiri Brahmans at the top, and the ostracised, degraded Pulayas (the main Kerala Harijan caste) at the bottom, was immense. It was concretised in what has become known as 'distance pollution'. In Kerala, unlike the rest of India where physical contact was necessary, a low-caste person could pollute a high-caste person merely by coming within a certain distance of the latter. In extreme cases, pollution could be transmitted by simply sighting a low-caste person.

The Nambudiri Brahmans, as I have said, occupied the summit of the hierarchy. Something of their exalted status, and of the ethos of the caste system, is conveyed in this late nineteenth-century description written – it may be worth noting – by a Tamil Brahman:

His [the Nambudiri's] tenants, all of them peaceful and contented on account of his unexacting nature, his genial manners, and considerate treatment, bow down to him not simply as a lord, but as their royal liege and benefactor, their suzerain master, their household deity, their very God on earth; and pay, their customary homage, with a good will and happy face generation after generation. His person is holy; his directions are commands; his movements are processions; his meal is nectar. He is the holiest of human beings. He is the representative of God on earth... Such is the popular estimation in which he is held. (Census 1875, Travancore: 191)

That such a picture could be drawn at all is, I think, significant. That it is, however, exaggerated can scarcely be doubted and nor is it the whole story: 'There, in the midst of their extensive estates, worshipped as gods by their innumerable tenants, and defrauded hourly by their astute agents and managers, they lead a life of opulent simplicity, unbounded hospitality and undisturbed indolence' (Census 1891, Cochin: 107). Some, indeed, would have seen the picture as wholly false; Chettur (1901: 135) described the Nambudiri landlords as 'very exacting' towards their tenants and attributed to them a major share of the blame for the Muslim rebellions in Malabar: 'is it a wonder that some tenants who are alien in faith and as such restrained by no religious scruples, take up arms against this sea of troubles and seek some momentary relief in shedding the life-blood of a dozen of them?' Certainly, during this century anyway, the Nambudiris' holy simplicity has tended more and more to be considered as exploitatary naïveté by many – not only Muslims – and in particular by the Nayars whose womenfolk afforded the Nambudiri men one of their principal founts of worldly pleasure. Forbes anticipated by almost a century an attitude that would become more or less universal among the Nayars: 'These shameless priests, not content with the dancing girls attached to the different temples, who are all prostitutes to the brahmins, have connections with the youngest and most beautiful women among the high tribes of Malabar...' (1813:

389). In fact (pace Forbes) temple prostitution was not prevalent in Kerala.

As empirical descriptions of the caste system, few of the travellers' accounts are factually correct. Most of them mention only a handful of the main castes and the complexity of the hierarchical relations between castes was not generally perceived. Of the earlier accounts, Barbosa's is again the best; he refers to eighteen castes, if we include the royal lineages as one, ranging from the Brahmans to the Parayas, with the addition of four immigrant castes in the country (1921: 70, n. 2.). (Exactly how many castes there are or were in Kerala is, of course, a meaningless question in any case (cf. Dumont 1970: 33), although the early Census Commissioners did try to find the answer; in the 1881 Census, the number of distinct castes and subcastes in Malabar was said to reach the grand and rather farcical total of 978 (Census 1881, Madras).)

Most travellers, however, noted that the Nayars were ranked below the Brahmans and the kings in the caste hierarchy, and few failed to comment on the position of the Pulayas at the bottom. Barbosa, though, was the only one of the early visitors to recognise explicitly the 'pollution line' separating the higher castes, such as the Nayars, from those below them (1921: 59). The lower castes are, or were, known as *tintal jati* – castes which pollute at a distance. The pollution rules, so extreme in Kerala, were naturally the subject provoking the most comment. Shaikh Zain al-Din remarked that the Nayars were, on account of these rules, 'subject to trouble without end', which meant that they were forever having to take purificatory baths (1833: 66). But most writers – with justice, I think the reader will agree – emphasised the rather greater problems of the low castes, in particular the Pulayas, who:

are not permitted to breathe the same air with the other castes, nor to travel on a public road; if by accident they should be there, and perceive a brahmin or a Nair at a distance, they must instantly make a loud howling, to warn him from approaching until they retired, or climbed up the nearest tree. If a Nair accidentally meets a Pooleah on the highway, he cuts him down with as little ceremony as others destroy a noxious animal: even the lowest of other castes will have no communication with a Pooleah. (Forbes 1813: 395)

The Nayars' right to kill immediately any Pulaya met on the road is attested to by virtually every visitor to Kerala, and there is little room for doubt about the accuracy of Forbes's account. According to others, for example, Buchanan (1807: 410), Nayars killed not only Pulayas but any member of the lower polluting castes, from Tiyyars (Izhavas) down. If this was so, it has a certain ghastly sense within the logic of the caste system, but it is not confirmed by other observers. Dellon, after noting too that Nayars could put Pulayas to the sword, went on to mention a still more horrific practice: 'If a Nayar wishes to test his martial skill, he is allowed to do so on any member, regardless of age or sex, of that unhappy lineage [i.e. Pulaya caste], without fear or remorse...' (1699: 123). Though others make no reference to this,

Dellon's assertion seems all too plausible. The low castes had some marginal protection, in that Nayars, when walking along the road, would normally warn others of their impending approach by shouting '*po!*', i.e. 'go away'. The former were then, as Forbes mentions, able to cry back to warn the Nayars: a practice compared – rather inaccurately, one feels – by Montaigne to the shouting of the gondoliers in Venice! (*Essayes*, bk. III, ch. 5; 1928, vol. V: 74)

Outcasteing was the punishment for transgressing caste rules, although in some circumstances it was followed by sale into slavery or even death. Because it was the most extraordinary of all, I shall briefly describe the outcasteing procedure reserved for a Nambudiri woman accused of illegitimate sexual relations. It was known as *smarttivicaram* and is described in detail by Iyer (1912: 210-14). If accused, a Nambudiri woman was lodged in a separate hut, for her presence inside the family house could pollute other members of her family. She was then brought before a caste court and interrogated. The court could only sit after the king had issued a summons, and it was held under his patronage. If the woman eventually confessed, or was judged guilty, she was asked to name all her lovers, of whatever caste. They were then brought before the court as well; their innocence or otherwise used to be determined through the use of ordeals, such as that with boiling oil. The accused plunged his hand into the oil; if it was burnt, he was guilty. Iyer (ibid.: 213) refers to a case in Cochin which at the time of his writing had taken place quite recently, and in which sixty-five men of the Brahman, Ambalavasi and Nayar castes were outcasted. (The Ambalavasis rank between Brahmans and Nayars.) The most famous trial of all, according to the stories which still circulate in Kerala, involved a notorious Nambudiri courtesan in Cochin in the 1920s whose case lasted for weeks as she proceeded to name virtually every man of substance in the city. Eventually, the raja stopped the trial because, according to all who recount the tale, his name was next on her list! Since then, so it is said, there have been no more of these trials.

Any contact, not only sexual, with a member of a polluting caste was a transgression of the rules and required appropriate action to be taken. Sometimes this would mean no more than a quick purificatory dip. But it could be more serious. Grose, who was in Calicut in the 1750s, recounts an extraordinary tale (1772: 189), the authenticity of which is a little difficult to assess. According to him, a Nayar and a Tiyyar happened to have a fight, 'in half jest, half earnest'. The Nayar was cut by the Tiyyar's sickle, and he 'no sooner saw his own blood, than he loosed his hold and entreated the Thyvee to make off as soon as possible, and to keep the accident a secret for both their sakes'. However, the secret leaked out and a Nayar caste council was called; the members of the council executed the offending Nayar with their swords. They then went to the Tiyyar's village with the ostensible aim of killing him and his fellows. However, the council had actually forewarned the Tiyyars of its intention and so by quitting their homes for a time, they escaped the massacre. The raison d'être of this action on the council's part appears to be that it was enough for the Nayars to be seen to be taking action, even though it was not efficacious.

The caste system was not invariably as vicious as I have portrayed it so far; it could also give rise to occasional humorous incidents. Gemelli Careri, for example, refers to the tribulations of Jesuit priests. (It is unclear whether Gemelli Careri actually saw, or only heard from others, what he relates.) The Jesuits accommodated themselves to the caste system; each priest lived as a member of a caste and tried to convert only members of that one caste. Thus, says Gemelli Careri (1704: 258): ' when two Fathers meet in the Street, one acting the Naires, and the other the Polias, they keep at a distance from one another, that they may not be suspected ' – of opposition to the caste system, presumably, rather than of their European origin which would be almost impossible to disguise. An amusing tale comes from the Journal of Roger Hawes, an English sailor and trader who was one of the factors, or agents, representing the first English fleet to attempt to trade with the Zamorin of Calicut, in 1615. The factors were in Kerala for most of that year, but were beset by the continual problem that the local merchants' promises to settle their debts were rarely realised: ' it is not the custome of best or worst in this countrey, to be as good as their word, being certain only in dissembling' (Hawes 1625: 604). Finally, however, they partly resolved their problem by exploiting their own polluting status:

> But the Governeur [the Zamorin's agent] and people continuing their wonted perfidiousnesse, the one more carefull of taking, the other of giving, bribes, than paying our debts: we used a strange policie to get some of them: for when we came to demand them at their houses, if they would pay us none, we would threaten not to depart till they paid us. And we had heard it reported that their custome is, neither to eat nor wash, whilst we are in their houses. By this means we sometimes got fiftie Fanos [local currency units] of one; one hundred of another; by no means would they endure us to lie at their houses, except one, where we waited three daies and nights, with three or foure Nayros: ... but we could get nothing. (ibid.: 605)

I have tried in this section to give a description of the caste system in Kerala as it appeared to visitors in the past. A more sober sociological account will be presented in the following chapter, but I hope that this impressionistic picture has imparted to the reader something of what struck visitors to the country. Today, though the caste system itself cannot be said to have disappeared, all its more extreme manifestations have vanished: few perceive the Nambudiris as ' gods on earth ', Pulayas need not fear for their lives on the roads, and outcasteing is extremely rare if not actually non-existent. It is not long, however, since many of these features were still in existence and old people in Kerala can yet remember the days when Pulayas were barred from public roads and outcasteing was common enough. The traditional system continues to have its observable effects on modern Kerala society.

On the character of the Nayars

This sketch of the Nayars and Kerala society may be closed by a few remarks on the character of the Nayars, on which most observers offered their opinion. As statements of objective fact, not many of the remarks have much value, but they do supply a quaint footnote to the history of European attitudes, if little else. Next to nothing emerges from any account of the character of Nayar women – in some ways, rather surprising given their position in society – and we have little about them apart from Sir Richard Burton's comments on their beauty. He visited Calicut around 1850 and tells of a chance encounter in the Zamorin's palace: 'we were gratified to catch a sight of Nair female beauty. The ladies were very young and pretty – their long jetty tresses, small soft features, clear dark olive-coloured skins, and delicate limbs... Their *toilette,* in all save the ornamental part of rings and necklaces, was decidedly scanty' (1851: 179).

The men, from nearly all accounts, emerge as proud and arrogant – a description which has not, of course, always carried the same negative connotations it bears today. Some attributed the Nayars' character to their blood, others to their martial prowess, others to their high caste rank and yet others to a combination of all these. Nieuhof recounts a tale which is hard to credit:

They [the Nayars] are very haughty, and at first pretended to dispute the Rank with the Portugueses, which occasion'd no small disturbance, till the Difference was agreed to be decided by a single Combat betwixt a Portuguese and a Nayros, in which the last being worsted, the Nayros ever since were forced to give way to the Portugueses; but all the other Malabars must give place to the Nayros. (1704: 272)

I have not, I confess, been able to find this story in any Portuguese source! And the credibility of parts of Nieuhof's account is not raised by his claim that: 'The Nayros scarce ever laugh, and that not but upon extraordinary Occasions; and if they see others laugh, they will look downward' (ibid.: 273).

Baldaeus (1704: 644) limited his remarks to stating that the Nayars were 'exceedingly haughty, proud and bold' while Correa noted that their pride meant that they never became Muslims – a pardonable exaggeration although almost certainly not quite true; 'they are people who are very refined in blood and customs, and separated from all other low people, and so much do they value themselves that no one of them ever turned Moor; only the low people turned Moors, who worked in the bush and in the fields' (1869: 155). Day, for some reason, clearly did not take to the Nayars at all; 'The Nairs are a proud and warlike race, arrogant to inferiors, subservient to superiors, profuse in promises, and slack in their performance. They occasionally officiate as accountants, but their statements must be received with caution, and additional testimony is generally advisable' (1863: 315). This last comment was made, of course, as the tide of European racialism

The Nayars Today

in India was begining to flow faster and faster, and it is in striking contrast to the impression made upon Dellon in the seventeenth century, with which I shall close: 'The Nayars are the nobility and the worthiest men in the land, as is shown no less by their bearing and courtesy than by their birth' (1699: 125).

2 Introduction to the Nayars in Central Travancore

In this chapter I shall present some basic information about the Nayars in Central Travancore. In the main, this is designed to serve as background to the detailed analysis, contained in the subsequent two chapters, of the kinship and marriage system of the Nayars of Ramankara, a village in Central Travancore in which I collected most of my field-work data. The area known as 'Central Travancore' – although it is all within the northern half of Travancore – more or less coincides with the modern administrative districts of Kottayam, Alleppey and Ernakulam (southern part). This chapter opens with a brief historical resumé of Kerala and Travancore and continues with some remarks about the geography of the region. I go on to describe the village of Ramankara, in particular the pattern of land-ownership and some of its sociological implications. The last part considers the nature of caste in the area and Nayar customs regarding purity and pollution.

Historical sketch[1]

Kerala has a long recorded history, but we need not go back beyond the early eighteenth century. Broadly, the political map of Kerala at that time was as follows. To the north of Calicut, i.e. in North Malabar, there were a number of fairly small kingdoms and chiefdoms, none of which was very strong or highly centralised. In Central Kerala – South Malabar and Cochin – four powerful kingdoms controlled the entire region. Of these, by far the most powerful – indeed the most powerful in all of Kerala – were Calicut and Cochin, their wealth being based on the respective ports. Inland were two smaller kingdoms, Walluvanad and Palghat, which at times came under the effective control of Calicut. South of Cochin, the region was divided into innumerable petty chiefdoms and weak kingdoms, over some of which Cochin claimed suzerainty. Others paid tribute to the Nayaks of Madurai, then the dominant power in the Tamil country.

One of the small kingdoms subject to Nayak exactions was Venad or Travancore, in the extreme south. In 1729, a young prince, Martanda Varma, acceded to the throne of Travancore. On his accession, the kingdom's internal affairs were in complete chaos. However, by the time of his death in 1758, Martanda Varma – through a series of brilliant but ruthless military campaigns – had gained control of the whole of southern Kerala, from Cape Comorin to the borders of Cochin. Most of the chiefs in the area were

17

defeated on the battlefield; the remainder were forced to accept Martanda Varma's terms of settlement. Martanda Varma's successor, Rama Varma, reigned until 1798; during his reign, in 1761, Cochin ceded yet more territory to Travancore which then stretched unbroken up to Cranganore, except for the small area surrounding the port of Cochin. Most of the Cochin state's territory was actually centred around Trichur, connected to the capital by Travancore territory.

Perhaps no community in southern Kerala was more affected by Martanda Varma's campaigns and policies than the Nayars. First, and most immediately, he ended the military careers of nearly all Nayars within his conquered territory by demobilising the armies of the defeated chiefs. Second, he annexed the lands of the former chiefs to his new state. Many of these chiefs were probably Nayars themselves – perhaps claiming high rank, as in Malabar. Their land was the principal source of their economic power, and Martanda Varma's action more or less destroyed it. By annexation is meant the transfer of *janmom* rights from individual chiefs to the Travancore state, thus reducing them to *kanamdars* of the state. For present purposes, *janmi,* one who holds *janmom* rights, may be translated as 'landlord' and *kanamdar,* one who holds land from the landlord on a type of lease known as *kanam,* may be translated as 'tenant'. As specialists will be aware, these translations are not entirely accurate and are, in some measure, misleading; however, I do not think that a more detailed analysis of Kerala land tenure is appropriate here.[2] Employing these translations, it will be seen that the state became the landlord in the conquered territories and the former chiefs became the state's tenants. The consequences of Martanda Varma's land policy were far-reaching; in particular, the fact that the state became the landlord for so much of the territory, in contradistinction to what occurred in Malabar under the British, is still exerting its effect on politics today. The combination of large absentee landlords and a great many tenants in Malabar was one factor in the Communists' rise in Malabar; conversely, the presence of a large owner-cultivator class and relatively few large landlords was a factor contributing to the Communists' relative failure in Travancore.

Martanda Varma's policies were an entirely new phenomenon in Kerala. He was the first Malayali king to fight his battles with the ruthless determination of European armies, and he was the first to execute recalcitrant enemies, demobilise opposing armies and annex conquered land. In the civil as well as the military sphere, he was a pioneer; he began to create a state of a recognisably modern character and, in particular, he laid the foundations of a modern bureaucracy, which although it employed some Nayars, was mainly administered by Tamil Brahmans.

The rise of Travancore meant, as we have seen, losses for Cochin. But the real blows to Malabar and Cochin were to come from the north. The Muslim king of Mysore, Haider Ali, first attacked Malabar in 1765 and for the next seventeen years, until his death in 1782, he and his troops repeatedly invaded Malabar. But he never gained complete dominance,

Introduction to the Nayars

and each time his armies withdrew, revolts broke out again. Haider's son, Tippu Sultan, continued his father's attempts to conquer Kerala. He added too a stronger strain of Muslim fanaticism, hinted at in the proclamation quoted in chapter 1. Although Tippu subjugated certain areas at certain times, he never gained undisputed mastery of the territory and, like his father, never managed to cross into Travancore - although attempts were made more than once. His final attempt, in 1789, resulted in his expulsion from Kerala. By then, Travancore had signed a treaty with the English East India Company. When Tippu attacked Travancore, the Company's troops, somewhat belatedly and initially ineffectually, began their assult on him. Three years later, in March 1792, Cornwallis (the Governor-General of India), who had taken command of the Company's troops, dictated peace terms; they included the annexation of Malabar by the British. So by the close of the eighteenth century, Kerala was formed of the British district of Malabar in the north, the now powerful, independent state of Travancore in the south, and the small, nominally independent state of Cochin in the centre. Travancore and Cochin, 'Native States' ruled by their own maharajas, had treaty obligations to the British Government. However, they were never legally incorporated into British India, although in 1947 when India became independent, Travancore and Cochin - like other, larger Native States such as Hyderabad or Kashmir - eventually acceded to the Indian Union.

A full discussion of the effects of the Mysorean invasions and British rule on Malabar is unnecessary here, though a brief summary of land policy may be helpful. After the British annexation, a large number of Hindu landlords who had fled from Malabar during the Mysorean invasions returned to claim their estates, many of which had been cultivated in their absence by Muslims. These landlords, and those rajas who had been reinstated by the British, were responsible for collecting the land revenue and remitting it to the sovereign power. The revenue assessment was very high and skirmishes between the Hindu agents of the rajas and the landlords, and the Muslim cultivating tenants, were commonplace. The situation was further exacerbated by the proclamation of 1793 which conferred on the landlords (*janmis*) full ownership rights, including the power to evict the tenants (*kanamdars*). These problems all came to a head in the 1830s when, for various reasons, there was a marked increase in the number and rate of evictions. These were followed by a series of violent outbreaks, mainly attacks by Muslim tenants on Hindu landlords. These rebellions, known as the 'Moplah riots' - 'Moplah' is the name by which the Malabar Muslims are often known - continued for almost a hundred years and culminated in the massive rebellion of 1921.

As a result of the 1793 proclamation, almost all the land in Malabar was held by a relatively small number of landlords - most of them extremely wealthy and most of them Brahmans, former rajas or high-ranking Nayars. In Travancore, by contrast, 80% of the cultivated and all the uncultivated land was, by the 1850s, held by the state. The situation in Cochin was intermediate: in the late nineteenth century, about 60% of the cultivated land was held by private landlords on the Malabar pattern, with the rest of the cultivated and most of the uncultivated land being held by the state on the Travancore pattern (Varghese 1970: 39, 44, 48).

A further radical revision of Travancore's land policy occurred in the 1860s. In 1865, the government conferred full ownership rights on all its tenants (*kanamdars*). In essence, this meant that the majority of Travancore's land became, overnight, a marketable commodity and the foundations for a capitalist agriculture were laid. In 1867, the Travancore government issued a proclamation forbidding landlords to evict their tenants which, following the example of their fellows in Malabar, they had begun to do. Whereas in Malabar, the British had conferred ownership rights on those at the top of the tenurial hierarchy, i.e. on the relatively small number of landlords (*janmis*), the Travancore government, by its 1865 proclamation, had conferred these rights on those in second place in the hierarchy, i.e. on the relatively large number of tenants (*kanamdars*) of the state. Further, the Travancore government had prevented the few private landlords who did exist from evicting their tenants — the opposite of Malabar's policy. (Cochin's policy was more like Malabar's than Travancore's — at least in effect, if not always in intention.)

I ought to point out that very few members of the low castes owned land anywhere in Kerala, despite these differences in land policy and the fact that the ownership of land was less inequitable in Travancore than in Malabar. The members of the lowest, Untouchable castes were, in fact, slaves until slavery was abolished — in Malabar in 1843, in Cochin in 1854 and in Travancore in 1855. But it is quite evident that even in 1900, most of the former slaves were still tied to their landowners in the old pattern.

Land, of course, was the most important form of wealth in Kerala by far — as indeed it still is, though to a lesser extent. The regional differences in land policy thus had significant effects on the way in which economic and political developments occurred in the late nineteenth and twentieth centuries. There is no space to go into this in any detail; briefly, the important fact is that capitalist development in Travancore was more rapid and far-reaching than in Malabar. This development was spearheaded by neither the Nayars nor the Brahmans, but by the middle-ranking communities — mainly the Syrian Christians in Central Travancore and Cochin; the Izhavas in some areas, especially Quilon in southern Travancore; and the Muslims, particularly in Malabar. The rising prosperity of these communities was perceived as a threat by many members of the higher, landowning castes, particularly the Nayars, and the threat was especially critical in Central Travancore, where the Syrian Christians had a leading role in what was the fastest economic development in Kerala. To cut a long story short — it is treated in more detail in the final chapter — the Nayars in Travancore, particularly in Central Travancore, began to argue that the patrilineal, nuclear-family organisation of the Syrians was a significant factor in their success, and that Nayars must therefore change their own matrilineal, joint-family system. An intensive campaign by Nayar leaders, which gathered strength after the formation of the Nayar Service Society (the Nayars' caste association) in Changanacherry, Central Travancore in 1914, finally brought about legislation permitting the break-up of Nayar joint families in Travancore. By this time, however, a large proportion of the families had already split. In Malabar and Cochin, the Nayars did not feel threatened, as they did in Travancore, and although legislation to permit partition of Nayar joint families was passed in the 1930s, the disintegration of the matrilineal, joint-family system took considerably longer there than it did in Travancore.

The Travancore Nayars were not only worried by the middle-ranking communities below them; they also perceived a threat to their progress in the shape of the Tamil Brahmans above them. Ever since Martanda Varma's establishment of a bureaucracy, Tamil Brahmans had maintained a virtual monopoly on the Government service, and the Nayars of the late nineteenth century considered it essential for their community's well-being that they be employed in large numbers in the service. Eventually, the Tamil Brahman monopoly was broken. Nayars were very successful in this sector and still are; today, even though the government has positively discriminated in favour of the lower castes since 1947, Nayars have about twice as many posts in the government service as would be expected on the basis of their proportion in the total population.[3]

The competition between the Nayars and the other Travancore communities in the late nineteenth century was one of the first important examples of communal politics in Kerala, although the sometimes bloody antagonisms between the Muslims and the Hindus in Malabar are part of the same political phenomenon. It is a mistake, however, to think that Kerala's politics can be explained solely in terms of inter-caste conflict. The political parties are not simply caste-based interest groups. Congress politics began in Malabar in the 1920s, as part of the all-India campaign against the British Raj. Travancore and Cochin, although not under British rule, could not remain immune to the reform movement led by Gandhi and the Congress, one of whose main aims was to break down the discrimination against the lower castes. In 1924, a campaign began in Vaikom, a town in Central Travancore, to open the roads around the great Siva temple, which were closed to the low castes. It lasted over a year, and Gandhi joined the demonstrators. Another similar campaign took place at the Guruvayur temple in South Malabar in 1931. These campaigns, it should be understood, were not merely religious affairs but attacks on the operation of the caste system itself, which in turn has significant political connotations. Changes in the caste system are better treated, however, in their context, and I shall discuss them later in this chapter.

During the 1920s and 1930s, many of the Congress leaders in Malabar – and their associates in Travancore and Cochin – became steadily more and more disenchanted with Gandhi's policies. The very serious effects of the Depression on Kerala, a country heavily dependent on the export of

The Nayars Today

primary products, hastened the radicalisation of these Congressmen, and in 1937 the Kerala Communist Party was clandestinely formed. During the same period, an intensive campaign against the autocratic nature of the Travancore government was pursued, although in 1938 a civil disobedience movement to demand universal suffrage was called off on Gandhi's urging. Political agitation in Travancore then subsided until after the war.

In 1947, Malabar became part of Independent India. Cochin acceded to the Indian Union at the same time, and Travancore followed suit one month later. The state of Kerala was formed in 1957; it comprised Malabar District, plus the Malayalam-speaking taluks (subdivisions of a District) of South Kanara, and Travancore-Cochin, minus the Tamil-speaking taluks in the extreme south. The Communists, whose strength still lay mainly in Malabar, came to power in the first elections held after the formation of the new state. Their government lasted just over two years, until it was brought down by a protest movement led by the Nayar Service Society and the Christian churches. They objected to the government's proposals to introduce radical land reforms and to take over the private schools run by the churches and the caste associations. The power of the N.S.S., most clearly demonstrated in 1959, has been a permanent feature of post-1947 politics in Kerala, but it would be erroneous to equate the N.S.S. with the Nayar caste as such. Although it tries to articulate politically the interests of the Nayars, it lacks strong support throughout Kerala - most of its strength is still in Central Travancore - and many Nayars are opposed to its policies. This is scarcely an adequate account of the role of the N.S.S. - on any count an important one - but all I wish to do here is point out that it cannot be regarded as the Nayar caste in its politically-organised incarnation.[4] Since 1959, Kerala has mostly been ruled by unstable Congress-led coalitions, alternating with periods of direct rule from New Delhi, although the present government (1975) - an alliance of the Congress, the right wing of the Communist Party (which split in 1964), the Muslim League and various other, small parties - has now been in power for more than four years.

Before leaving this severely truncated account of the exceptionally complex politics of Kerala, it is worth mentioning Krishna Menon, almost certainly the most famous of all Nayars, although he did in fact spend little of his life in Kerala. Vengalil Krishnan Krishna Menon was born in Calicut in 1896. His parents, interestingly, were one of the first couples to break the traditional interdiction on marriages between Nayars from North and South Malabar (George 1964: 14-19). Sixty-one years later, after being, amongst other things, an editor of Pelican Books and India's first High Commissioner in London, he became India's Minister of Defence, Nehru's closest ministerial confidant and, it was popularly said, 'the second most powerful man in India'. He was also regarded by some as a 'crypto-Communist' and 'the evil genius of Independent India'. In 1962, after the debacle of the war with China, he was forced to resign his office. In October 1974, he died - forgotten, I suppose, by most non-Indians. Let

Table 1. *Average monthly rainfall in Kottayam District*

	(mm)	(in.)
January	31.2	1.2
February	27.0	1.1
March	59.5	2.3
April	133.1	5.2
May	237.4	9.3
June	585.8	23.0
July	628.0	24.7
August	412.4	16.2
September	263.5	10.4
October	330.8	13.0
November	213.6	8.4
December	72.2	2.8
Total	2994.5	117.9

Source: G.O.K. 1972: 5.

no-one say, however, that the Nayars are mere curiosities in the anthropological catalogue.

Geographical and demographic background

Geographically, Kerala divides into three zones: highland, midland and lowland. Ramankara lies in the midland zone (elevation approximately 25 ft to 250 ft; 8 m to 75 m) and the red laterite soil is generally fertile. The economy of Central Travancore, like that of the rest of Kerala, is still predominantly agricultural, and the principal crops cultivated in the Ramankara region are coconut, rubber and tapioca. These are all grown on dry (or garden) land, which accounts for around 95% of the land in Ramankara. On the small amount of wet land, paddy is cultivated – two crops a year is usual. Dry land is watered only by rainfall, nearly all of which falls during the two monsoons: the south-west monsoon, which brings most of the rain, between June and August and the north-east monsoon in October and November. Table 1 shows the average annual rainfall by month in Kottayam District, in which Ramankara is situated.

The monsoon is sometimes up to a month late and occasionally even more, but it never fails altogether in Kerala. Although poverty and malnutrition are widespread in the state, this means that devastating drought – bringing in its wake serious food shortages or famine – never strikes as it still does in many other parts of India.

The poverty of Kerala's people, given its predominantly agricultural economy, is mainly attributable to the excessive population in relation to the available land. Table 2 shows population growth rates for Kerala,

The Nayars Today

Table 2. *Population growth in Kerala, Travancore, Kottayam District and India*

Year	Kerala Pop. (m.)	Kerala % decennial incr.	Travancore Pop. (m.)	Travancore % decennial incr.	Kottayam District Pop. (m.)	Kottayam District % decennial incr.	India % decennial incr.
1836	2.64	—	1.28	—	—	—	—
1854	—	—	1.26	—	—	—	—
1875	5.06	—	2.31	—	—	—	—
1881	5.22	—	2.40	—	—	—	—
1891	5.82	11.49	2.56	6.67	—	—	—
1901	6.40	9.97	2.95	15.23	0.47	—	—
1911	7.15	11.72	3.43	16.27	0.56	19.15	5.75
1921	7.80	9.09	4.00	16.62	0.65	16.07	− 0.31
1931	9.51	21.92	5.10	27.50	0.89	36.92	11.00
1941	11.03	15.98	6.07	19.02	1.08	21.35	14.22
1951	13.55	22.85	—	—	1.32	22.22	13.31
1961	16.90	24.72	—	—	1.73	31.06	21.51
1971	21.35	26.33	—	—	2.09	20.81	24.78

Sources: Kerala and India: Turlach 1970: 23 and Census 1971a: 1, 3. Travancore: Aiya (1906: II, 1), who states that the 1836 and 1854 figures must be regarded as unreliable; Census 1911, Travancore: 24; Census 1921, Travancore: 3; Census 1931, Travancore: I, 6; Census 1941, Travancore: 10; Kottayan: Census 1971b: 56.

Travancore (until 1941) and Kottayam District (taking account of boundary changes).

The table shows that in every decade, Kerala's percentage population increase has exceeded that for India as a whole. Between 1901 and 1941, the number of persons living in the land revenue unit (used as the unit in censuses) in which Ramankara lies rose from 6588 to 21275, and by 1961 it had reached 28684 - a rise of about 335% compared with 164% in the state over the same period. The population growth rate was exceptionally high in the 1920s and 1930s; during this period, the population of Changanacherry taluk, which contains Ramankara, almost doubled, mainly owing to the prosperity brought by the boom in rubber prices, at least until the Depression (Census, 1941, Travancore: 18).

But it is the density of population which is truly astounding. In 1971, the density of population in Kerala as a whole was 549 persons per sq. km (approx. 1405 per sq. mile). In the lowland zone along the coast, it was no less than 1385 per sq. km (approx. 3540 per sq. mile) and in the midland zone 778 per sq. km (approx. 1990 per sq. mile). In the midland zone of Changanacherry taluk, the density in the rural area was 875 per sq. km (approx. 2240 per sq. mile) (Census 1971b: 36-7). One way of putting these figures into some kind of perspective is just to glance at a conventional atlas, in which all areas with a population density exceeding the comparatively puny figure of 200 persons per sq. km (512 per sq. mile) are shaded red. Areas with densities higher than this are not differentiated in such atlases, but in any case very little of the world is tinted red. The Kerala population density figure, alternatively read, means that in 1971 the per capita area of land in the state was about 0.46 acres. In 1961, it was 0.57 acres (Census 1961: 81) but only about 0.40 acres in the Ramankara land revenue unit. The implications of these figures are worsened when we discover that in 1969-70, only 2.1% of all the land in Kerala was classified as cultivable waste (G.O.K. 1972: 9). There is significantly less waste land in Travancore than in Malabar and Cochin, and in the Ramankara land revenue unit, even in 1908, only 0.01% of the land was cultivable waste. The pressure of population on the land has worried all those concerned with Kerala and more than a century ago, when Travancore's population was only a fifth of what it would be today, the Dewan (Prime Minister), Mahdeva Rao, warned of the serious problems attendant on its rapid growth (G.O.T. 1869: 120).

Introduction to the village of Ramankara

The settlement pattern in almost all of Kerala is dispersed; the houses are scattered across the countryside more or less haphazardly, rather than arranged in streets and clustered together in nucleated villages, as is the case in most of the rest of India. It is not easy, for one lacking the novelist's skill, to portray accurately the appearance of the Kerala countryside. The overwhelming impression is one of dense greenness. Paddy fields and tapioca plots apart, the land is almost entirely covered in trees, especially coconut palms. The palms stay green throughout the year and rubber trees only lose their leaves for a couple of months in the cool season. The land in the midland zone is gently undulating; this means that except from a few high points, the typical view embraces very little but trees, with probably only a couple of houses visible. Houses are often hidden in quite inaccessible places and no-one without local knowledge could locate quickly all the houses in any given area. The contrast between Kerala and the rest of India is dramatic - especially with the neighbouring state of Tamilnadu, as seen from a train or aeroplane bound for Madras, where houses are mostly huddled together in compact villages set in the midst of an apparently endless brownish plain dotted with a handful of palm trees. It is of course an illusion, but one easily understands why Malayalis sometimes claim that the rest of India is a desert in comparison with their own land.

In much of Kerala, including the Ramankara region, a well sunk twenty feet or so through the soil is likely to provide enough water for a household's domestic and agricultural needs throughout the year. The ready availability of water, although it can hardly be accounted the cause of

The Nayars Today

1. A group of people, made up primarily of Nayars, in Ramankara.

2. A typical lane in the village of Ramankara.

Introduction to the Nayars

the dispersed settlement pattern, is almost certainly the most important single factor promoting it (Janaki 1953: 45). The dispersed pattern means that there are no visible boundaries between villages (*karas*). Indeed, in the Ramankara region at least, if by 'boundary' is meant a line which can be drawn on the ground or a map, there are no boundaries between villages; all that exists is a sort of rather vague boundary zone separating them (cf. Miller 1954: 411). The structural definition of the villages is a complex question which is irrelevant here and I shall not discuss it in any detail.[5] Given that Ramankara, like other neighbouring villages, has no definite boundaries - nor is it an administrative unit - it is impossible to state its precise size or population. However, its approximate area is three square miles and it contains about 650 houses, which means that its population numbers around 4000.

A brief description of the houses might be desirable here. Those of perhaps half the people - the better-off half - are built of local bricks, i.e. blocks of dried red laterite. The houses of the other half are constructed from mud and thatch. The size and type vary enormously and are primarily a function of wealth. Those of the poorest people are one-roomed huts with a mud floor, sides of mud or thatch and a thatched roof. (The thatch is made of plaited palm leaf.) The occupants will own a few cooking utensils, mats for sleeping on and perhaps one bed, and maybe a bench or chair. A kerosene lamp or two will provide them with light, and an odd religious print or calendar the only decoration. The houses of the better-off have walls of brick and roofs of thatch or tiles, and vary in size from two small rooms up to perhaps six rooms with a verandah and outhouses. The wealthy live in spacious buildings which, if old, are often decorated at the front with elaborate wood-carving. Houses are not distinguishable by the caste of their occupants, although most Hindu homes have a brass lamp which is lit at sunset, set on the verandah or in front of the granary (usually located in the centre of the house). Scenes from Hindu epics and portraits of the most popular gods - together with those of Indian patriots such as Gandhi and Nehru - hang on the walls of most Hindu houses. Calendars, for some reason, are very popular in Kerala and almost every house has several. All houses, including those of the poorest, are kept scrupulously clean. Except for those of the very poor, every house has its own well, but only the rich and modern-minded have bathrooms and lavatories. For the majority, the ground behind the house and water from the well provide the necessary facilities and the thick trees provide adequate privacy.

Ramankara is about eight miles from Changanacherry, an important market town in Central Travancore, with a population (1971) of 48 545 (Census 1971a: 95). Along the main road from the town, which passes through the south of the village, around one hundred buses run each way every day - an indication of just how far Ramankara is from being an 'isolated village community' in 'traditional' India. Another main road, with a less frequent bus service, links the village to Kottayam, also a market town and the administrative centre of the district. Its population

The Nayars Today

(1971) was 59 714 (ibid.: 95). Like most villages in the region, Ramankara has an electricity supply, and there are a few telephones in the village. Newspapers and mail are delivered to houses daily, and several small shops in and around Ramankara sell most commodities in daily demand. Newspapers are read avidly by all Malayalis and the people of Ramankara are no exception. Official figures give the literacy rate, on the total population, for the Ramankara land revenue unit as 65.2% in 1961 (G.O.K. 1966: A, 54). Even within Kerala, the most literate state in India, this is a high figure and contrasts strikingly with the all-India figure for 1961 of 28.3%.

Caste and landownership in Ramankara

On the basis of the local council's list, I estimate that about 35% of the 650-odd households in Ramankara are Nayar. Nayars form the largest single community in the village; other sizeable communities are the Syrian Christians, the Izhavas, the Parayas and the New Christians, i.e. Christian converts from the low castes. About ten other castes are represented in the village by a few households. I am unable to present precise figures because I did not carry out a census survey of all of Ramankara, but only of a sample of 209 households.[6] The caste-wise breakdown of these is given in table 3.

In order to avoid a lengthy digression into the concept of 'dominant castes' in rural India, I hope the reader will accept that control over the land is the most crucial factor. Srinivas (1955: 18) introduced the concept of 'dominant caste'; since then, he and others have extended his original discussion. Briefly, the dominant caste in an area is the caste whose members have preponderant economic and political power. In Central Travancore, Nayars and Syrian Christians own most of the land and are thus the dominant communities. In Ramankara, the position belongs to the Nayars alone. There are no up-to-date figures showing landownership by caste, except for the households covered by my sample census. But it is worth quoting figures calculated from the report of Travancore's only land settlement, carried out in the Ramankara land revenue unit in 1908.[7] Table 4 shows the areas owned by the different communities at that time and indicates plainly the virtual landowning monopoly enjoyed then by the Nayars and Syrians, although since that time, the Nayars have certainly lost a considerable part of their lands.[8]

In table 5 is shown the distribution of landowning by caste for the households in my sample census of Ramankara. It, together with table 6, indicates that the Nayars, in this sample, own twice as much land as their proportion in the population would suggest and thus the overwhelming majority of the land in the village.

Table 7 displays the distribution of landownership by amount of land owned – something over half the land being owned by less than one tenth of the households and 43% being owned by only seven households, all of them Nayar. Because the distribution is so skewed, the picture presented

Table 3. *Ramankara sample census: household by caste*

Caste	No. of h'holds	% of total	No. of persons	% of total	Mean no. per h'hold
Nayar	91	43.5	511	41.5	5.6
Izhava	37	17.7	234	19.0	6.3
Syr. Christian	27	12.9	182	14.8	6.7
Paraya/Sambavar	22	10.5	110	8.9	5.5
New Christian	12	5.7	57	4.6	4.7
Ashari	4	1.9	43	3.5	9.3
Vilakkittala N.	4	1.9	21	1.7	4.3
Thandan	3	1.4	22	1.8	7.3
Ulladan	3	1.4	18	1.5	6.0
Kallan-Ashari	2	1.0	8	0.6	4.0
Kollan-Ashari	1	0.5	12	1.0	12.0
Vannan	1	0.5	8	0.6	8.0
Kannadiyan*	1	0.5	4	0.3	4.0
Pulaya	1	0.5	2	0.2	2.0
All castes	209		1232		5.9

* In this household, the husband is a Kannadiyan and the wife a Pulaya.

Table 4. *Ramankara land revenue unit, 1908: landownership by caste*

Caste, etc.	Area (acres)	Area (% of total)
Brahman	644.58	5.8
Ambalavasi	1.44	0.1
Nayar – Illam subcaste	3 556.25	31.8
Nayar – Itasseri subcaste	2 924.48	26.2
Syrian Christian	3 112.86	27.8
Muslim	18.99	0.2
Artisan castes	61.13	0.5
Izhava	125.79	1.1
New Christian	86.88	0.8
Kangazha landowner (Nayar)*	560.32	5.0
Government	80.44	0.7
Kottayam C.M.S.†	11.84	0.1
All castes, etc.	11 185.00	100.0

* This landowner lived outside the revenue unit.

† Kottayam Church Missionary Society – land on which New Christian C.M.S. converts settled.

The Nayars Today

Table. 5 *Ramankara sample census: landowning by caste, household table*

	Area of land owned								
		Cents‡		Acres					
Caste	0	1–50	51–100	1.01–2.50	2.51–5.00	5.01–10.00	10.01–15.00	15.00	Total
Nayar*	2	17	10†	13	19	13	9	7	90
Izhava	6	16	7	7	1	—	—	—	37
Syrian Christian	6	6	3	5	3	2	2	—	27
Paraya/Sambavar	4	17†	—	1	—	—	—	—	22
New Christian	6	6	—	—	—	—	—	—	12
Ashari	2	2	—	—	—	—	—	—	4
Vilakkittala Nayar	1	2	1	—	—	—	—	—	4
Thandan	3	—	—	—	—	—	—	—	3
Ulladan	2	1	—	—	—	—	—	—	3
Kallan-Ashari	2	—	—	—	—	—	—	—	2
Kollan-Ashari	—	1	—	—	—	—	—	—	1
Vannan	1	—	—	—	—	—	—	—	1
Kannadiyan	1	—	—	—	—	—	—	—	1
Pulaya	—	1	—	—	—	—	—	—	1
All castes	36	69	21	26	23	15	11	7	208

* One household's landowning is unknown and excluded.
† Includes one household holding land on *otti* tenure.
‡ One hundred cents = one acre.

Table 6. *Ramankara sample census: landowning by caste*

	Households in sample		Land owned	
Caste	No.	%	Acres	%
Nayars	90	43.3	566	86.4
Syrian Christians	27	12.9	56	8.5
Izhavas	37	17.8	24	3.7
Others	54	26.0	9	1.4
All	208	100.0	655	100.0

Table 7. *Ramankara sample census: cumulative table of landownership*

Owning up to (acres)	Households		Area of land	
	No.	%	Acres	%
0	36	17.3	0	0
0.5	105	50.5	16	2.4
1.0	126	60.6	34	5.2
2.5	152	73.1	79	12.1
5.0	175	84.2	169	25.8
10.0	190	91.3	271	41.4
15.0	201	96.6	374	57.1
over 15.0	208	100.0	655	100.0

in table 7 is markedly dependent on the figures for the wealthiest households; as these are subject to error, the table must be treated with caution. I am unsure, too, whether my sample census is typical of Ramankara as a whole in this respect. Official figures concerning landownership are notoriously inaccurate and are, in any case, not broken down by caste. Comparative data are thus unavailable from this source. Although, as we have seen, nearly all households with large landownings are Nayar, I must also point out that the majority of Nayar households are not wealthy and nearly half of them own less than 2½ acres. The income generated by an acre of land is highly variable, but generally it falls within the range Rs 500-1000 (£25-50) per annum (1971-2).

In fact, most Nayar households in the sample census – 53 of the 90 (59%) – do not depend solely on their land, but have members employed in various occupations. These range from doctors and lawyers, through school teachers, clerks and military personnel, to shopkeepers, artisans, manual workers on the railways, roads, etc., rubber-tappers and agricultural labourers. But few fall into the last category and the only three households with members engaged in labouring jobs all own less than half an acre of land. At the other end of the scale, there are twelve households with members having higher professional occupations; of these, nine own more than five acres and seven more than ten acres. (By 'higher professional occupations', I mean doctors, lawyers, college lecturers, gazetted officers in the government service, factory managers, etc.)[9] Most other jobs are taken by members of households from all categories of landowning. The reason why higher professional jobs are mainly restricted to those from wealthier households is quite simple: these jobs demand higher educational qualifications and only the fairly well-to-do can afford to send their children to colleges. Only primary schooling is free in Kerala; for this reason, many poorer children never finish secondary education and even fewer finish higher education. Education is regarded by nearly all Malayalis as the only real

The Nayars Today

escape route from poverty, and by the better-off it is also considered to be the only exit from the agricultural economy, from which escape has become an urgent necessity during the last twenty years as a consequence of land reform policies, which have fixed a maximum area of landowning for the household.[10] For those with large landownings, the reforms have destroyed the traditional notion that land is the best security and agriculture the most prestigious occupation. A good job now takes the place that land once held.

Landowners and labourers

We have seen that very few Nayars in Ramankara are labourers, most of whom belong, as in almost all of Kerala, to the Harijan or other low-ranking castes. Most labourers are landless or own only tiny plots; few Nayars are in this situation. Nayars, however, also loathe working on even their own land if they can afford not to; this disinclination to 'get their hands dirty' is something to which they readily admit. It is certainly the case that, other things being equal, Nayars work less on their farms than do, for example, Syrian Christians. Broadly speaking, male members of a Nayar household owning more than six or seven acres will not normally work on their land, whereas those owning less than this will have to out of necessity. Only in very poor households, where the men go out to work, will Nayar women labour on the land.

A full analysis of the relationship between landowners and labourers and its wider connotations, in terms of the rural class structure, is not feasible here.[11] A brief summary, though, is probably desirable. But first I should state that there is no *jajmani* system in Central Travancore villages today. (The *jajmani* system is the traditional economic system of the Indian village, in which households are linked to each other by hereditary ties of exchange. Services, e.g. carpentry, are exchanged for other services, e.g. barbering, and/or for payment in kind. Amounts of payment are fixed by custom, not contractually.) Given the pattern of agriculture, especially the importance of cash crops, it is possible that a system of a more contractual type, such as that reported by Harper (1959) for Malanad (Mysore) may have obtained in this area too. Artisan and service castes have been paid piecework rates in cash for at least the last twenty years and maybe longer, and they no longer have any ritual obligations to the higher castes.

Labourers, too, are paid in cash, except for paddy harvesting and, sometimes, tapioca harvesting, when they are paid a fixed proportion of the harvest. Cash wages are fixed for a day's work. (In 1971-2, male labourers were paid about Rs 5 (25p) per day, female labourers about Rs 3.50 (17p). In 1975, the rates had risen to Rs 7 (35p) for men – and Rs 5 (25p) for women.) Households owning more than around seven acres – in the case of Nayars – normally have their land entirely worked by hired labour; those owning less employ labourers only when there is too much work to be carried out by household members alone. These latter, smallholding households do, of course, make up the overwhelming bulk of the landowning households in the sample, as they do in the village as a whole. Only about one tenth of all households are large landowners, and they provide employ-

Introduction to the Nayars

ment for most of those who need it. These few large landowners therefore have, for obvious reasons, considerable power over the labourers. They can almost literally deprive the latter of their means of subsistence, and until quite recently — when land reform legislation put a stop to it — a landless labourer could also lose his home if his landlord chose to evict him from his land. The landowners' power appears quite nakedly in the case of casual labourers, who find work wherever they can; between them and their employers, relations are governed almost entirely by the cash nexus, and mutual dislike and distrust is often apparent. Between a landowner and one who works for him regularly, the relationship is a little different; the landowner in this case usually has an attitude of paternalistic responsibility, exemplified by his payment of bills for medical treatment incurred by the labourer or his family, or by the gifts presented when there is a marriage or funeral in the labourer's family. In general, though, antagonism between landowners and labourers is on the increase in Kerala, and Ramankara is unlikely to remain immune; strikes have already taken place in neighbouring villages within the last few years.

Smallholders do not work for the large landowners and only occasionally employ labour. As a function of their position in the agrarian system, they neither dominate others nor are subject to others. This means that in the power structure of the village, to the extent that this is a function of landownership, the majority of the population is actually independent of this structure, which has some important political implications. To mention just one of these, the manner in which the smallholders react in a situation of conflict between large landowners and labourers can materially affect the outcome. Because, as is certainly true in Ramankara and probably more widely, the smallholders, like the large landowners, tend to belong to the higher castes, they are on the whole likely to support the latter against the labourers, who are mostly low-caste. Although caste is not the only consideration, it is still, perhaps, the most critical one in such situations and what is, in essence, a class-based conflict can easily become one centring on caste as well.

The Castes in Kerala

Various aspects of the Kerala caste system have already been touched upon; however, I have not yet presented a straightforward account of it. To do this is not easy, for there is a problem of levels — ranging from all Kerala at one extreme down to individual villages, such as Ramankara, at the other. Despite the inherent dangers of over-simplification, it may be most helpful to begin at the widest level and list all the principal Kerala castes in order of status. The order below is that given in the majority of older works (e.g. Logan 1887; Aiya 1906: II; Iyer 1909, 1912), but it is worth stressing that it is not enshrined in any legal or religious code, nor is it immutable. There may be, and often are, disputes as to the relative status of various castes. With these reservations, I present the following list in order of decreasing status:

The Nayars Today

Nambudiri Brahmans
Other Brahmans
Kshatriyas
Samantans
Ambalavasis
NAYARS
Vilakkittala Nayars, Veluthedathu Nayars
Kammalas – including Asharis, Thattans, etc.
Izhavas – also called Tiyyans, Thandans and Chovans
Kaniyans or Kanisans
Mukkuvans and Arayans
Pulayas or Cherumans
Parayas
Tribal peoples

I have already mentioned the tiny, exclusive caste of Nambudiri Brahmans several times, and I shall return to them again in discussing their role in the Nayar marriage system. Like many other castes, the Nambudiris are divided into a number of mutually-ranked subdivisions, but these need no discussion here. (Modern data on the Nambudiris may be found in Mencher 1966b; Mencher and Goldberg 1967.) The category ' Other Brahmans' includes non-Nambudiri Malayali Brahmans, ranked below the Nambudiris, and also 'foreign' Brahmans, those of predominantly Tamil or Konkani origin. The Kshatriyas and Samantans are both minute castes and their membership is practically confined to those belonging to the various royal and chiefly lineages. Despite their pretensions, they are, in my opinion, best regarded as super-eminent Nayars, and we shall meet them again in discussing Nayar marriage. The name ' Ambalavasi' is applied to the grouping made up of several distinct castes, each with its traditional duty in the temple, such as the Pushpakans – who bring flowers to the temples – and the Marans – who act as temple musicians and sweepers. All Brahmans, with the exception of one or two localised communities, and some Ambalavasi castes are patrilineal. Kshatriyas, Samantans and the remaining Ambalavasi castes are matrilineal. In certain areas and in certain periods, male members of the above castes have all had sexual access to Nayar women. The Vilakkittala and Veluthedathu Nayars, barbers and washermen respectively to the upper castes, each have the same status, but are not usually considered as ' genuine' Nayars. They are both matrilineal and endogamous.

Like Ambalavasi, the name ' Kammala' is applied to a grouping of several castes. These are the artisan castes: Ashari (carpenter), Kallan (stone-carver), Kollan (blacksmith), Mushari (brass- and coppersmith) and Thattan (goldsmith). These five group themselves together and may intermarry; nowadays, they sometimes call themselves Visvakarma Brahmans and claim Brahman status (cf. Kramrisch 1959). This claim appears to have originated in the Tamil country around the beginning of the century; the

Introduction to the Nayars

Malayali artisans began to emulate their Tamil fellows a decade or two later (Aiya 1906: II, 389-91; Pillai 1940: I, 829). There are also several other artisan castes such as, to confuse matters further, the Kammalas, who are stonemasons. In modern Central Travancore, at least, all the artisan castes regard themselves as having equal status. In the past, they were treated as polluting castes (*tintal jati*); in Cochin the Brahmans, for example, were polluted if they approached within 24 feet of the Kammalas.[12] By no means all of the members of these castes practise their traditional occupation; on the other hand, it is true that virtually every carpenter, for instance, is a member of the Ashari caste. These castes are all patrilineal.

The Izhavas form the largest single caste in Kerala. They are also known as Chovans in South Cochin and North Travancore, Thandans in South Malabar and North Cochin, and Tiyyans in North Malabar. The Tiyyans and the Travancore Izhavas are mainly matrilineal; the rest are mainly patrilineal (Aiyappan 1944: 16). The Izhavas' traditional occupation is toddy-tapping, but it is literally incredible that a fifth of the population of Kerala can all have ever been engaged in alcohol production. In fact, most of them have probably always been, as they still are, small farmers and agricultural labourers. The economic and political power of the caste has grown considerably during this century, and nowadays many Izhavas dispute their traditional rank below the Kammalas and claim a status second only to the Nayars. (The Izhavas have been described extensively by Aiyappan (1944; 1965).) At about the same place in the caste hierarchy - like the Kammalas and the Izhavas, they formerly polluted Brahmans at a distance of 24 feet - come the Kaniyans or Kanisans, whose traditional occupation is astrology, though again the majority is probably engaged in agriculture.

Ranked below these latter castes are the Mukkuvans and the Arayans, most of whom still work in their traditional occupation of fishing. (They feature prominently in Klausen's (1968) ethnography of a southern Travancore fishing village.) They could pollute a Brahman in Cochin at a distance of 32 feet. At the bottom of the hierarchy, there are two major Harijan castes: the Pulayas (Travancore or Cochin) or Cherumans (Malabar), and the Parayas, who today prefer to be called Sambavars. The Pulayas traditionally rank slightly above the Parayas and, in Cochin, polluted Brahmans at 64 feet, whereas the distance for Parayas was 72 feet. Older authorities, however, usually mention the endemic disputes between Pulayas and Parayas - and other very low castes - as to relative status; it was normal for these castes mutually to refuse to accept food from each other. (See e.g. Iyer 1909: passim.) In my own experience, though, such disputes are infrequent today and members of the Harijan castes evince little interest in questions of relative status. Until the mid-nineteenth century, most Pulayas and Parayas were slaves; today, most of them are still landless labourers. All the lower castes are patrilineal. Still lower than the Parayas in the hierarchy, are the tribal peoples who have been steadily incorporated into the caste system over the centuries, although they still remain partially independent of it.

The Nayars Today

As well as the non-Malayali Brahmans, there are a number of communities of Tamil origin in Kerala; the main ones are the Vellalas, the Chettis and the Nadars (Shanans). The former two are ranked somewhere below the Nayars but above the Izhavas; the latter has a rank approximately equal to that of the Izhavas.[13]

Two sizeable non-Hindu communities exist in Kerala: the Christians who are mainly concentrated in Travancore and Cochin, and the Muslims who are mostly to be found in Malabar. Both communities are internally divided into several distinct groups, ranked according to various criteria — particularly the caste of the original converts. Much of my own experience in Kerala was with Christians in Central Travancore; they are divided into Syrian, Latin and New Christians. The Syrians claim descent from Nambudiri Brahmans converted by St Thomas the Apostle in A.D. 52 and are ranked just below the Nayars. The possibility that St Thomas visited Kerala cannot be entirely ruled out, although it has to be admitted that there is no certain evidence one way or the other. It is, however, indisputable that there were Christians in Kerala by the sixth century at the latest. Some Syrian Christian legends do claim an origin in Syria itself, but this is dubious. More certain is the link with the Antiochene church of Syria, demonstrated by the use of Syriac as the liturgical language — the reason, of course, for their name. Nowadays, the majority of Syrians belongs to the Church of Rome, although they continued to use Syriac until the church adopted the vernacular. The rest are communicants of various independent and semi-independent sects, some with links to Eastern Christian churches. The Latin Christians, nearly all Catholics with the Latin rite, are for the most part the descendants of members of the fisher castes converted by St Francis Xavier in the sixteenth century. The New Christians are descended from members of low castes — mainly Izhavas, Pulayas and Parayas — converted by missionaries in the nineteenth and early twentieth centuries. Many New Christians belong to Protestant churches, though there are New Christian Catholics as well. Latin Christians have a rank more or less equal to other fisher castes; New Christians are of similar status to other low castes, although some sources state that converts to Christianity were exempt from some of the more rigorous aspects of the pollution system as it was applied to the Hindu low castes. The relation of the Christian community to the Hindu caste system is complex, but as it is irrelevant to the subject matter of this book, I shall omit any discussion of it. From the available literature, it is plain that the position of the Muslims in the caste system is equally problematic, but it too may be ignored here. I have no first-hand knowledge of the Malabar Muslims and think it unwise to attempt a brief discussion of them on the basis of the not wholly consistent data which exist.[14]

Table 8 shows the populations of the main castes and the proportions of the total population which they represent, for Travancore, Cochin and Malabar in 1931 and for Kerala in 1968. I decided to use the 1931 Census material as no data on caste are available for Malabar in 1941, although they are for Travancore and Cochin. The information available on Malabar,

Table 8. *Caste populations (main castes only)*

Caste	1931 Travancore No.	%	1931 Cochin No.	%	1931 Malabar No.	%	1931 Travancore + Cochin + Malabar No.	%	1968 Kerala Caste grouping	No.	%
1. Brahman	68072	1.3	41324	3.4	60612	1.7	170008	1.7	1. Brahmans, Ambalavasis, etc.	353329	1.8
i. Malayali	16774	0.3	7163	0.6	26333[b]	0.7	50240[h]	0.5			
i. Nambudiri	8481	0.15	5918	0.5	—	[e]	—	[e]			
ii. Non-Malayali	51298	0.8	34161	2.8	36289[c]	1.0	121748[h]	1.2			
2. Kshatriya	3673	0.07	2128	0.2	—	—[a]	5901	0.06[kj]	2. Nayars, Samantans, etc.	2905775	14.5
3. Samantan	97	—[a]	571	0.05	—	0.15[f]	—	0.05[k]	3. Vilakkittala N, Veluthedathu N etc.	435396	2.2
4. Ambalavasi	8155	0.15	9211	0.8	—	0.5[f]	—	0.4[k]			
5. Nayar	868411	17.1	142637	11.8	494882	14.0	1505929	15.3	4. Asharis (Kammalas)	756178	3.8
6. Vilakkittala N.	30603	0.6	3699	0.3	—	—[a]	35199[h]	0.4	5. Vellalas, Chettis, etc.	151150	0.8
7. Veluthedathu N.	14878	0.3	3922	0.3	897[b]	0.1	22219[h]	0.2			
8. Kammala	209068	4.1	45546	3.8	3419[b]	0.4[g]	—	2.7[k]	6. Izhavas, etc.	4457808	22.2
9. Vellala	70705	1.4	5299	0.4	—	0.4[g]	—	0.9[k]	7. Kaniyan, Arayan Mukkuvan, etc.	851603	4.2
10. Chetti	17422	0.3	5339	0.4	—	0.9[g]	—	0.5[k]			
11. Izhava + Tiyyan	872174	17.1	276649	22.9	—	24.6[g]	—	20.4[k]	8. Scheduled castes (Parayas, Pulayas, etc.)	1578115	7.9
12. Kaniyan/Kanisan	15652	0.3	3841	0.3	—	0.5[f]	—	0.4[k]			
13. Mukkuvan + Arayan	58135	1.1	6574	0.5	—	0.7[f]	—	0.9[k]			
14. Paraya	142364	2.8	11562	1.0	11730	0.3	165656	1.7	9. Ezhuthacchan, Maravan, etc.	260042	1.3
15. Pulaya + Cheruman	365150	7.4	82043	6.8	231194[d]	6.5	678387[h]	6.9			
16. Kuravan	95295	1.9	—	—	—	—[a]	95295	1.0[j]	10. Syrian Christian, Anglo-Indian, etc.	3214278	16.0
17. Thandan	41214	0.8	—	—	—	—[a]	41214	0.4[j]	11. Latin Catholics	731207	3.6
18. Nadar (Shanan)	402555	7.9	—	—	65894	1.9	402555	4.1[j]			
19. Christian*	1604475	31.5	334870	27.8	65894	1.9	2005239	20.4	12. Sched. Caste converts to Christianity	301912	1.5
i. Syrian	948514	18.6	225367	18.7	23672	0.7	1197553	12.2			
ii. Non-Syrian	655961	12.9	109503	9.1	42222	1.2	807686	8.2			
20. Muslim	353274	6.9	87902	7.3	1163453	33.0	1604629	16.3	13. Muslims	3842322	19.1
Total population	5095973		1205016		3533944		9834933		14. Scheduled tribes	253519	1.3

* Figures for Syrians and non-Syrians unreliable. In Malabar, Christian converts included as Christians; in Travancore and Cochin, they are also included under caste, thus low-caste Christians appear in two categories. [a] Less than 0.1% of population. [b] In all Madras Presidency. [c] Tamil Brahmans only. [d] Pulaya population (23378) in all Madras Presidency. [e] Unknown. [f] % calculated on population of caste in all Madras Presidency, Census 1921. [g] % of population in Census 1921. [h] See notes b, c, d. [j] Figures and % possibly slightly low, see note a. [k] See notes f, g.

Sources: Census 1931, Travancore: II, 153–63 (Imper. table XVII); Census 1931, Cochin: II, lxxii–lxxiv (Imper. table XVII); Census 1931, Madras: II, 306–10 (Imper. table XVII); Census 1921, Madras: II, 110–23 (Imper. table XIII); G.O.K. 1971: Appendix XVIII.

The Nayars Today

however, is nothing like as detailed as that on Travancore and Cochin, and so, where possible, I have filled gaps in the 1931 Malabar figures with estimates based on those for 1921. The 1968 data come from a sample census taken by a Kerala government commission (G.O.K. 1971: App. XVIII); there has been no complete caste census undertaken since Independence. The Nayars form some 15% of the total population; only the Izhavas, with around 22%, are a larger caste. The number of Brahmans is very small and of these only a minority are Nambudiris. Pulayas and Parayas constitute about 9% of the population; most of those listed as Scheduled Castes[15] (Harijans) - nearly 8% of Kerala's population in 1968 - belong to one or another of these two castes. The numerical discrepancy is accounted for by Scheduled Caste converts to Christianity - 1.5% of the population. In Travancore and Cochin, Christians make up approximately 31% of the population, but there are few of them in Malabar; Muslims, on the other hand, form around 33% of Malabar's population but only about 7% of Travancore's and Cochin's.

The Nayars, like the Izhavas and the Pulayas, are distributed more or less evenly throughout Kerala. Together, these castes account for nearly 50% of the people in the state. Other castes and communities, however, are not all distributed so evenly, and this is one major cause of regional differences in the empirical form of the caste system. The uneven distribution of the Nambudiri community, despite its minuteness, is perhaps most significant in this respect; Nambudiris are concentrated most heavily in Central Kerala, and it is there that the wealthiest *illams* were located. There too, at various times, Nambudiris have wielded considerable political influence. Although it is hard to specify, this has probably given to the caste system in Central Kerala an extra rigour which it lacked elsewhere.

Nayar subdivisions

Before closing this general description of the Kerala castes, I should, I think, provide some information about the internal structure of the Nayar caste. I have discussed this subject in some detail elsewhere (Fuller 1975); here I shall summarise the main points of that paper.

The Nayars were formerly divided into a relatively large number of named subdivisions (*vibhagam*). My interest in this topic was first aroused by the apparent discrepancies between the data published in some of the early census reports and the standard descriptions presented in the gazetteers. In the 1901 Travancore census (the most detailed on this subject), more than 130 subdivisions were discovered by the enumerators, compressed into 44 distinct subdivisions in the final report (Census 1901, Travancore: 321). For Cochin and Malabar, the fullest data were given by the 1891 census; 55 subdivisions were enumerated in Cochin (Census 1891, Cochin: 111) and 138 in Madras (Census: 1891, Madras: XIII, 222). By contrast, Aiya (1906: II, 348-9) lists only 17 subdivisions for Travancore, Iyer (1912: 14-18) lists 18 for Cochin, and Innes (1908: 116-20) lists 20 for South Malabar. These

Introduction to the Nayars

latter three sources present very similar pictures which, significantly, bear a striking resemblance to the description given in the *Jatinirnayam* (Menon 1933: 192-5), according to Iyer (1912: 15) a 'work of some authority, which gives an account of Malayali castes'. Hardly different is a modern description, Gough's (1961: 308-12) for Central Kerala. In table 9, I have summarised the standard descriptions, together with the *Jatinirnayam's* version.[16] Apart from the *Jatinirnayam*, each of these accounts separates the high-ranking Nayar subdivisions from those of lower status, all of which are said to have had traditional occupations; further Iyer, Innes and Gough – but not Aiya for Travancore – separate from the others the lowest three or four subdivisions, which apparently formed a distinct group of Nayars whose touch polluted those above them.

Squaring the picture emerging from the census reports with that presented by the standard descriptions poses a double problem. Firstly, and most obviously, there is the discrepancy in the number of subdivisions. The problem deepens, though, when it is discovered that some of the subdivisions listed in table 9 are not to be found in the census reports at all, while others are recorded with only tiny populations. I submit that the explanation for this paradox is that each of the standard descriptions stems ultimately from the *Jatinirnayam*, which embodies an ideal model of the subdivision system. Like the earlier authorities, Gough is, I think, mistaken in presuming that the system she outlines ever accorded with the historical reality.

From the census figures presented in table 10, it is clear that the majority of Nayars belonged to the five higher-ranking subdivisions of Kiriyam, Illam, Svarupam and Purattu and Akattu Charna and, of those who did not, that most were included in the Itasseri and Chakkala subdivisions (Travancore) or the Pallicchan, Vattakkatan and Asthikkuracchi subdivisions (Cochin and Malabar). These few subdivisions accounted for around 90% of all Nayars in each of the three provinces. Most of the other subdivisions enumerated in the census reports had very small populations. Many had less than one hundred members, several had less than ten and not a few had but one solitary representative.

It follows fairly obviously from this that the Nayar subdivisions cannot all be groupings of a single sociological type. An analysis which treats the Illam subdivision in Travancore – population over 325 000 – as identical to the Itattara subdivision in the same state – population 1 – is clearly mistaken (cf. Dumont 1964: 98; Gough 1959a: 28). Omitting a certain amount of the argument which I have put forward elsewhere, I would suggest that the key to the problem is to recognise that there are a number of analytically distinct categories within the system of Nayar subdivisions. The first of these categories is made up of the handful of populous subdivisions, such as Illam or Pallicchan. This first category of subdivisions can be visualised as forming the stable 'core' of the system, and it seems sensible to term these subdivisions 'subcastes'. Around the core is a 'fringe' comprised of a large number of very much smaller subdivisions. The fringe is more volatile than the core, and these smaller subdivisions are (or were) being created and

Table 9. A list of Nayar subdivisions

Jatinirnayam	Aiya	Iyer	Innes	Gough
1. Kiriyam	1. Kiriyam	1. Kiriyam	1. Kiriyam	1. Kiriyam
2. Illam	2. Illam	2. Illam	2. Purattu Charna	2. Purattu Charna
3. Svarupam	3. Svarupam	3. Svarupam	3. Akattu Charna	3. Akattu Charna
4. Padamangalam	4. Padamangalam	4. Purattu and Akattu Charna	4. Illam	4. Pallicchan
5. Tamil Padam	5. Tamil Padam	5. Menokki	5. Mutta	5. Illam
6. Itasseri	6. Itasseri		6. Taraka	6. Vattakkatan
7. Maran	7. Maran	6. Maran	7. Ravari	7. Otattu
8. Chempukotti	8. Chempukotti	7. Padamangalam	8. Anduran	8. Anduran
9. Otattu	9. Otattu	8. Pallicchan	9. Otattu	
10. Pallicchan	10. Kalamkotti	9. Vattakkatan	10. Pallicchan	9. Asthikkuracchi
11. Matavan/Puliyath	11. Vattakkatan	10. Chempukotti	11. Urali	10. Veluttetan
12. Kalamkotti/Anduran	12. Pallicchan	11. Otattu	12. Chempukotti	11. Vilakkittalavan
13. Vattakkatan/Chakkala	13. Asthikkuracchi	12. Itasseri	13. Vattakkatan	
14. Asthikkuracchi/Chitikan	14. Chetti	13. Anduran	14. Asthikkuracchi/Chitikan	
15. Chetti	15. Chaliyan	14. Asthikkuracchi	15. Kulangara	
16. Chaliyan	16. Veluttetan	15. Tarakan	16. Itasseri	
17. Veluttetan	17. Vilakkittalavan	16. Vilakkittalavan		
18. Vilakkittalavan		17. Veluttetan	17. Veluttetan	
		18. Chaliyan	18. Vilakkittalavan	
			19. Kaduppattam	
			20. Chaliyan	

Sources: Menon 1933: 192–5 for *Jatinirnayam*; Aiya 1906: II, 348–9; Iyer 1912: 14–18; Innes 1908: 116–20; Gough 1961: 308–12.

Traditional occupations of lower-ranking subdivisions: Itasseri, herdsmen; Maran, temple-drummers; Chempukotti, coppersmiths; Otattu, tile-makers; Pallicchan, palanquin-bearers; Matavan/Puliyath, servants to Brahmans and Ambalavasis; Kalamkotti/Anduran, potters; Vattakkatan/Chakkala, oilmongers; Asthikkuracchi/Chitikan, funeral priests; Chetti/Tarakan, traders; Chaliyan, weavers; Veluttetan, washermen; Vilakkittalavan, barbers; Urali, masons; Kulangara, minor temple priests; Kaduppattam, schoolmasters.

Table 10. *Populations of Nayar subdivisions*

	Travancore 1901	Cochin 1891	Madras 1891
Total Nayars	536 186	101 691	393 767
Kiriyam	25 164	23 017	115 125
Illam	325 125	23 279	42 429
Svarupam	103 123	—	—
Purattu Charna	—	} 9 096	109 396
Akattu Charna	—		32 446
Total higher subdivisions	453 412	55 392	299 396
% of total	85	55	76
Itasseri	24 332	—	—
Chakkala	15 173	—	—
Pallicchan	—	18 568	16 668
Vattakkatan	—	8 452	30 980
Asthikkuracchi	—	4 553	13 689
Total all listed subdivisions	492 917	86 965	360 733
% of total	92	86	92

Sources: Census 1901, Travancore: 321; Census 1891, Cochin: 111; Census 1891, Madras: XIV, 69–70.

eliminated by several social processes, of which three may be analytically distinguished. The first of these is the process by which lower-ranking groups – castes or sections of them – are absorbed into the Nayar community as part of a process of upward mobility. The second is the process in which exogamous lineages are joined together to form localised subdivisions, which may sometimes remain distinct subdivisions, sometimes coalesce with larger subdivisions, thereby eliminating the previously existing smaller subdivisions. In the third type of process, relatively very small sections of the community – *taravads* or sections of them – split off to create subdivisions in the context of a 'status game' played at the highest-ranking levels of the community, a process intimately associated with the hypergamous marriage system.

Space precludes any detailed discussion of the difficulties posed by my analytical categories, or of the ethnography relating to the various processes isolated above. Briefly, though, it would appear that certain low-ranking subdivisions, such as the Veluttetan and Vilakkittala, have risen to the status of Nayar over a long period of time (Mencher 1966a: 160; cf. Dumont 1964: 98; Iyer 1912: 18) – a transition exactly paralleled elsewhere in India, for example among the Patidar of Gujarat (Pocock 1972: 54). How common subdivisions made up of a number of exogamous lineages are or were is difficult to say; the only detailed description of this process is by Unni (1958: 63–7). His data were collected in two South Malabar villages, but I do not know how typical they are. Essentially the process consisted of the formation of a subdivision from a number of *taravads,* usually in the same village, which had equal status and which only exchanged *sambandham* partners with each other. The third process is the one which has attracted most attention from previous writers; it involved not only Nayars, but also Brahmans, Kshatriyas and Samantans. The status of a Nayar, Kshatriya or Samantan *taravad* was in part determined by the statuses of the men who tied the *talis* for the *taravad's* girls, and of the *sambandham* partners taken by the *taravad's* women. Conversely, for whom a man tied a *tali* could affect his own *taravad's* status, although his choice of *sambandham* partners had little effect. Among the Kshatriyas, Samantans and high-ranking, aristocratic Nayars, all relations set up by the *tali*-rite and the *sambandham* union were hypergamous; i.e. a girl's *tali*-tiers and *sambandham* partners were from families of status superior to her own, whereas men only acted as *tali*-tiers for, and took *sambandham* partners from, families of status inferior to their own. As I consider this third process in much greater detail in chapter 5, I shall omit any further discussion here.

Much of what is outlined in this section is now part of history. Concrete data, as opposed to general impressions, are sparse on the subject of Nayar subdivisions in modern times, and few generalisations applicable to all of Kerala can be hazarded. I do, however, have some data for Central Travancore, although they are almost certainly atypical because the Nayar Service Society, which as I have mentioned has its strength in this region, has unceasingly campaigned for the abolition of subdivisions within the Nayar community, arguing that only as a united community could Nayars become a powerful political force. The N.S.S. has encouraged intermarriage between subdivisions, although even now it is still very rare (cf. Pillai 1940: I, 858). In Central Travancore today there are four subdivisions: Illam (to which almost all Nayars in Ramankara belong), Svarupam, Itasseri, and Chakkala, as well as the Veluttedathu and Vilakkittala Nayars (Veluttetan and Vilakkittalavan). The latter two are not considered by other Nayars to be 'real' Nayars at all. Turning to the other subdivisions, the reader will recall (in table 10) that these four, with Kiriyam, were by far the largest subdivisions in Travancore in 1901 and that together they accounted for over 90% of all Nayars in the state. Kiriyam, though, was mainly confined to the area of Travancore bordering on Cochin.

It is conceivable that these four are the only subdivisions which have ever existed in the Central Travancore region. More likely, I think, is that other smaller subdivisions have been absorbed into the four largest ones. Gough (1961: 308) and Mencher (1966a: 161) both refer to the current tendency towards amalgamation of Nayar subdivisions, although it must be admitted that they produce little hard evidence to support these statements. Further research would be necessary to resolve this problem satisfactorily.

Introduction to the Nayars

The subdivision system illustrates an important characteristic of the Nayar caste which ought to be stressed. This is that in many respects the Nayars do not form a completely homogeneous community, and they certainly do not constitute a solidary, corporate block. Further, the Nayar caste is not a bounded group, for it can be 'infiltrated' at the bottom, while at the top there is also a certain degree of vagueness, as aristocratic Nayars cannot always be clearly distinguished from Samantans or Kshatriyas. Within the caste, too, as we have seen, there is considerable status mobility and flexibility. (These features are by no means unique to the Nayars; they are all characteristic, for instance, of the Patidar caste in Gujarat (Pocock 1972).) My remarks in this paragraph may seem to conflict with my comments on the rigidity of the Kerala caste system, but this is not really so. It is important to distinguish between the rigid structure and the less rigid behavioural patterns which can exist within that structure. To oversimplify somewhat, rigidity was more a feature of relations between castes, and flexibility more a feature of relations within castes. In the next section, I shall be concerned mainly with relations between castes and the effect of caste differences on behaviour.

Caste in Central Travancore and Ramankara

The special feature of the Kerala caste system was, as we saw in the first chapter, 'distance pollution' – the notion that impurity could be transmitted through the air, rather than only by contact. In that chapter, I quoted a number of accounts describing certain aspects of the system and the consistency of these reports is such that there can be little doubt as to their overall veracity. Rather than continue our discussion at the all-Kerala level, I think it would be wise for us to look at some features of caste at the more localised level of Central Travancore and the village of Ramankara, and I shall begin with distance pollution.

I have already mentioned once or twice the distances over which pollution could be transmitted, e.g. a Pulaya could pollute a Brahman at a distance of 64 feet. But such descriptions are somewhat mystifying, as Mencher remarks: 'Writers about Kerala commonly speak of distance pollution in terms of feet, conveying the strange impression of men walking around with footrules. In fact, the distances relate to places, e.g., the gate of one's compound, the courtyard, or the first step on the verandah' (1966a: 154). So at the house of a Ramankara Nayar belonging to the Illam subcaste, for instance, another Illam Nayar could enter and eat in it; a lower subcaste Nayar could enter some of the rooms but not eat there; a Syrian Christian could come onto the verandah; an artisan or Izhava could come into the courtyard surrounding the house; a Harijan could only come up to the outer gate. Mencher points out that in the past these rules were not particularly difficult to observe in the villages, and that there were methods of circumventing them when necessary, such as when a carpenter came to work in the house. But elderly informants did tell me that communicating instructions to labourers was difficult, for the Nayar landlord had to stand on his verandah, shouting to his Harijan workers who remained outside the wall of the compound. Just beyond the wall was a hut known as the *kuliparambu* – ' wage place ' where the landlord would leave the paddy for their wages when the labourers were out in the fields. On returning, he would bathe to remove the pollution contracted by entering this hut. Nayars walking along village paths would shout to warn any low-caste persons of their impending approach. The latter could then get out of the way. Old Nayars told me that this aspect of distance pollution was one of its most inconvenient features, though ' inconvenience ' is no doubt rather too mild a description for the problems caused to members of the lower castes. (All ' public ' roads in Travancore were opened to all castes by Proclamation in 1870, but it was a ' paper reform ' for many years, in many places (Jeffrey 1973: 112–13).)

Today, in Central Travancore, most of these caste practices have vanished; or at least, they would seem to have done. The roads and paths are used by all, and Nayars no longer parade around proclaiming their progress, nor do they shout their orders to labourers from the verandah. In the past, it used to be possible to identify a person's caste by his dress. This cannot be done today either. Indeed, Tampi states that it had become impossible by 1941 and that touch and distance pollution had been almost completely eliminated (Census 1941, Travancore: 143–4). Only after some time, in fact, does the visitor to Kerala become aware of any behaviour reflecting caste distinctions. As we have seen, there is scarcely even any residential segregation by caste. Restaurants and tea-shops, in villages as well as towns, are open to everybody, and all customers are served alike; no Harijan is expected to eat outside or drink from special cups, kept apart. Everyone is served identically at shops, and there is no segregation by caste on the buses.

However, as I realised after living in Travancore for several months, things are not as simple as they seem at first. What happens in and around houses is rather more complicated, and it is made yet more so by the tendency of almost everyone to deny that caste differences do still affect behaviour. Caste differences are practically a taboo subject; surprising though it may be to readers familiar, at first-hand or through the literature, with rural India, the fact is that in modern Travancore distinctions of caste are only reluctantly discussed with outsiders. Thus the data below come mainly from my own observations and from what a handful of informants – those I judged to be most frank – told me.

The gate, the courtyard, the verandah and the interior of the house still operate as pollution ' thresholds '. When a low-caste labourer comes to his high-caste employer's house to ask for instructions, he is likely to lean on the gatepost while the employer remains seated on the verandah. Now this is not something which either party consciously notices, and if asked about it, both would probably deny that there was anything significant in it. Nonetheless, it seems clear to me that what is signified is the real, even if tacit and unspoken, acceptance by both employer and labourer that the distance between the verandah and the gatepost should be maintained between persons of their respective statuses.

However, such behaviour is not determined solely by caste; it is also determined by class. Beck (1972: 156ff) has brought out the distinction clearly in her study of Konku (Tamilnadu). There, she explains, food exchange is the critical medium for caste ranking and seating arrangements for master-servant relations. There is, she insists, a patent difference between the two types of relation; for example, a cook is inferior to his employer on the master-servant scale but equal on the purity-pollution (caste) scale, whereas a low-caste official might be equal on the former scale, but he is inferior on the latter. Food exchange and seating are also relevant media for expressing these forms of ranking in Travancore, but not in anything like such a consistent and explicit manner as in Konku. In many houses, both eating and seating arrangements are casual: persons of lower caste often do eat in the houses of higher caste people, and rich landlords not infrequently sit on the floor while their less wealthy, less powerful guests have the chairs.

To some extent, a clear pattern only emerges when there is simultaneously a caste and class difference - most commonly between a high-caste landlord and a low-caste labourer, as in the example given above. When there is not a distinction on both scales, it is hard to predict what might happen. This is partly due to another important factor - changing attitudes. Irrespective of status on either scale, the old are more likely to observe these distinctions than the young. Political attitudes are relevant too; conservatives tend to observe status distinctions more than radicals. In fact, radicals - especially active Communists - sometimes act deliberately to confuse caste and class rankings. Communist low-caste labourers, armed with the knowledge that high-caste employers can no longer actually do anything to enforce observation of caste differences, do on occasion step up to their employer's verandah, instead of waiting respectfully at his gate. Such deliberate confusion of caste and class ranking is perhaps most clearly seen in the demonstrations which have periodically occurred to assert the rights of the low castes to enter temples which have previously been closed to them. Throughout India, the vast majority of temples were closed to the low castes. Nowadays, all temples are, at least legally, open to all castes. Communists, despite their nominal atheism, have often taken an important role in such demonstrations. (See, e.g. Gough's excellent account of one (1970).) Conversely, demonstrations of this type, although initially concerned with a caste-cum-religious issue, seem to have sometimes generated wider political radicalism. One of the founders and leaders of the Kerala Communist Party, Krishna Pillai (a Nayar), received his first political education when he saw the demonstrators at the 1924 Vaikom temple demonstration being beaten by henchmen of the Brahmans (Krishnan 1971: 6).

The situation, as the reader will now be aware, is confusing and in a state of flux. The caste system does not affect behaviour either consistently or explicitly, as it used to or as it still does in much of rural India. There is, in modern Central Travancore, no pattern of systematic food exchange (on the basis of which a 'matrix analysis' could be produced) expressing and maintaining caste distinctions. That is to say, in contrast to many Indian villages, there is no systematic pattern in which members of one caste will accept food or water from members of certain castes, but not from others, in a manner which reflects their rank, vis-à-vis those other castes. Caste differences are confused, sometimes deliberately, with class differences, and attitudes vary between individuals according to age and political persuasion. Finally, the situation is rendered yet more complex by informants' insistence that caste differences no longer matter.

One or two further points may be mentioned here. Low-caste persons are able to draw water from wells owned by members of higher castes; I saw this occur on many an occasion in Ramankara, and informants stated that no-one would deny access to a well on grounds of caste. Students of rural India may well be astonished by this, but it is nevertheless the case, although I myself suspect that there are at least some high-caste households which deny low-caste people the use of their wells. Whether or not the temples in Ramankara, and in Central Travancore generally, are actually open to and used by members of the low castes, I am unsure. Informants, of course, insisted that they were. But I was unable to check their assertions, as I did not live near a temple nor, as a non-Hindu, was I allowed inside one. (Throughout Travancore, non-Hindus are barred from the temples.) Barbers' shops are now open to all following the enactment of legislation some fifteen years ago. After initial opposition from the barbers, the change was made quite smoothly. (No doubt, the prospects of an increase in trade influenced the barbers' attitude.) Washermen, however, still refuse to clean the clothes of the lower castes (i.e. artisans (?), Izhavas, and those of lower rank); this was the sole case of quite open caste-based discrimination that I encountered. In other public places, as I have said previously, there is no discrimination. The situation as I saw it in Central Travancore seems to resemble closely enough that observed elsewhere in modern Kerala (cf. Gough 1970 and Aiyappan 1965: 79-91 on two Central Kerala villages).

The evidence suggests that the norms governing caste behaviour in Travancore were subject to radical change in the 1920s and 1930s. In 1941, Tampi wrote that 'caste is now in a nebulous condition', with prediction of future developments impossible (Census 1941, Travancore: 132-3). The year 1924-5 was the year commonly quoted by my older informants as marking the beginning of the end of the rigid caste system. That this was the year 1100 in the Malayalam era may not be irrelevant, but the main event of that year was the Vaikom temple satyagraha, referred to briefly above. (The term 'satyagraha' is used for the non-violent demonstrations pioneered by Gandhi.) This satyagraha was aimed at opening the roads around this famous Siva temple to Harijans, and it lasted from

Introduction to the Nayars

the spring of 1924 until the autumn of 1925. Gandhi participated in its later stages and was able to gain some concessions through his negotiations with the Travancore government. Although the Travancore Temple Entry Act was not passed until 1936, the Vaikom demonstration clearly had a tremendous impact in the state, and it is an event still remembered well by older Nayars in Ramankara. Vaikom is less than thirty miles from Ramankara, and some Nayars had probably visited the temple. 1925 was also the year in which the Nayar Act, permitting the division of the joint families, was enacted. There is no direct connection between the latter and changes in the caste system, but both are related to the economic and accompanying social developments sweeping through Travancore at this time. Aiyappan's contemporary account indicates the inconvenience of rigid caste observances under modern conditions, and he emphasises too the effects of education and wider employment opportunities (1944: 43–50). The old system's inconvenience was always stressed by my informants as well. There were more shops to visit and more journeys to the towns in connection with official and commercial business to be made. It had not been very difficult to maintain strict rules of caste behaviour in the villages, but it was becoming much less easy now that travel had become so frequent. The simple, pragmatic nature of informants' explanations as to why these rules were relaxed – their growing inconvenience – should not lead us to discount them as naive; the history and ethnography of India are replete with examples of caste observances being dropped and bent when too troublesome. As Crooke pithily expressed it, ' Hinduism is elastic enough to ignore its own rules when they are practically unworkable...' (qu. in O'Malley 1932: 108).

But while behaviour concerned with caste differences has changed dramatically, belief has not. No doubt, there has been some alteration, but it has not paralleled that in behaviour. The subject of belief is even more difficult to discuss than that of behaviour, for one has to rely almost entirely on what people say. Firstly, as I have mentioned, most people tend to deny that caste matters any more – except in marriage, to which I shall come shortly. Secondly, there is an inclination on the part of many richer members of the higher castes to say there is no discrimination against the low castes but, at the same time, to state that if there is, then it is because low-caste people are feckless and do not work hard enough; in other words, to transfer the issue from a caste to a class context and rationalise caste discrimination on economic grounds. More than once, I have been told by a high-caste landowner how much has been done for the Harijans and how all Malayalis are now equal. In the next breath, he has gone on to say, with clear contempt in his voice, how dirty, lazy and spendthrift modern labourers are. It was crystal clear at the time that low castes and labourers were being equated and that the clear distinction between caste and class, which we may wish to make, was not present in the speech of these high-caste landowners. The other side of the coin is that low-caste people, especially young radicals, tend to see their position

The Nayars Today

as being directly caused and perpetuated by poverty. There are considerable problems involved in interpreting statements such as these, and the reader may well feel sceptical about any claim that they provide convincing evidence on attitudes to caste. Perhaps more conclusive evidence that beliefs about caste have changed but little comes from those few, very frank informants who were prepared to talk about the subject directly. Although a tiny minority, I am convinced that what they told me is nearer the truth than is the assertion by the majority that caste is no longer important. The absence of change was most vividly summed up for me by a highly sophisticated Nambudiri Brahman lawyer, who had sat in the Kerala Legislative Assembly as a Communist member; he told me that in spite of the fact that he would never discriminate between persons of different castes in his behaviour, and in spite of his total opposition to the caste system intellectually, he could never prevent himself feeling strange and uncomfortable if a low-caste person came too close to him or touched him.

Purity and pollution

Intimately connected with caste, of course, is the system of purity and pollution, and in this too there has been considerable change during recent decades. This section is based on my data collected from Nayars in Ramankara and concentrates on the three main types of pollution resulting from bodily conditions: birth, death and menstruation.

After she has given birth, a Nayar mother is polluted for fifteen days. Birth pollution does not affect other members of her matrilineal descent group (cf. Gough 1952b: 87 and Mencher 1965: 185 for Central Kerala Nayars). During this period, the mother may not enter the kitchen, and she eats separately in a special room. She should not touch others in the household, although this rule does not apply to her baby and other children under six years old, for it is considered that they cannot transmit the mother's pollution. Her clothes should be kept apart from those of others. She is not allowed to enter the temple for 56 days after the birth. Among Nayars in Ramankara, and I think in Central Travancore generally, birth pollution, unlike death and menstrual pollution, is still strictly observed. This is undoubtedly related to the fact that it does not cause great inconvenience. It affects only the mother, who in any case is expected to observe a fairly long period of convalescence, during which she should not do any hard work at all and should take a variety of ayurvedic preparations thought to promote the recovery of her strength. (Ayurveda is the indigenous Indian system of medicine, based mainly on herbal remedies.) A woman always returns to her mother's home for the birth of her first child and may do so for subsequent ones as well.

Traditionally, death pollution lasts sixteen days for Nayars, but it is becoming more common for it to last only ten. It is supposed to affect *all* members of the deceased's matrilineal descent group, but this has always been subject to the limitation that the number of Nayars acknowledging a matrilineal link with the deceased depends to some extent on the latter's position in society. More people will observe pollution on the death of a rich man of high status than on that of a poor man of low status. In exceptional cases, when the deceased was particularly prominent, pollution might be observed for a whole year, although no informant could quote an instance of this actually happening. All my informants maintained that the range of persons observing death pollution was steadily declining, i.e. people only fairly remotely related to the deceased were less and less likely to observe it. There has also recently been a move by some Nayars to reduce the amount of money spent on the feast (*antubali*) marking the end of pollution. While suffering death pollution, a Nayar is subject to quite a catalogue of prohibitions. He (or she) must sleep on the floor, not on a bed, must abstain from sexual relations, must not shave, must eat identical curries each day, must avoid bitter condiments (especially tamarind), must not use oil on the hair or body, must not cross rivers, nor, of course, enter the temple; this does not exhaust the list of what must and must not be done. Death pollution is thus inconvenient and not especially pleasant and that, according to informants, is why it tends to be observed by fewer people for less time nowadays. Along with this trend has come another development, at first sight contradictory. This is for death pollution to be observed by members of a household in which some are affected, even though they themselves are not. For example, if a woman (and thus her children) were subject to death pollution, her husband would observe it too although he cannot, of course, be matrilineally related to the deceased as well. The explanation for this extension of the range of pollution is again that of convenience; for households without servants – the majority today – it is just too much trouble to have to prepare two separate meals or to bring in an outsider to cook for unaffected males. Similar changes are recorded for Central and North Kerala Nayars by Gough (1959b: 269). As before, I am inclined to accept informants' pragmatic explanations for changes in the observance of death pollution, modern socio-economic developments having increased the inconvenience caused by this type of pollution.

Nayar women in Ramankara no longer observe menstrual pollution. It was abandoned in the area some ten years ago, though I understand that in other communities and in other areas of Kerala, it is still observed. In the past, a menstruating woman was barred from the kitchen and the granary for four days and her touch, or even her shadow according to some, was held to damage crops. She was not allowed into the temple for seven days. Again the explanation given for its abandonment was inconvenience. Menstrual pollution would also be a problem in the modern nuclear household, for life becomes difficult if the only adult woman is unable to cook for a few days every month. Few Indian men – at least those I met – have any culinary competence. But in nuclear households which remain orthodox, men do sometimes cook while their wives are menstruating.

The Nayars Today

Birth, death and menstrual pollution all illustrate a common pattern – a tendency, in modern times, to reduce the inconvenience of their observance, whether this inconvenience is caused by the number of persons affected, or by the strictness of the prohibitions, or by the frequency with which they occur. Over the last few decades, there has plainly been an overall decline in the extent to which the rules of purity and pollution in general are observed; this is demonstrated not only by the bodily pollutions I have just discussed, but also by the alterations in behaviour influenced by caste differences which were noted above. But in marriage, the iron rules of caste and subcaste endogamy seem to have corroded hardly at all. Even now and even in the towns, the overwhelming majority of marriages are between two persons of the same caste. Most of the inter-caste matches which do occur are 'love marriages', decided upon by the individuals concerned and not arranged by their parents. In my sample census of Ramankara, I came across only two inter-caste or subcaste marriages: one between an Illam Nayar male and an Itasseri Nayar female, and one between a Kannadiyan male and a Pulaya female. Why the norms governing marriage have seemingly remained unaltered, in the face of a general decline in the strictness with which the rules of caste – and of purity and pollution – are observed, is evidently a crucial problem. This is hardly the place to attempt an answer, but it is surely connected with the belief that purity is ultimately transmitted in the blood, especially the blood of women (Yalman 1963). Marriage implies, on the one hand, the progeniture of legitimate children in which the blood of the father and mother are combined, and, on the other, socially approved sexual intercourse, involving a highly intimate form of bodily contact and also the emission of extremely polluting substances (cf. Stevenson 1954). It is hence the social relationship wherein the dangers of pollution are potentially greatest. There is too the hazard that 'anomalous' children may be born if the mother and father are not of the same caste.

For a number of reasons, my information about Nayar, and Hindu, beliefs concerning purity and pollution is inadequate. The topic is, however, difficult to discuss in any case. I have referred to the Nambudiri lawyer's feelings about low-caste people; it is my impression that such feelings – which clearly have to do with the whole sphere of purity and pollution, not merely with inter-caste relationships – are common enough, at least among members of the higher castes. It may be worth noting that purity and pollution beliefs are not, in the way we as Westerners are likely to understand the word, obviously 'religious'; often, they seem very much more akin to our 'manners'. In the same way, it is unwise to think that purity is a religious concept clearly distinct in practice from secular cleanness. Philosophically, it may be; empirically, one is confronted with statements of the kind which assert that Harijans are dirty – not so easy to interpret. These remarks are in no way meant to excuse lacunae in my data, but merely to draw attention to an exceptionally difficult problem underlying any investigation in this field.

3 The Nayar kinship system in Ramankara

In this chapter, I discuss the kinship system of the Nayars of Central Travancore: the structure of the property-owning group and the household, and the inheritance system. The data refer, except where otherwise stated, to the Illam Nayars of Ramankara, and the period with which I am concerned is, approximately, the last one hundred years. During the present century, the kinship system of all Nayars, including those in Ramankara, has undergone dramatic changes, and much of my analysis will be taken up with considering the form and cause of these changes. Without an understanding of them, the way in which the marriage system has altered, to be discussed in the next chapter, cannot be understood. Change, of course, is a continuous process, but for convenience I have divided my analysis into three periods: the 'old order', the 'interregnum' and the 'new order'. Exact dates cannot be given, but we may say that the interregnum began around 1920 and ended around 1940. The watershed was 1925, the year in which far-reaching legal changes were brought about in Travancore by the enactment of the Nayar Act. I want to make it clear that by the 'old order' I do not mean the 'traditional system'; if the latter term is to have any useful meaning, then its use should be confined to describing the system which existed before the series of modifications brought about, directly or indirectly, by Martanda Varma in the eighteenth century. Certainly, the kinship and marriage system of the Nayars was changing significantly during the nineteenth century. The 'old order' thus refers to the system as it existed around the turn of the century.

I begin this chapter by considering, in more detail than I have done above, what is meant by the Malayalam word *taravad* and mention some features of Nayar matriliny. Some relevant background information on the Ramankara Nayars will be presented, and I shall then proceed to the detailed analysis of the data.

The taravad, matriliny and the Ramankara Nayars

Anthropologists would translate the word *taravad*, as it is used by the Nayars, as 'matrilineal descent group'. All those who can, or claim to be able to, trace descent matrilineally from a common ancestress, form one *taravad*. All segments of this group, whatever their size, are referred to by the same word. However, when used without qualification, the word *taravad* usually refers to that segment of the descent group which consti-

The Nayars Today

3. A traditional joint-family house in Central Kerala, in which about 75 people live together.

4. Some of the younger occupants of the joint-family house in Central Kerala. They are typical in appearance of Nayar children throughout modern Kerala.

tutes (or rather did constitute) the matrilineal joint family, whose members owned property collectively and lived together in one house. This house was also referred to by the word *taravad*. There is another word – *tavazhi* – that is also employed by the Nayars to refer to any segment of the *taravad*. It can only be defined relative to *taravad*; which segment it refers to depends on which segment the word *taravad* applies to in the context. But unqualified, it refers to a segment of the joint family headed by one of the elder women and including herself, her children, her daughter's children, etc.

I shall term the group owning property collectively the 'property group'. If there is no possibility of confusion, I shall occasionally use the word *taravad* to refer to units in which the 'property group' and the household (i.e. the residential group) are congruent, i.e. where they have identical memberships, and are thus equivalent to a joint family. However, I shall refer to the largest matrilineal unit, i.e. the one comprising all those claiming a common ancestress, as a 'clan'. Sometimes, the 'clan' and the property group/household will be coextensive; on other occasions, there will be distinguishable segments intermediate between the clan and the property group/household. I shall refer to these latter segments as 'subclans'. The justification for these analytical distinctions will emerge below.[1] We must remember, however, that these are analytical distinctions and that they do not accord precisely with native categories.

The clan is exogamous. No two persons with an assumed common matrilineal ancestress, however many generations back she may have been, are permitted to marry each other. Sexual relations within the clan are forbidden as well. The exogamous unit is also the community of pollution. By 'community of pollution' is meant the group of people who all observe pollution together for the same occurrence; for example, if someone dies, all those who consequently observe death pollution form a 'community of pollution'. The example is particularly apposite here, for if any member of the clan dies, then all other members of his or her clan are, in theory, polluted. (In Ramankara, birth pollution was not thought to be transmissible through the whole clan.) As Gough expressed it: 'The two concepts, of exogamy and of community of pollution, are inextricably interlinked. Among Nayars, both these concepts are associated with that of descent from the same ancestress' (1952b: 87).

Each clan has a name, which forms part of the name of each individual member of the clan. In practice, any two people living in the same area bearing the same clan name are assumed to have a common ancestress, even though the connections between them are unknown. There are cases, though, of subclans dropping their original clan name, even when it has not been forgotten that the sections belong to one clan. In a large clan, there may be many subclans, each with its own name. For example, in the Vadakkil clan – the largest in Ramankara – there are subclans such as Kunnam in which the clan name has been dropped, and others, such as Vadakkil Puthenveedu, in which a section suffix has been added. One subclan retains the original name without any addition.[2]

The Nayars Today

The clan is not corporate and its members assemble together but once a year, on the occasion of an annual ritual held at the clan's *sarppukavu* (serpent grove). Offerings are made to the serpent deities, represented in the *kavu* by stone images. These *kavus* are the only parts of the old *taravad*-house compounds still surviving in Ramankara. Other than this, the clan's functions are limited to defining the span of exogamous restrictions and the community of pollution. Many smaller clans are localised, with all their members living in one village, but this is not always true, especially with the larger clans. The status of a clan (*paramparyyam*) has some significance in marriage, but otherwise the clan will feature but rarely in the remainder of this chapter and the next.

The Nayars refer to their matrilineal descent system by the word *marumakkattayam,* from *marumakan* – 'sister's son' and *tayam* – 'share, inheritance'. (The patrilineal descent system of, for example, the Syrian Christians, is referred to by the word *makkattayam, makan* – 'son'.) Questions of inheritance and residence will occupy most of this chapter; here I wish to make some brief remarks on other aspects of descent.

A male Nayar has four names: his clan name to which reference has been made; an inherited personal name; a given personal name; and a caste title. In the past, the inherited personal name was his mother's eldest brother's given name, but nowadays it is usually his father's. There is a range of caste titles, but two predominate in Ramankara. Members of two of the four principal clans in the village (Vadakkil and Kizhakkil) bear the name Kurup (Malayalam-*kuruppu*), and those belonging to the other two (Tekkapuram and Padinjerapuram) bear the name Nair (the normal anglicisation of *nāyar* when used as a name). Like the clan name, this title is always inherited matrilineally. In this, it differs from the personal name which, as I have just stated, used to be inherited matrilineally but is now inherited patrilineally. A typical Nayar man's full name might, therefore, be Vadakkil Narayana Krishna Kurup; if he was born more than about twenty years ago it is likely that Narayana was his mother's brother's name, if less than this time ago his father's name. He would normally be known as either Krishna Kurup or (V.) N. K. Kurup.

A female Nayar has only three names, as she does not bear the caste title. Her clan name is inherited matrilineally, of course, and in the past she also took her mother's name before her given name. So a Nayar woman born more than twenty-odd years ago might be called, to give an illustration, Vadakkil Lakshmi Parvati – Lakshmi being her mother's name. But today, instead of the mother's name, Nayar women take their father's name – for example, Vadakkil Rama Parvati, if Rama was her father's name. Again there has been a change from matrilineal to patrilineal inheritance of names, but in this case it involves a change of sex as well. She may be known as V. R. Parvati, although modern married women quite often add the caste title of their husbands and give their name as, say, Mrs Parvati Nair.

Formerly, authority over children was vested mainly in the *karanavan*,

The Nayar Kinship System

the head of the *taravad* (see below), who was often the mother's brother, but today it is almost entirely vested in the father. He is responsible for day-to-day discipline in the home and also for major decisions taken on behalf of the children, such as the arrangement of their marriages. On the other side of the coin, nowadays it is the father who gives his children the traditional gifts at the festivals of Vishu and Onam, whereas in the past the mother's brother gave them to his sisters' children. At the same time, there has been an alteration in the relative statuses of men and women. Today, husbands dominate their wives in a way which was intrinsically impossible when they did not live together, but men also seem to have greater power over women in general than they used to (cf. Mencher 1962). Male–female relations appear to have grown more and more like those typical of high-ranking patrilineal castes, and this development is associated with an increased emphasis on stable, monogamous marriage.

With the exception of some recent immigrants, all Nayars in Ramankara claim membership of the Illam subcaste. They are divided into some thirty different clans; of these, four have a special position in the village and hence in my study.

I have christened these four the 'big four' clans because they are by far the wealthiest in Ramankara and because informants, if asked for the names of the most powerful clans in the village, will always quote these four: Vadakkil, Tekkapuram, Kizhakkil and Padinjerapuram. Whether or not they also have higher status than other Ramankara clans is somewhat problematic; it will be discussed in the context of marriage where it has some significance.

Vadakkil is certainly the largest, but it is impossible to specify the size of its membership. In the 1908 Settlement Report, the names of ten distinct sections of this clan appear, but no-one knows how many sections there are today. It has proved impossible to reconstruct the genealogy of the whole Vadakkil clan, as informants' statements about the relations between the various subclans were vague and contradictory. That the order of segmentation is not clearly recalled is correlated with the fact that it is irrelevant to property reversion in the rare cases of *taravads* becoming extinct, as there are other means of solving this problem (cf. Gough 1952a: 76; 1961: 326), and also with the fact that there are no differences in status between subclans based, for instance, on the relative seniority of apical members. Together, the various property groups within the Vadakkil clan owned more land than those within any other clan in Ramankara, but its very large membership meant that each group did not necessarily own very much land. And one subclan, Kunnam, in fact owned more than half the total Vadakkil land in 1908. The members of most sections of this clan resided in Ramankara, as many of them still do, but one subclan migrated to another village some eight miles away. Vadakkil is the only one of the big four clans with an important section owning land and residing outside Ramankara.

The Tekkapuram clan was actually only a single property group in 1908,

and the clan is now extinct, for the last *karanavan* – who died in about
1920 – had no matrilineal heirs. He adopted an heir from another, fairly
poor clan called Vilangu which was said to have been a section of the
Tekkapuram clan originally. The young *karanavan* of Vilangu was married
to a daughter of the Tekkapuram *karanavan* and the property of the two
groups amalgamated. The Tekkapuram group owned more than 1000 acres
in Ramankara, as well as land outside the village, especially in the nearby
town of Changanacherry. The latter land was eventually given to the second
wife of the Tekkapuram *karanavan*. Being so few in number, the members
of the Tekkapuram-Vilangu clan were undoubtedly the richest Nayars in
Ramankara, but it so happened that the adopted heir turned out to be a
profligate spender, who lost many hundreds of acres of land. Nonetheless,
those who have inherited from the original Tekkapuram property group are
still among the richest people in the village.

It is an anthropological commonplace that the amount of accurate
genealogical information which can be obtained from informants about
any particular descent group, in almost any society, is partly dependent on
the group's 'social importance', in the broadest sense of the phrase. This
commonplace holds in Ramankara and, as in many other societies, 'social
importance' there is to a large extent a function of wealth. My genealogical
data are thus best for the wealthiest sections of the big four clans, and this
explains why it has not been feasible to make estimates of the actual size
of the various clans. Many poorer subclans may well have been completely
forgotten like other, poorer Ramankara clans; I was unable to collect more
than fragmentary genealogies for any of these. Much of the following analysis
is therefore based on information gathered on the richer sections of the big
four clans. It may not apply to poorer clans and subclans, but this is not
always easy to deduce.

The old order

In the old order, the property group and the household were usually congruent. This group consisted of a matrilineal segment residing in one house,
and it is to this segment that the word *taravad* normally refers. The *taravad*
was thus a prototypical matrilineal joint family. Husbands visited their
wives at night and did not live in the latter's houses. Property was held
jointly by all members of the group, including minors, in the name of the
legal guardian who was the oldest male member. He was known as the
karanavan and his role is discussed in more detail below. The time-depth
of these groups was rarely greater than four generations in Ramankara;
according to my oldest informants, who were brought up in such *taravads*,
they normally comprised a set of siblings, their mother if she were alive,
the sisters' children and the sisters' daughters' children. The average size
of *taravads* was around thirty or forty, the largest one of which I heard in
Ramankara had something over fifty members and the smallest had only
eight.

The Nayar Kinship System

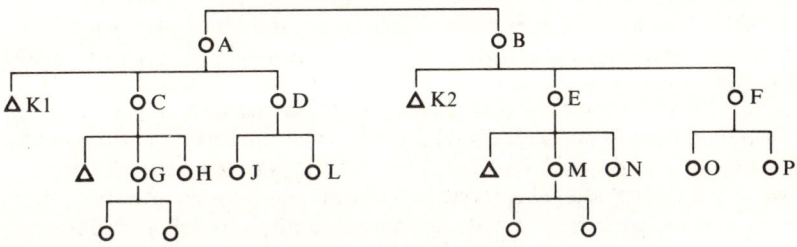

Figure 1 – A *taravad* at the point of partition

Clearly, if a *taravad* is headed by a set of full siblings which includes more than one sister, partition must be effected every generation if it is always to be headed by a set of full siblings. During this period, partition of the household sometimes took place before partition of the property group, although the divisions were often simultaneous. I have examples of both types of division and do not know which, if either, was the commoner. When partition was not simultaneous, the cause was usually disagreement over division of the property.

Figure 1 represents a hypothetical *taravad* at the point of partition. A and B, two sisters, are both elderly and have no surviving brothers. G, A's eldest daughter's eldest daughter and M, related similarly to B, have both borne children who are still young. H, J, L, N, O and P have no offspring, The elder of K1 and K2 is the *karanavan*. As my informants were only children when *taravads* of this size and type existed, it was difficult to obtain precise details of when and how they split. I suggest, however, that it was at a point in the *taravad*'s development similar to that represented in figure 1.

The three critical features are: one, the birth of children to G and M; two, the probable desire of both K1 and K2 to become *karanavans*; and, three, the age of A and B for after their deaths the *taravad* would probably divide anyway. The first factor was the one most often quoted to me as being the most important, for it seems that the lateral extension of the group resulting from the births of these children was, during this period anyway, considered too great. I suspect the second factor to have been significant as well, although it was infrequently mentioned to me; Gough (1961: 344) refers to its importance in the division of *taravads* in Central Kerala. No further explanation of the third factor is needed, as it is plain that the deaths of A and/or B will cut the connection between the two halves of the *taravad*. The division of the group's property was stirpital (by branches of a family) and therefore could not occur if, in this case, a mother, mother's brother or brother of A and B were alive (cf. ibid.: 343). It could happen, however, if a brother of A and B, who would have been the *karanavan*, retired from this office; such retirements did occasionally take place in Ramankara. I know of one instance in which the equivalents of A and B continued to reside together, although the division was stirpital. This seems to have been simply because the two old sisters wanted to remain together, and it does not affect the general principles of *taravad* division.

It is important to note that the process of partition, with which we are concerned here, is not an individual partition of property, i.e. it was not a division of property between individual members of the *taravad*, but between matrilineal segments (*tavazhis*) of it. It is not necessarily true, therefore, that the concept of a matrilineal joint family was being seriously undermined by this species of partition. As Nayar reformers in Travancore at the time recognised, the distinction between the two types of partition is extremely significant, and this will become clearer below.

In Central Kerala too, by the close of the nineteenth century, property groups were apparently splitting in a manner very similar to that described above (Gough 1961: 343-4). However, according to Gough (ibid.: 334), before 1800 or thereabouts, property groups in Cochin had had a time-depth of up to six generations and had partitioned less frequently. Mencher (1962: 232) reports that in Ernad (South Malabar), the groups ' of all but the poorest Nayar retainer families ... had a time-depth of six to eight generations'. The possibility that groups of a similar size and depth had once existed in Ramankara too cannot be ruled out but nor, on the other hand, is there any evidence that they did.

After partition of the household, a new house would be built on land owned by the *taravad*; as each of the wealthy ones owned large estates, there would have been considerable choice about a site for the new house. During this period, however, most of the large houses were constructed in a fairly small area of Ramankara bordering on paddy fields – such a site usually being preferred.

Reference has already been made to the fact that a division of the household sometimes occurred before a division of the property group. If this happened, a de facto partition of property would most likely be made in practice, with the *karanavan* allocating part of the estate to the new household. Partition of the property would, I think, always be legally finalised before the next partition of the households. It is fairly clear that there existed a strong ideological norm favouring the congruence of the property group and the household. The concept of the *taravad* in the old order necessarily implies such a norm, for it was supposed to comprise a group of people owning property collectively for their own maintenance under the guardianship of the *karanavan*. It is in the role of the *karanavan* that the contradiction, implicit when the property group and the household are not congruent, is most patent; he cannot take full responsibility for the junior members of his family, if he does not have full control over the property on which the family depends (cf. Nakane 1962: 18).

The role of the *karanavan* in the old order must now be considered in more detail. The word *karanavan* means literally ' man with responsibility, authority'. Aiya (1906: II, 363) has concisely summarised the *karanavan's* role, and I can do no better than quote from his account:

The eldest male member of ... a taravad is by legal right the karanavan or managing head and is succeeded by the next senior male member to whatever branch of the family he may belong. Every member, male or female, has an equal interest in the taravad, but cannot claim his or her share of it. The karanavan is legally responsible for the well-being, control and management of the taravad members, and is bound to meet their wants arising from their social status. But he has no right to alienate the immovable property of the family without the consent of all the members, at least of all the adult male and female members. The internal management of the taravad is vested in him ... The disposal of the moveable property of the family is solely under his control, and he is not bound to account except when he habitually wastes the property or does not administer it for the benefit of the other members, in which case a suit may lie to dispose him from the karanavanship. An individual member cannot claim any specific portion of the property as his share, nor will any debts incurred by any junior member of the family or for the matter of that by the karanavan himself, except for the benefit of the family, be binding on the property. Partition of family property can be effected only with the consent of all the grown up members of it.

The *karanavan*'s power was in theory, and frequently in practice, absolute. Informants often compared the *karanavans* of the past to petty rajas. With the probably rather hypothetical exception of legal action, there was no means by which the junior members of the *taravad* could rid themselves of their *karanavan*, even if he were incompetent or senile, deranged or totally irresponsible. (Gough (1959b: 245-6), however, notes that supernatural sanctions could be brought to bear: '... lineage ghosts were probably particularly effective in punishing or setting to rights misdemeanours of the *karanavan* himself'.) Nowadays, a fair picture of the *karanavan*-ship is hard to obtain as no modern Nayar has a good word for it, at least in Ramankara. Stories of *karanavans* who squandered the *taravad* fortune on toddy, gambling, womenfolk or spectacular weddings and temple festivals are legion – the adopted heir of Tekkapuram was one such. Very occasionally, I was told, the junior members might rebel against a *karanavan* and, if agreement could be reached, he might be persuaded to leave the *taravad* by the gift of a piece of land for his personal use. Amongst his other responsibilities, the *karanavan* had to organise cultivation of the *taravad* estate; if he were competent, the junior members could expect to lead lives of pleasant idleness.

As Aiya says, the agreement of all adult members was required before the *taravad* estate could be partitioned. However, as informants pointed out, such jural democratic principles had little sway in the autocracy which was the *taravad*; if the *karanavan* and perhaps the one or two other important men in the group decided on partition, then the nominal agreement of other junior members could be counted upon. Shea's argument (qu. in Mencher 1962: 232) that the unanimous agreement of all *taravad* members to a partition was almost impossible to obtain and that it was therefore infrequent traditionally, seems untenable given the authority structure of the *taravad*.

The *karanavan* represented his *taravad* in the local caste council. These councils were responsible for the behaviour of local caste members; in particular, they were charged with the enforcement of caste rules, such as those proscribing cross-caste marriage. However, it is not clear what role these councils (known as *karayogams*) played in this period in Central Travancore, for they were reorganised as local branches of the Nayar Service Society in the early part of this century. Further north, *karanavans* were also members of local caste councils; the political structure of Travancore after Martanda Varma means, however, that the hierarchy of power, by which a *karanavan's* authority was, to some extent, guaranteed by the chiefs and ultimately the king in Central Kerala (Gough 1961: 339-40), cannot have obtained here.

Aiya mentions succession to the office of *karanavan*; as he says, the heir is the next eldest male, irrespective of which segment he belongs to. This rule, of course, means that men tend to be fairly old by the time they succeed to the *karanavan*-ship. A total absence of men in the *taravad* must have been very rare, but were it to occur, then the oldest woman became *karanavan* (cf. Mencher 1962: 234).[3]

Taravad property, as we have seen, was held collectively and no individual member had any right to claim his or her share of it. There is thus, ipso facto, no system of inheritance of property between individuals. In practice, however, there is a problem to be considered; it arises out of the attempts by men, especially *karanavans,* to transfer some of their *taravad's* property to their own wives and children. The *karanavan,* with complete control over this property, was evidently in an excellent position to make such transfers without detection by junior members, and informants insisted that *karanavans* had always tried to do this. In the interregnum, as we shall see, such transfers became practically universal and approvable. This makes it difficult to interpret my informants' statements for there is an obvious possibility that they are projecting onto the distant past the behaviour and motives of men of more recent times. It is not possible to reach a conclusion on this question in the absence of sufficient evidence. Junior members could attempt to prevent their *karanavans* from transferring land out of the *taravad* – if they found out about it – by suing in the courts, but the difficulties were the same as those attending any other attempt to oust the *karanavan* through legal manoeuvres.

In speaking of 'property', I have meant primarily landed property. Even today, land is still the most important form of wealth for most people in the villages, and fifty years ago this was even more true. Except for the house, no form of property possessed by the *taravad,* or its members, had anything like the importance of its land. When the land was divided between segments of a *taravad,* the value of the house to the segment continuing to occupy it was probably taken into account. In the old order, an individual's self-acquired property was also supposed to revert to the *taravad* on his death, but in fact, despite the controversy surrounding this prescription in the early years of this century, it was not a problem

The Nayar Kinship System

of major significance to Nayars in Ramankara, where opportunities for acquiring property were poor. This latter point must be emphasised, for it contrasts strongly with the situation in the Central Kerala villages studied by Gough (1952a: 79) and Mencher (1962: 233-4), where men were acquiring property for themselves on a significant scale. Such a man then used his property to found a new matrilineal joint family that would trace its descent from his wife. This did not happen in Ramankara, where men neither acquired much new property nor tried to start new *taravads*. These comparative questions, and the wider backcloth against which the changes in Ramankara were occurring, will be discussed in greater detail in chapter 6. Here I shall concentrate on the Nayars in Ramankara and now move on to look at developments in the interregnum period.

The interregnum

The crucial process taking place during the interregnum was the development of a concept of individual property, i.e. property owned by an individual, not by a corporation such as the *taravad*.

I begin by considering a case history — that of the Kunnam *taravad*. This was the second wealthiest in Ramankara and is therefore atypical, but unfortunately it was the only one for which I was able to obtain detailed and self-consistent information. However, the general pattern revealed by this case is the same as that which emerged from many discussions with other informants about the break-up of *taravads*, and I feel fairly confident that the outline below is not inaccurate in its essentials.

In the early years of this century (precise dates are unavailable), the Kunnam *taravad* was headed by two brothers — Aiyappan (G21), the *karanavan*, and Rama (G22) — and their three sisters — Narayani (G23), Kalyani (G24) and Mani (G25); see chart 4. All five were born and raised in one house. After marrying, the brothers left the family house to live with their wives in homes which were probably built on the latter's land. Aiyappan later built a new house on his own land, but this was probably after the death of his first wife and his subsequent remarriage. The eldest sister, Narayani, remained with her husband in the family house, and the two younger sisters went to live with their husbands in new houses constructed on land owned by the Kunnam group. The *tavazhis* of Kalyani and Mani, i.e. the matrilineal segments of the *taravad* headed by these two sisters, took new names to distinguish them from the *tavazhi* of Narayani which kept the old name, and from each other. The Kunnam *taravad* seems to have owned about 320 acres. Each of the five siblings was now living in a separate household and therefore the *taravad*'s land was divided into five. Responsibility for the partition was the *karanavan*'s, and Aiyappan allocated about 50 acres to each of his siblings and kept the remainder for himself. Informants stressed that it was more or less universal for the *karanavan* to keep a greater share for himself than he allowed to his brothers and sisters. Now this property division was de facto, not de jure, and thus the property group, comprising the five siblings and their descendants, was no longer congruent with the household, which had split into five parts. The shares of the *taravad* land allocated to the *karanavan* and his brother were supposed to revert to the *taravad* on their deaths; in Malayalam, these brothers' shares are known as *jivanamsam* – 'life-share'. The income of any particular household thus derived from two sources: the *jivanamsam* of the husband and the wife's share of her *taravad*'s property.

The division of property in the interregnum marked the transition from a partition between matrilineal segments to a partition between individuals. In fact, it was both. The ultimate partition of the former type is a division between siblings (and their matrilineal descendants); inevitably, therefore, it involves a division between individual brothers. We can thus see how repeated partition of a matrilineal joint family's property can lead to the development of individual property and the creation of an inheritance system.

The general pattern may be summarised quite simply. We see that the household, in the old order a joint family consisting of a matrilineal segment, splits into *tavazhis*, i.e. shallow matrilineal segments, which become the new households with the addition of the husbands of adult female members. The old order household was a matrilineal segment; the interregnum household was a matrilineal sub-segment plus husbands. In the old order, husbands and wives did not live together, whereas post-marital residence in the interregnum was normally uxorilocal, though we should note the relevance of Nakane's comment that in this situation, uxorilocal residence resulted from the disintegration of the *taravad*: 'It should be treated as a different problem from the uxorilocal residential patterns of other matrilineal systems' (1962: 23). It is worth remarking too that as, in many cases, both husband and wife were natives of Ramankara, a house might well have been built on the husband's land if there were advantages in so doing.

In the interregnum, as we have just seen, the property group and the household ceased to be congruent. Households, however, did control property, even though they did not own it, and they were responsible for its cultivation and had absolute rights over its fruits. Now, as I have said, a man's *jivanamsam* ('life-share') was supposed to revert to his *taravad*, i.e. to his sisters and sisters' children, after his death. Reference has also been made to *karanavans'* attempts, even under the old order, to transfer *taravad* property to their wives and children. In the interregnum, these transfers came to be made quite openly and, in most cases, were sanctioned by Nayar public opinion. Naturally, in any one case, there were opponents: ego's sisters' husbands, who had a vested interest in defending the matrilineal norm in ego's (their wives') *taravad*, while advocating its abolition in their own *taravads*. But informants' statements reveal that a clear shift occurred; at the beginning of the interregnum, around 1920, the proportion of the *jivanamsam* which reverted to matrilineal kin was relatively high. But towards its end, this proportion had dramatically fallen, and by 1940, the *jivanamsam* was going in its entirety to the wife and children.

The Nayar Kinship System

The changes during the interregnum clearly altered the role of the *karanavan*. Although at the beginning, he was still able to control the property and divide it how he wished, by the end of the interregnum this was no longer true. A man became able to transfer property to his own wife and children but, of course, as he did this, he was simultaneously diminishing the amount of *taravad* property and thus lessening his power. The control of his sisters' property was steadily passing to their husbands, and, in a more general sense, a man, while increasing his control over his own wife and children, was correspondingly relinquishing it over his sisters and sisters' children. What occurred in Ramankara is theoretically familiar to anthropologists: a strengthening of the marital bond, as exemplified in the changing pattern of property transmission, is directly correlated with a weakening in the unity of the matrilineal joint family.

The reader should find it easier to understand exactly what was happening during the interregnum after I have explained what is the situation today; it is to this that I now turn.

The new order

In the new order, the property group as such no longer exists, for property is owned by individuals. But the members of a household do own all the property on which their household depends; unlike the situation during the interregnum, no household depends on or controls property whose legal owner is not one of its members. The household is also, of course, a production and consumption unit. The question of property and inheritance will be returned to later; I begin with a breakdown by household type of 91 Nayar households in my Ramankara sample census (see table 11).

The table shows that 53% of households are nuclear (type 1) and that 90% of households are nuclear or variants on the nuclear type (types 1-5), as opposed to only 9% which are joint families of various types (types 7, 8, 11). Of these joint families, only one (type 7) is collateral; the other seven are lineal joint families which, as we shall see, are characteristic of a certain stage in the developmental cycle of the household. The *taravad*, of course, was the archetypal collateral joint family. (The collateral joint family in the sample is said to be a temporary arrangement by its members.) There can be no doubt that the norm today - both ideologically and statistically - is the nuclear family. The comparative implications of the above with data on household types in Malabar and Cochin will be taken up in chapter 6.

We must now look at the developmental cycle of the modern Nayar household, and I shall begin from the point at which a recently married Nayar couple have set up home together. Eventually, their children grow up, and their marriages are arranged. Sons should be married in age order, as should daughters, although there is no objection to marrying daughters before their older brothers, and this happens often enough. When husband

Table 11. *Household types among Ramankara Nayars (after Kolenda)*

Type	No. of households	% of households
1	48	52.8
2	23	25.2
3	8	8.9
4	1	1.1
5	2	2.2
7	1	1.1
8	6	6.6
11	1	1.1
12	1	1.1
All	91	

The classification is that suggested by Kolenda (1968: 346–7).[4] No households fall into her categories 6, 9 and 10.

and wife come from different villages, there is a tendency today to prefer virilocal marriage, but this is not a strict rule and there is considerable variation in post-marital residence (see tables 16–18, pp. 91–3); a variation correlated with the fact that both husband and wife are likely to own land.

As marriages may be either virilocal or uxorilocal, let us - for the purposes of illustration - assume that all the sons of our couple marry virilocally and all the daughters uxorilocally. That this is unlikely does not materially affect the following argument. The first child to marry will bring his or her spouse to live in the parents' house, and the whole household - parents, the newly-married couple and unmarried children - will form one economic unit. It is very rare indeed for any Nayar household, or a household of any other community in this region of Kerala for that matter, not to form a single economic unit. The newly-married couple will remain in the parents' house until the next child marries and brings his or her spouse to the parental home as well. Shortly after this, the first couple will move out to a new house. They may or may not have children by now; this is not a relevant consideration. In their new house, they form a separate economic unit. How they obtain land from which to earn a living will be discussed shortly; for the present, we need simply assume that they receive land from one or both sets of parents. This process continues through the sibling group, with the second couple moving out after the marriage of the third child, and so on. Finally, the last child will marry but will not move out. On this last child will devolve the responsibility for looking after the parents in their old age, and after their deaths this child will inherit the parental house; there thus exists a sort of ultimogeniture with respect to the inheritance of the house.

It is, of course, unlikely that all sons will marry virilocally and all daughters uxorilocally. As there is now a preference for virilocal marriage, it is becoming more and more common for the youngest son to inherit the house, but many older people still express a preference for uxorilocal marriage and told me that they intend their youngest daughter to inherit their house. Not infrequently, the eldest daughter inherits it; this is especially likely to occur if she has had to look after her parents for many years. In such a case, those of her siblings who marry after her will move to new houses immediately following their marriages. Theoretically, if all sons married uxorilocally and all daughters virilocally, a situation might arise in which no-one was in a position to inherit the family house. But this is highly improbable, as a house is a valuable asset for which there is more likely to be competition than a reluctance to occupy it. There are one or two cases in which all the children of a couple living in Ramankara live elsewhere because of their jobs, but even in these cases it has usually been decided who will inherit the house eventually, as it is assumed that the emigrants will wish to retire to their native village.

Of the 23 households of type 2 (table 11 above), nine are households including the husband's parent and five the wife's parent. In the light of my description of the developmental cycle, it is not surprising that eight of the nine former households are built on the husband's land and all five of the latter on the wife's.

In order to proceed any further, I shall have to explain how the members of a household obtain the property on which they depend. For the purposes of inheritance among the Nayars today, land is divided into two categories. These are: land which is vested in the family as defined matrilineally, in other words a *taravad* or *tavazhi*; and land which is vested in the individual. Following the lawyers (Derrett 1963: 353), I term the former ' family property' and the latter ' individual property', although ' family land' and ' individual land' would be more accurate as we are concerned *only* with land in this discussion.[5]

Family property is that property inherited by a *woman from any matrilineal relative.* For the most part, this now means her mother, but were she to inherit from any other matrilineal relative such as her brother, sister or mother's brother, then that property too would be family property. Family property is for the maintenance not only of the woman in whose name it is held, but also for all her matrilineal descendants, i.e. her children, daughters' children, etc. In other words, she holds it on behalf of all her matrilineal descendants, as well as herself. Without the consent of all her adult matrilineal descendants, she may not alienate it, and if there are minor matrilineal descendants at the time of alienation, provision must be made so that each of them receives upon adulthood a plot of land equal in value to that which would have been their share at the time of alienation, or cash in lieu. Family property is equivalent to the Sinhalese category that Leach (1961a: 109) calls the ' entailed inheritance of the mother'. When partition takes place, family property must be divided equally between all matrilineal descendants; in practice, this usually means between the woman's children and her daughters' children. A pregnant daughter should receive a share for the unborn child. For example, suppose at the time of partition, a women has two sons and two daughters and that one daughter has two children, then the woman's family property must be divided into six. The daughter with the two children will receive three shares – half the property – which she holds for herself and her children. If one of the sons were dead, the property would be split into five, and no share would go to his widow or children. Similarly, if the daughter with the children were dead, the property would be divided into five, and her two children would each receive one-fifth of the property. The partition, in other words, is strictly per capita between all living matrilineal descendants.

Individual property is that property obtained by a woman by any means *other* than inheritance from a matrilineal relative, and the property of a man; how he acquired it is of no consequence whatsoever. Individual property is equivalent to Leach's (idem.) Sinhalese category of 'acquired property', and there is no equivalent of the Sinhalese 'entailed inheritance of the father'. Individual property is freely alienable, and no person other than the owner has any right to interfere in its disposal; in this respect, it is clearly distinguished from family property which, as we have seen, is only alienable with the consent of all adult matrilineal descendants of the holder. Consequently, the rules governing the inheritance of family property outlined above are enforceable in the courts, whereas those governing individual property, which I describe below, are not. To deprive a child of a share of family property is illegal; to deprive a child of a share of individual property is not. From the definition of individual property which has been given, it will be seen that if a woman inherits land from her father, it will be individual property. But if she then hands this down to her daughter, it will be for the latter family property, because it is property held by a woman which has been inherited from a matrilineal relative. Thus the size of the 'pool' of family property does not decline simply as a result of the operation of the inheritance system, and particular pieces of land which are family property in one generation may be individual property in the subsequent generation and vice versa.

The rule governing the inheritance of individual property is basically that it should be divided equally between all the children. If any child is dead, then its descendants should receive the share that would have been the deceased's. In other words, the division is stirpital. There are several variations on this basic rule. For example, a woman will often amalgamate all her property, both family and individual, and partition it according to the rules governing family property; she is most likely to do this when the majority of her property is family property. Alternatively, if most of it is individual property, she may divide it as if it were all individual property; strictly speaking, such a partition is illegal, but I have never heard of a court case over such an action. A man often has all his property transferred to his wife, either before or after his death, and it is then up to her to decide how it will eventually be divided. Sometimes a man divides his property between his wife and children, but never, I am certain, would he give shares to his daughters' children. Finally, it is quite common for husband and wife to amalgamate their property and, for the purposes of partition, consider it all as one unit. In this case, whether or not daughters' children receive shares is likely to depend on the proportion of family property in the whole. Just occasionally, it happens that a child is denied a share of his parents' property if, for example, he or she refuses to marry someone whom the parents have chosen as a spouse. But such occurrences are extremely rare.[6]

No dowry (*stridhanam*) is paid by Nayars in Central Travancore. Because both men and women own property and inherit from their parents, it would, say informants, be illogical to pay dowry, which is regarded as a daughter's share of the parental estate.[7] A gift of gold may, however, be given to a bride by her parents, but this is seen as more akin to our wedding present than it is to a dowry. Inheritance of the house has been mentioned in the context of the developmental cycle. Domestic animals such as cows and hens, and all household furniture, kitchen equipment, etc. are considered as part of the house and are inherited with it. Jewellery and clothing, such as saris, are usually left by women to their daughters. Informants said that there were no rules about the inheritance of cash, as no-one ever left much!

The mode and timing of partition are directly related to the developmental cycle of the household. Nowadays, it is rare for land to remain unpartitioned until after the death of the owner, and in general we can say that land tends to be partitioned earlier than it used to be; by earlier, I mean earlier in the developmental cycle of any particular household and earlier in the lifetime of any particular individual. An owner has the sole right to decide how and when land is partitioned and, even today, so informants told me, women jealously guard this right and rarely yield it to their husbands. A considerable amount of personal choice, which cannot be fully analysed, is therefore involved, but, at the same time, there is a variety of pressures on owners, which may be identified.

I have said that after the second child, of our typical family, has married, the first child will leave the parental home, and that in their new house this first child and his or her spouse form a separate economic unit. It is probable that the new house will be built near the parents' house on land belonging to them, and thus it is almost inevitable that a husband's parent, in a virilocal marriage, and a wife's parent, in a uxorilocal marriage, will be the first to have to partition his or her land.

Suppose, for the sake of illustration, that the four parents each own x acres of land and that each of the two couples has six children, which is statistically approximately the norm. Ignoring the slight discrepancy which may arise because daughters' children inherit part of the mothers' family properties, it can be seen that each child will inherit a total of

$\frac{1}{3}x$ acres from its parents, and that a married couple will own a total of $\frac{2}{3}x$ acres, or one-third of the area owned by their respective parents. If x is large, then $\frac{2}{3}x$ may be considerably more land than is actually required by a young couple with perhaps only one or two small children. In such a case, there may be no need for them to obtain all their four shares immediately. But if x is small, then even $\frac{2}{3}x$ – all they can hope to inherit – may be hardly sufficient for the young couple to live on. What is plain is that the pressure exerted on their parents by this couple, to give them their shares straight away, will be inversely proportional to the size of x. Now the median landowning of a Ramankara Nayar household is between 2½ and 5 acres, and thus the median value of x lies between 1¼ and 2½ acres; $\frac{2}{3}x$ is therefore approximately 1–2 acres, and the median size of each of the four shares to be inherited from the four parents is between 25 and 50 cents. An acre of land is likely to yield an annual income of Rs 500–1000 (1972), which even in Kerala represents a low standard of living. However, my aim here is to suggest to the reader the intensity of the pressure, which is necessarily exerted on parents to divide their land quickly and let their children take their shares. Today, both parents' land is in fact usually divided at this time, that is upon the setting-up of a new household by the first of their children. But in the past, when land was more plentiful, this did not always happen, and even today rich families are less likely to partition all their parental land at this time. The general trend, though, is plain; the decline in the average landowning is forcing the division of parental land to occur earlier in more and more cases.

There is, however, a countervailing tendency associated with a certain conflict of interests, which informants often discussed with me. As family property is divided between children and daughters' children, it may be in the interests of a woman to have the partition of her mother's family property postponed, until she has borne all her children. Conversely, it is in the interests of sons to have it done before any of their sisters give birth. Sisters' interests are also likely to conflict: elder sisters desiring partition before their younger sisters have too many children and younger sisters wanting partition delayed. I think it probable that in a virilocal marriage, sons are more likely to be able to persuade their mothers to divide the family property early, whereas in a uxorilocal marriage, daughters may have more influence. I should say that this suggestion is my own speculation; it was not expounded to me by informants.

An actual partition may be made in several ways. Firstly, it may be de jure or only de facto. In a de jure partition, the legal title to the land is transferred from parent to child; whereas in a de facto partition this is not done, and there is only an informal agreement between the two. In the latter case, legal transfer may not take place until all children have become adult or until after the death of the parent. Not infrequently, adult children may receive legal title to their shares, particularly if they intend to sell it, while younger children only obtain their shares de facto. Informants state that when partition takes place, all heirs should be allocated their shares at one and the same time, even if some of them are only children. In practice, however, a parent may give his older children shares without working out the division of the remaining property. The critical principle underlying partition, whatever its particular form may be, is that it should be fair, i.e. that all those entitled to equal shares should receive *exactly* equal shares. This is why shares should be allocated to all heirs at the same time, for in this way the possibility of some heirs receiving more than others is said to be minimised. I must make it clear that 'equal' does not necessarily mean equal in terms of area. The criterion employed is that of equal income generation – shares should generate the same amounts of money in, say, one year. Some attempt may also be made to compensate for the differing values of plots according to their location, as land close to a road is, for example, worth more than land further away – other things being equal. The partition necessarily has a rough and ready element in it and can engender bitter disputes between siblings, especially if partition takes place after the death of the parent who, in his own lifetime, would have had the moral authority to impose his decision on his heirs. For the purposes of partition, wet and dry land are always considered separately, as they are not thought to be truly equatable.

Secondly, there is considerable variation in how the material wants of the parents will continue to be met. There are three basic methods of arranging this. The first is for the parents to keep one category of property for their own use and partition the remainder. For instance, the parents may keep the husband's property and divide all the wife's; this retained property will be split after the parents' deaths. The second way is for the parents to keep a portion of the land and divide all the rest, in other words, to make a division between themselves and their heirs. Again, the retained land will be divided after death. This portion is known as a *jivanamsam,* a 'life-share'. (The reader will recall the word from earlier discussion.) For example, a man may have five children and own five acres. He may keep one acre for himself and his wife, and give 80 cents to each heir. After his death, they will each receive a further 20 cents. Although not absolutely certain, I am fairly sure that this type of *jivanamsam* is freely alienable by the parent, who has not relinquished any of his rights over it (assuming it is individual property). In the third way by which parents' needs are met, their *jivanamsam* is not alienable at will. Here all the land is divided between the heirs, but the parents retain the right to take a part of the income generated by the inherited land from each heir. Almost always, this income is that produced by the trees – coconut and areca-nut palms, rubber trees and pepper vines – and not from seasonal crops such as paddy, tapioca and bananas. The logic is that in the case of the non-seasonal tree crops, the previous owner has spent many years tending them and thus has a right to continue to enjoy the income from them, whereas he has not contributed to the cultivation of seasonal crops after handing over the land. The income received by the previous owner under this arrangement is known as *meladayam,* from *mela* – '(what is) above', i.e. in reference to the trees, and *adayam* – 'income'. In this latter type of *jivanamsam,* the land may only be alienated with the agreement of both the previous owner and the heir. Finally, the parents may solve the problem by a combination of more than one of these basic modes; for example, by dividing some of their categories of property but retaining a proportion of others.

These general principles of partition were explained to me by many informants, and the inclusion of case studies would not materially aid the exposition. The ideological norm which states that all heirs are entitled to equal shares is so strongly adhered to that it is hardly ever broken, and I have never heard of a case in the Ramankara Nayar community.[8] I am convinced that, in practically all partitions, heirs receive shares which are at least thought to be precisely equal. Of the Sinhalese in Pul Eliya, Leach writes that: 'The individual's inheritance prospects are at times wildly unpredictable' (1961b: 143). Quite the opposite is the case in Ramankara, although of course birth, death and the timing of partitions are hard, if not impossible, to prophesy. Nevertheless, if a man has five siblings and his father has six acres of land, he can be almost 100% certain that he will eventually inherit one acre from his father.

I stated above that the mode and timing of partition are directly related to the developmental cycle of the household. The connection lies in the disfavour with which economic co-operation between households is viewed; it is extremely rare for two households to co-operate in production and to share in consumption, even if they are the households of father and son, or of brothers. When it does happen, it is almost always a very temporary phenomenon. There exists, too a strong objection to the presence of more than one married child in the parental home at the same time; when it does occur, it is again almost always a temporary phenomenon except among the very poor, who may be unable to build a separate house. The latter was the explanation for the existence of the only such household in my sample.

Conclusion

In this chapter, it has been shown that during the last hundred years or so, the household has changed from being a large joint family consisting of the members of a matrilineal segment, through a stage in which it comprised a matrilineal sub-segment plus husbands of female members of the sub-segment, to the modern type which is basically a nuclear family, although at certain periods in the developmental cycle it is likely to become a lineal joint family. In the old order, the property group was congruent with the household, but in the interregnum this ceased to be so. This, I suggest, can be viewed as an internal contradiction in the system which could only be resolved if the *taravad* ceased to be the property group. I have argued that there existed in the old order a strong ideological norm

Table 12. *'Maternal' and 'paternal' features of Nayar kinship system*

Feature	Old order	Interregnum	New order
Property group	Matrilineal joint family (*taravad*)	Matrilineal joint family (*taravad*)	None (nuclear-type household)
Inheritance	No individual property	Male → Ch+Z/ZCh Female → Ch/DCh/etc.	Male → Ch Female (Individual) → Ch (Family) → Ch/DCh/etc.
Household	Matrilineal joint family (*taravad*)	Matrilineal segment (*tavazhi*) + H's of adult fems.	Nuclear/(lineal joint family at certain stages)
Residence	Duolocal (visiting husbands)	Uxorilocal	Viri-/uxori-/neolocal
Clan (def. of exogamy)	Matrilineal descent group (M → Ch)	Matrilineal descent group (M → Ch)	Matrilineal descent group (M → Ch)
Death pollution community*	Clan (M → Ch)	————————→†	Clan (M → Ch) (ideological norm). Also immediate affines (behavioural norm)
Clan name	M → Ch	M → Ch	M → Ch
Inherited personal name	M → D ME1B → ZS	————————→	F → S F → D
Caste title (males only)	MB → ZS	MB → ZS	MB → ZS
Authority and responsibility	MB (*karanavan*) → ZCh H ↛ W	————————→	F → Ch H → W

* Discussed in more detail in chapter 2.
† Arrows through interregnum indicate no distinct mode in this period.

favouring the congruence of the household and the property group; it therefore seems reasonable to conclude that the absence of such a congruence during the interregnum was perceived as an internal contradiction which needed to be resolved. The resolution took the form of a dissolution of the property group, so that property came to be held only by individuals and so that a household depended solely on the property owned by its members, who in turn owned no property on which another household depended.[9] I have insisted previously that the development of individual property in land has been the most significant factor in the total set of changes which has occurred, that it is, so to speak, the 'dynamic' underlying the process. In the following chapter, where I discuss marriage, the reader will see that this same dynamic underlies the set of changes which have occurred in that sphere of Nayar social organisation. It is worth noting what has *not* happened. There has been no transfer of property from women to men, nor from matrilineal descent groups to patrilineal descent groups. Nor does the statement that 'matriliny' has given way to 'patriliny' either describe or explain anything of significance in this context, as I hope the reader will agree on looking at table 12 above which summarises the principal changes that have taken place.

Finally, what will happen next? The development of any strongly patrilineal system seems highly improbable, for that would require the abolition of women's rights to property. There is no sign of such a development. In 1972, however, it seemed likely that the development of individual property would continue to its logical conclusion: namely, the abolition of the category of family property. There were indications that this was occurring in some families, where women had not given shares to their daughters' children, and many young Nayar men expressed their opposition to the giving of such shares. Three years after I completed fieldwork, the Kerala Hindu Act, 1975, was passed; this Act, I understand, has abolished daughters' children's rights to any of their grandmother's land. 'Paternal' features may continue to grow in importance, e.g. virilocal marriage may become the norm, to a much greater extent than it is now. In other words, relations between men and women among the Nayars may approach still closer to the high-caste Indian norm. But no certain predictions can be made, for the issue of inheritance is likely to be affected by many economic factors, for example, and the question of the development of 'paternal' features by the growing influence of other ideas, especially modern Western ones, about the proper relations between men and women.

4 The Nayar marriage system in Ramankara

In the previous chapter, I discussed property ownership, inheritance and residential patterns among the Ramankara Nayars, and argued that the most significant change during the last century or so has been the development of individual property in land. The data on marriage 'dovetail' with those presented in the last chapter, and the division into old order, interregnum and new order is again appropriate. My information comes mainly from genealogies and informants' statements, and some census data are also pertinent. Both the evidence and my analysis of it principally pertain to the 'big four' clans – the wealthiest and highest-status descent groups in Ramankara. I have already alluded to the near impossibility of collecting genealogies for the other, poorer clans.

Marriage in the old order was characterised by preferential marriage between a *muraccherukkan* ('right man') and a *murappennu* ('right woman'), and part of my analysis will be concerned with explaining exactly what this means. This type of marriage is associated with repeated inter-marriage between the 'big four' clans and with a tendency towards village endogamy (cf. Nakane (1962: 25), who refers to the same tendency among Cochin Nayars and remarks on its convenience for visiting husbands – a point also made by my informants). Marriage in the new order is characterised by the reverse: today a *muraccherukkan* should preferably *not* marry his *murappennu,* and there is a tendency towards village exogamy.

Nayar marriage: some general remarks

Before proceeding further, I must make clear what is meant by 'marriage' in the present context. In the 'traditional' system, there were, as we saw briefly in chapter 1, two types of union which could be called 'marriage'; although in chapter 5, where I discuss the traditional system in more detail, I shall argue that this terminology is misleading. The first of these unions was that between a prepubescent girl and a man (the *tali*-tier) inaugurated at the *tali*-rite; the second was that between a mature Nayar woman and a man of status equal or superior to her own, which was known as *sambandham*. However, further discussion of these two types is unnecessary here, for the *tali*-rite seems to have died out in Ramankara by the turn of the century, or even earlier, and not even my oldest informants were able to give a first-hand account of it.

The Nayars Today

The marriages which I shall be discussing in this chapter are more or less stable and usually monogamous unions between mature adults – in other words, marriages as they are normally recognised in the rest of India. As I shall show in chapter 6, it is clear that such unions have been the norm in Travancore at least since the beginning of this century. At that time, these marriages were still referred to as *sambandham*; Aiya (1906: II, 357) says that the *sambandham* was the 'marriage proper' in Travancore, and his opinion is shared by Panikkar (1918: 220) and Subramanya Aiyar (Census 1901, Travancore: 330). For the Nayar reformers, however, the word *sambandham* had a connotation of immorality, and today it is never used. Marriage is referred to as *kalyanam* (the word also employed in Tamilnadu) or, less commonly, as *vivaham* (the Sanskrit term used by the Nambudiri Brahmans). (For more details on the significance of these terms, see Mencher 1962: 238; 1965: 179.)

Two rules operate in all the marriages, past and present, with which we shall be concerned in this chapter. First, there is the rule of exogamy which prohibits marriage within the matrilineal descent group, i.e. between any two persons thought to have a common matrilineal ancestress. In practice, this is mainly determined by clan name: if two persons have the same clan name, then it is assumed that they have a common ancestress even if, as is often the case, the genealogical connection between the two has been forgotten (cf. also Nakane 1962: 21). Marriage to the patrilateral parallel cousin is also prohibited, although I am uncertain about the lateral extent of this interdiction, which is probably relatively defined according to circumstances. (Sister's daughter's marriage is self-evidently prohibited; Gough (1952b: 90) states that brother's daughter marriage occasionally occurred in Central Kerala, but I have never come across a case in Ramankara.) Second, there is the rule that a husband must be older than his wife, a universal rule in India which, in this context, carries the implication that the husband's status must be higher than his wife's. I know of no marriage in Ramankara which violated either the rule of exogamy or that of relative age – although even if they had occurred, it is quite likely that I would not have found out. The eternal Indian preference for fair-skinned wives – fairness being the most important determinant of beauty – is, of course, shared by Nayars.

The vast majority of Ramankara Nayars belong to the Illam subcaste, the highest-ranking of the four Central Travancore Nayar subcastes (see chapter 2). Except for marriages between Nambudiri Brahman men and Nayar women and, recently, a handful of marriages across subcaste boundaries, all marriages in Ramankara have been within the subcaste. I have some evidence of a rather inconclusive nature, which suggests that the other Nayar subcastes are not as strictly endogamous as the Illam subcaste; if this evidence were correct, it would correlate with an expected pattern of greater concern with purity in the highest subcaste. However, it is important to note here the strong ideology of endogamy present among Illam Nayars, and indeed, as we shall see later, there exists a positive preference for isogamous union, i.e. for unions in which both spouses' families are of equal status. There is no emphasis on or preference for hypergamy, where the husband's family ranks higher than the wife's.

It is clear that in Central Kerala the institution of *enangans* or 'linked lineages' was structurally very significant (Gough 1959a: 25-32; 1961: 327-30; Mencher 1965: 170-71; Dumont 1961: 20-24). The institution evidently existed in parts of Central Travancore too (Panikkar 1918: 264). According to Aiya (1906: II, 353), however, in much of Travancore, *talis* were tied by members of specially-designated families known as *macchampikkars*. These questions are dealt with in more detail in chapter 5; here I wish only to record the fact that my informants had never heard of either *enangans* or *macchampikkar* families. So far as they knew, a Ramankara girl's *tali* had been tied by her *muraccherukkan*, to whom it was handed by a Nambudiri. I was unable to obtain any information about the status of these Nambudiris.

In the past, Ramankara Nayar women sometimes married Nambudiri Brahman men, although genealogical evidence shows that this was never common. But by about 1925, such marriages had ceased, as Nayars were refusing to allow their womenfolk to marry Nambudiris. Previously, such unions had been thought to enhance the status of the Nayar woman, her children and her *taravad,* but Nayar reformers and the Nayar Service Society began to urge them to regain their 'self-respect', and to stop degrading themselves by permitting their women to be exploited as concubines by Nambudiris. (As one informant put it: '*sambandham* (to a Nambudiri) was really *asambandham* (a mockery)'.) More pertinently, Nayars began to object to Nambudiri refusal to contribute towards the upbringing of the children they fathered. For the Nambudiris to have made such contributions would, of course, have been to negate the very raison d'être of the system from their point of view. Relevant too is the fact that by this time, Nambudiris themselves – especially younger sons and some women – were beginning to campaign for the right of all Nambudiris to marry within the caste. (The reform movement started in South Malabar around 1917 (Mencher 1966b: 192).)

The old order

In the paragraphs above, I have given some of the background for the following analysis. In the old order, as we have already seen, *taravad* members had no individual ownership rights over any part of the *taravad*'s property, but only a right to maintenance. Throughout their lives, both men and women lived in their own *taravad*-houses, and their material wants were met only from their own *taravad*'s income. Husbands visited their wives at night; a man had no claim on his wife's *taravad,* or vice versa. Thus the economic standing of any one Nayar depended solely on the resources of his or her own *taravad,* and not at all on that of his or her spouse. This means that in marriage arrangements, economic factors are utterly irrelevant;

The Nayars Today

when arranging a match, the amount of property owned by a prospective spouse's *taravad* is of no consequence.

When individuals own and transfer property, the situation is totally altered. There is evidence that *karanavans* have always sought to transfer some of their *taravad*'s property to their own wives and children, and if this is the case, then the 'ideal' picture I drew above has never applied. Economic factors must always have been important, at least in *karanavans*' marriages. But relatively anyway, these factors cannot have had anything like the importance under the joint-family system that they grew to have later, when each and every adult Nayar came to own property individually – a development which began, as we know, during the interregnum.

The overall argument of this chapter is that economic factors have become increasingly significant in the arrangement of marriage: developing from, ideally, zero importance in the old order to the most important single factor today. At the same time, status – in the old order perhaps the most significant element – has nowadays become little more than a delimiting factor.

I have already mentioned that marriage in the old order was characterised by a rule which stated that a *muraccherukkan* should preferably marry his *murappennu*. The Dravidian root *mura* means 'right according to custom'. The *muraccherukkan* is thus the 'right man or boy' and the *murappennu* the 'right woman or girl'.[1] To simplify matters for the reader, I shall refer throughout to the 'right man' and the 'right woman'. I shall discuss only the case of male ego, for that of female ego is, mutatis mutandis, identical. A man should preferably marry his 'right woman'; therefore the first condition is that he should be unmarried and, conversely, no married woman can be his 'right woman'. (A man, of course, has no 'right men'.) The second condition is that only women younger than ego can be his 'right women'. Given that these conditions are satisfied, the defining criterion for a woman to fall into the category of ego's 'right women' is that she be 'related' to him. I deliberately use the vague word 'related', because whom a Nayar reckons as his relatives cannot be defined absolutely; it depends, for example, on genealogical knowledge which is itself contingent on factors such as wealth and status. The set of all relatives is equivalent to what Mayer (1960: 4) has aptly called the 'kindred of recognition'; broadly speaking, this is a larger grouping for the rich or those of high rank, than it is for the poor or those of low rank. But one element is fixed: the 'right woman' must be related to ego through *at least one* affinal link (other than a patrilateral parallel link), for were there only matrilineal links ego's 'right woman' would be a member of his own descent group and therefore unmarriageable.

Now it is critical that the direction of the relevant affinal link(s) is of no consequence. For instance, if at some time in the past, A, a male member of descent group X had married B, a female member of descent group Y, then another man of X – a matrilineal kinsman of A – would expect to have among his 'right women' women of Y – matrilineal kinswomen of

The Nayar Marriage System

B. At the same time, a man of Y would expect to have among his 'right women' women belonging to X. Exactly what is meant by a descent group's status is discussed below; here we need only know that each descent group does have a particular status. Suppose descent group X had higher status than Y; in this case, a marriage between a man of Y and a woman of X would imply that the wife-takers were of lower status than the wife-givers. We know, of course, that such a hypogamous marriage – a *pratiloma* union – is anathema in India. Therefore, the fact that the direction of the affinal link connecting a 'right man' and a 'right woman' is irrelevant necessarily implies that X and Y are of equal status, that there exists a rule of isogamous marriage.

Among the Ramankara Nayars, the isogamous rule is actually made explicit, and they insist that those who exchange women must be of equal status. For these Nayars, isogamy is a strongly stressed ideological norm.

It should now be clear what the rule is stating: that if the marriage between A and B satisfied the criterion of equal status, then a marriage between any two of their matrikin must also satisfy this criterion. Further, it is plain that there is no logical limit beyond which this cannot be extended. For if B had a brother, C, who married a woman, D, belonging to descent group Z, then a marriage between a man of Z (a kinsman of D) and a woman of X would also satisfy the criterion, as would a marriage between a man of X and a woman of Z. Whether or not a member of X would in practice recognise the existence of 'right men' or 'right women' in Z would depend on circumstances; as I have said, the kindred of recognition has no pre-determined boundaries.

This marriage rule, it should be noted, is not prescriptive, even at the ideological level. It does not state that ego must marry a 'right woman', but only that a 'right woman' is a better choice than an unrelated woman. For any unmarried ego, there are three categories of women: those he may not marry, those he should preferably marry and those he can marry. Marriageable women are, so to speak, divided into first-choice partners and second-choice partners.

I must emphasise that the 'right man' and 'right woman' categories, and the associated rule of marriage, are completely egocentric, i.e. they only refer and apply to individuals, not groups or categories. If two unmarried brothers, Govinda aged 26 and Gopala aged 20, had two unmarried mother's brother's daughters, Kalyani aged 23 and Karthiyani aged 17, then Kalyani and Karthiyani are both 'right women' of Govinda, whereas only Karthiyani is a 'right woman' of Gopala. This example indicates the crucial distinction between the 'right man' and 'right woman' categories, and those of cross-cousins.[2]

Cross-cousin kinship terminologies, i.e. those in which the category of cross-cousins is clearly distinguished from the category of siblings and parallel cousins, are prevalent throughout South India and Sri Lanka, where they are referred to as 'Dravidian' terminologies. Such terminologies are usually associated with a preferential rule of cross-cousin marriage, which states that ego should marry a woman falling into his category of cross-cousins. In such a system, both Kalyani and Karthiyani of our illustration would be in Govinda's and Gopala's cross-cousin category. Although terms for cross-cousins do exist in Malayalam (*macchunan, macchunicchi*), they are never used by Ramankara Nayars, whose kinship terminology thus lacks the standard Dravidian cross-parallel distinction.

These remarks will probably mean more to the specialist readers than others. However, at the risk of stretching the tolerance of the non-specialist still further, I should, I think, conclude my discussion of the difference between the Ramankara Nayar rule and a cross-cousin marriage rule, by pointing to the contrasting ways in which the two systems should formally operate. Suppose there are three descent groups X, Y and Z, between all three of which there have been marriages at some time. The operation of the Ramankara preferential marriage rule could lead to further intermarriages between any two of X, Y and Z, but *in no particular order.* Formally at least, the operation of a matrilateral cross-cousin marriage rule in such a situation should lead to a 'long cycle' linking the three groups; of a patrilateral cross-cousin rule to the formation of 'short cycles' between the groups; and of a bilateral cross-cousin rule – between two groups – to direct exchange between them. All these latter are marriage systems which come about because the marriage rule specifies a relation between *groups*. Our rule, on the other hand, does not specify a relation of this sort, but only the preferred spouses of *ego*; at the formal level, it can only generate random intermarriage between the three groups. It may well be that the genealogies of Ramankara Nayars look exactly like those collected in communities with a cross-cousin marriage system, but this is a separate problem. It must not be allowed to disguise the fact that the empirical similarity has emerged despite formal dissimilarities, not because of any formal identity.

Let me now leave kinship theory and return to the Ramankara Nayars. All Illam Nayars, of course, have equal caste status. Both their preferential marriage rule and the preference for village endogamy helped to maintain the purity of the subcaste, insofar as they discouraged marriages with Nayars whose subcaste status could not be so easily guaranteed. Informants told me that the preference for village endogamy was, in the past, explicitly linked to a concern for the maintenance of subcaste purity, the fear apparently being that lower-subcaste Nayars in stranger villages may have sought to pass themselves off as Illam Nayars, when marriages were being arranged. I was told that until the 1920s, or thereabouts, a cross-subcaste marriage would have led to outcasteing of the offender from the Illam community.

Apart from caste status, there is another type of status which matters in marriage; it attaches to clans or subclans and is referred to in Malayalam as *paramparyyam*. The nearest English translation would be 'ancestry' or, more precisely, 'pedigree', though the latter term has unfortunate connotations. The ancestry of a descent group is determined by the prestige and achievements of its past and, to a lesser extent, its present members. A Nayar clan whose forebears had distinguished themselves as servants of the rajas or as military leaders, as scholars or as sannyasis, would be one with good ancestry; ancestry thus depends on the number and magnitude of ancestral achievements. Such a notion is not foreign to us; when we say, for instance, that the Churchills are a 'distinguished family', we have in mind the number of members of the family who have made their mark in various spheres of life which we recognise as important. The Nayars do not confuse ancestry with caste status. They make it clear that two descent groups belonging to the same subcaste have equal caste status, i.e. are equally pure ritually, but may have quite different ancestries. Because ancestry is attached to a clan or subclan, it is transmitted unilineally and the clan name acts as its 'marker'.[3]

An objective measure of ancestry is intrinsically impossible. If the members of one descent group claim higher status and others accept their claim, then they have high status; if others reject it, they do not. Usually, informants – members of the 'big four' clans and others – would opine that the ancestry of the 'big four' was equal, but higher than that of all other Ramankara clans. However, if discussion turned to the number of marriages between members of the 'big four' and other, supposedly lower-status clans, then an informant was quite likely to assert that the status of all Ramankara clans was actually the same. The former statement was often given to me as unsolicited information; nevertheless, it may be tendentious to claim that it is more 'correct' than the latter. One can conclude that the ancestry of the 'big four' is equal or superior to that of the other clans; certainly no-one ever suggested that the 'big four' had a status lower than that of any other clan.

Conceptually, wealth and ancestry are sharply distinguished by all informants; ancestry, they pronounce, is in no way dependent on wealth. Nor do Nayars accept that wealth and ancestry can be weighed against each other as, for instance, Syrian Christians do. But it is patent from the way Nayars talk and act today that the two are not empirically independent. As I have said, clan names are the markers of this type of status. When collecting genealogies, I met many people claiming to belong to clans or subclans to which they did not actually belong, according to the rules of matrilineal descent. In particular, there were many people claiming membership of the Tekkapuram clan, although it had in fact become extinct after the death of its last *karanavan*. The Kunnam section of the Vadakkil clan also attracted a lot of 'fraudulent' claims. Claims of this sort were always established by tracing descent through the father, mother's father or mother's mother's father, rather than strictly matrilineally. A direct question about the ancestry of Tekkapuram or Kunnam will always elicit the assertion that it is identical to that of all other 'big four' clans and subclans. But these 'fraudulent' claims demonstrate that this latter value statement is not the only basis for action and that the enormous

The Nayars Today

wealth of Tekkapuram and Kunnam has its influence. In other words, there is an economic component within the notion of status. It is possible that this is a relatively recent development and that, in the past, ancestry and wealth were empirically distinct. But this is not easy to discover, for in informants' statements about the past there was frequently, I feel, a tendency to project today's conditions onto previous times.

Unfortunately, I have next to no empirical data on marriage in the old order, for the maximum depth of the genealogies collected was about five generations overall. The marriages of those in generation one took place in the last years of the nineteenth century. Members of this generation spent most of their adult life in joint families and men only visited their wives at night. But by the time those in generation two had reached maturity, the joint families were beginning to split up. Members of this generation lived most of their adult life in smaller residential units which included their spouses.

My argument concerning the relevance of status and economic factors to marriage in the old order is therefore not founded on genealogical data, but on a logical analysis of the implications for marriage of the joint-family system in the old order and of the preferential marriage rule. In the 'ideal' type of joint-family system, I have contended, economic factors must be irrelevant to marriage arrangement. Even though the empirical situation may not have accorded precisely with this 'ideal' picture, it is plain that the significance of economic factors must inevitably have been slight, compared with their significance later, when individuals had come to own property. It has been shown, too, that the question of status was a crucial element in the marriage rule defined by the 'right man' and 'right woman' categories, for it embodied a rule of isogamy and also defined the preferred spouse by reference to a previous marriage, which had satisfied the status criterion.

The marriages in generation one took place in the old order, and they constitute the only data available on marriages from this period. Little can be said about them, except that they in no way contradict my assertion that economic factors were of next to no relevance. For example, the last *karanavan* of the Tekkapuram *taravad*, which owned over 1000 acres according to the 1908 Land Settlement Report, married a woman from the Kizhakkil *taravad* which owned only 250 acres (B11, D11), and his brother married into the Vadakkil Puthenveedu *taravad* which owned less than 100 acres (B12, F12). (The numbers locate individuals on the genealogical charts.) So far as I know, there is no reason why the Tekkapuram brothers could not have married into the Kunnam *taravad*, which owned over 600 acres and was the second greatest landowner in Ramankara.

The interregnum

During the interregnum, economic factors became increasingly significant in marriage choice, although status factors still played an important role.

5. A fairly wealthy Nayar farmer in the village of Ramankara.

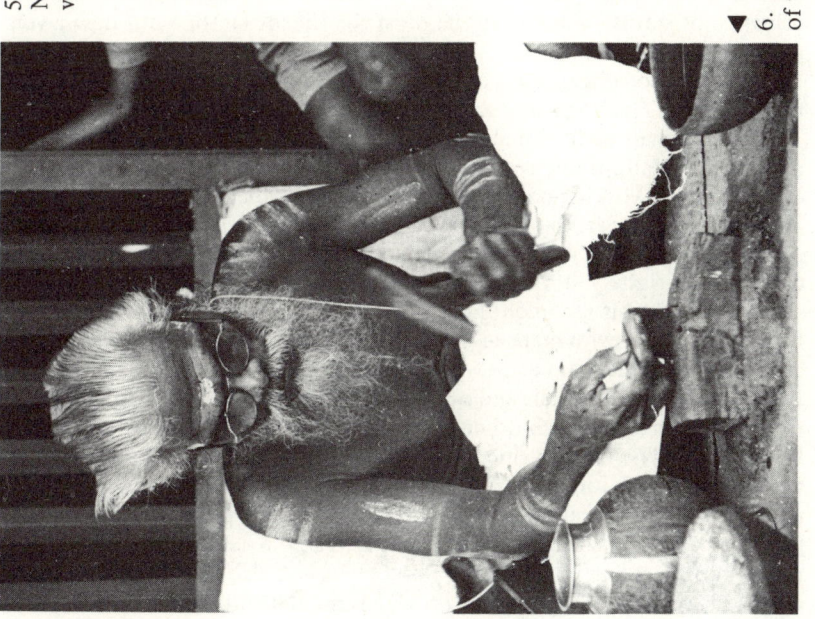

6. A village goldsmith of the Thattan caste.

The Nayars Today

Analysed synchronically, marriage arrangement in the interregnum reveals a pattern in which economic and status factors are of approximately equal significance. During this phase, as I explained in chapter 3, both men and women began to own property individually, while collective ownership by the *taravad* disappeared. If men and women both own property and if they live together sharing its fruits, it is evident that the economic standing of a man is partly dependent on that of his wife, and vice versa. A man will want to marry a woman owning the greatest possible amount of property. As we are concerned with a community in which almost all property takes the form of land, this marriage ' preference' may be re-formulated as follows: if he can, a man will wish to marry a woman whose landowning exceeds his by the maximum amount; if he cannot marry a richer woman, then he will want a wife whose landowning is less than his by the minimum amount. Mutatis mutandis, a similar pair of propositions will apply to woman as well. Of course, young men and women did not arrange their own marriages. The responsibility was theoretically the *karanavan*'s, i.e. usually the mother's eldest brother, but the father also had a say, and his opinion gained more and more influence during this period. Today, the mother's brother's right to a say is only nominal. However, the marriage preference, as I expressed it, may stand – if it is understood that in fact the choice of spouse rested with the father or mother's brother. What I hope to demonstrate is that marriage in the interregnum is best seen as the result of an attempt to maximise a conjugal pair's landowning, within the constraint set by a principle of status – previously the most significant factor – but now giving way to economic considerations.

I was able to collect fairly complete and coherent genealogical information on six clans and subclans: Tekkapuram–Vilangu, Vadakkil, Vadakkil Puthenveedu, Kunnam, Kizhakkil and Padinjerapuram. Considering only generations one to four inclusive (many in generation five are only children), and working only with those sections which are, to my knowledge, accurate, the genealogies include a total of approximately 350 persons. About 100 of them definitely married into one of the 'big four' clans; by 'definitely' I mean that I located both partners in the genealogies.[4] In table 13 is recorded the proportion of persons for generations one to four inclusive, who married into one of the 'big four' clans, into one of the other Ramankara clans, or outside Ramankara. Note that these figures refer to individuals and not to marriages. As most of those in the first column married each other, the figures for marriages would clearly be different. The table excludes people who either remained unmarried or on whom no information is available; there were, respectively, 7, 5, 4 and 23 such individuals in generations one, two, three and four. An obvious pattern emerges from table 13: a steady decline in the proportion of persons marrying into the 'big four' clans and also into other Ramankara clans (except for generation one on which the data are limited), as opposed to a large rise in the proportion of persons marrying outside the village. There is, it is true, a bias in the figures, for those in earlier generations who

Table 13. *Marriages of 'big four' clan members*

Generation	Married into 'big four' clan		Married into other Ramankara clan		Married outside Ramankara		All cases
	No.	%	No.	%	No.	%	No.
1	8	80.0	2	20.0	—	—	10
2	16	45.7	17	48.6	2	5.7	35
3	42	35.9	44	37.6	31	26.5	117
4	38	25.7	45	30.4	65	43.9	148
All	104	33.6	108	34.8	98	31.6	310

married outside the village are more likely to have been forgotten than those who married within it. However, my information convinces me that this bias does not significantly affect the observed trend. As marrying outside the village has become most prevalent in modern unions, I shall defer consideration of the reasons for it until later.

I did attempt to analyse the data on intermarriage between the 'big four' clans in terms of, firstly, a pattern of marriage alliance between the clan sections and, secondly, the genealogical relationships between husbands and wives. The first attempt was wholly futile, and I refrain from giving details here; there is certainly no systematic intermarriage pattern between these clan sections.

Seventeen of the marriages between members of 'big four' clans were between cross-cousins. Men married their MBD in 5 cases; MBDD: 1; MMBDD: 1; MMBDDD: 1; MMMBDDD: 2; MMMBDDDD: 1; FZD: 2; FZDD: 3; and, FZDDD: 1. Gough (1961: 365-6), Mencher (1962: 241) and Nakane (1962: 25) all report an increase in the frequency of cross-cousin marriage after the break-up of the *taravads*, relating this to its economic function of re-uniting property divided by inheritance – a function which cannot, of course, pertain when property is owned collectively by the *taravad*. A similar explanation was given to me by some informants, and it may be that a rise in the frequency of cross-cousin marriage did occur in Ramankara during the interregnum. Without accurate knowledge of the previous situation, however, no certain conclusion can be reached. I do not, though, think that the pattern of marriage in the interregnum can be accounted for simply in terms of the economic function of cross-cousin marriage; the marriages of this type which did occur are rather, I contend, special cases in the general pattern to be discussed below, and I submit that an analysis of this pattern in terms of cross-cousin marriage alone is in error. (The argument of this paragraph might be considered redundant in any case, given that the Ramankara Nayars never had a cross-cousin marriage system.)

The Nayars Today

I shall now look at marriage within the village in greater detail; the analysis has to focus closely on the particulars of the genealogical charts, and I shall be mainly concerned with marriages in generations two and three. Although I do not know exactly when these latter marriages took place, there is adequate justification for regarding them, admittedly a little arbitrarily, as having occurred in the interregnum. To draw out explicitly all the relevant information from the genealogies would require an excessive amount of space and would probably strike the reader as unutterably tedious; a judgment that will, I hope, be suspended in the case of the page or so of explication which I feel must be presented. The sceptical reader is unlikely to be convinced by the assertion that the pattern revealed below is general; nonetheless, I shall make that assertion, although it is true that the evidence is less patent for the clans and sub-clans whose genealogies are incomplete.

Let us begin by looking at the Vilangu clan (chart 2). Comparing the sisters A23 and A24, we see that A23 married into a 'big four' clan and of her seven children, three made similar marriages and one married into another Ramankara clan; A24, whose husband was from Ramankara though not from a 'big four' clan, had five children of whom only one married into a 'big four' clan and two into other Ramankara clans. A23 and A24 are daughters of A11, who also married into a 'big four' clan. Her sister, A13, about whose marriage nothing is known, had three daughters. One daughter, A25, probably married into Vadakkil Manimalaveedu,[5] and she bore five children, of whom one married into a 'big four' clan and two married into other Ramankara clans.

Turning our attention to Kizhakkil (chart 3), we see that D24, who was married to the Tekkapuram-Vilangu *karanavan,* had seven children of whom six married into 'big four' clans, while another sister, D23, married into another Ramankara clan, as did one of her two daughters. (About a third sister, we know nothing; a fourth sister died before marriage.) Their mother, D11, was married to the last *karanavan* of Tekkapuram. D12, whose husband is unknown, had two daughters: D29 married into Kunnam and of her five children, three married into 'big four' clans and one into another Ramankara clan; D210's husband is unknown and, of her three children, two married into 'big four' clans. D13's husband was from one of the Ramankara clans, and she bore four daughters. The first, who married into Padinjerapuram, had six children all of whom married into Ramankara clans. The second married into a Ramankara clan, as did three of her five children. The third married likewise, and of her five children three made similar marriages and one married into a 'big four' clan. The fourth also married into one of the Ramankara clans and so did seven of her eight children.

In the Vadakkil Puthenveedu subclan, F12, who was the wife of the Tekkapuram *karanavan*'s brother, bore six daughters but no sons. The first married into a Ramankara clan as did one of her five children, with two marrying into the 'big four' clans. The second also married into a Ramankara clan and so did one of her two children. The third married the Kizhakkil *karanavan,* but had no children. The fourth married into one of the Ramankara clans, and one of her two children married into a 'big four' clan. The fifth married into a 'big four' clan, as did one of her four children, while the sixth married a Nambudiri Brahman - one of her children married into a 'big four' clan and one into another Ramankara clan.

These three examples suggest that, during the interregnum, the probability of a Nayar marrying into one of the 'big four' clans was higher if his or her mother also did so, and - to a lesser extent - if his mother's mother made such a marriage. A similar conclusion applies to marriages into other Ramankara clans. Now this is, of course, no more than a restatement of the role of status in marriage arrangement and, particularly with respect to intermarriages between the 'big four' clans, of the operation of the preferential marriage rule. The evidence presented above gives some indication of the pattern realised empirically by the operation of this formal rule; clearly, the correlation between the two levels is imperfect, and I shall try to isolate some of the other variables.

One pertinent question is whether the role of status in marriage arrangement is identical for all members of the 'big four' clans. Evidence from elsewhere in India (Dumont 1970: 109ff) suggests that there may be differences between men and women, between brothers of different ages and between first and subsequent marriages. This question may be investigated by looking at the marriages of *karanavans* - the eldest brothers in a sibling group - and their siblings. (Marriages of the *karanavans* and their siblings into 'big four' clans are shown on chart 1.) All seven *karanavans* took their wives from one or other of the 'big four' clans; how many of their brothers and sisters did likewise is indicated in table 14. (The Tekkapuram and Vadakkil Puthenveedu *karanavans* are in generation one; all the others are in generation two.) From so few cases, it is impossible to draw firm conclusions, and random factors such as the sex ratio and the age order of siblings are clearly involved too. Nevertheless, the figures do suggest, firstly, that brothers are more likely to marry into 'big four' clans than sisters - including the *karanavans* themselves, 11 out of 13 brothers made such marriages as opposed to 4 out of 12 sisters - and, secondly, that the eldest brother is more likely to make such a marriage than are younger brothers. Both these conclusions accord with the typical Indian pattern. Three of these *karanavans,* B11, G21 and C22, had more than one wife: B11 and C22, two each, and G21, three. None of these four secondary wives belonged to a 'big four' clan and only one of them seems to have come from Ramankara. The lower status of secondary wives, also predictable in the Indian context, is apparent too in other cases of subsequent marriages appearing in the genealogies.

In generations two and three, I have argued, two of the variables - which have to do with status - affecting marriage arrangement are, first, to whom a person's mother and mother's mother were married and, second, a person's relative age and sex. Some of the marriages in generation four also reflect

Table 14. *Marriages of the karanavans' brothers and sisters*

	Brothers		Sisters	
	No.	W from 'big four'	No.	H from 'big four'
Karanavan				
1. Tekkapuram (B11)	1	1	—	—
2. Vadakkil Puthenveedu (F11)	—	—	2	1
3. Vilangu (A21)	1	1	2	1
4. Vadakkil (E21)	—	—	1	0
5. Kunnam (G21)	1	1	3	1
6. Padinjerapuram (C22)	2	1	2	0
7. Kizhakkil (D27)	1	0	2	1
All	6	4	12	4

the influence of these variables, but they have not been considered here because the large majority of them occurred after the end of the interregnum. Evidently, the spread of ages in each generation is considerable. I suggest that further relevant status factors cannot be isolated; the principal outstanding factor is economic, and I now turn my attention to it.

The reader will recall that, in generation two, spouses lived together and that households based on these conjugal pairs controlled the property on which they depended, although the share brought by the husband was still regarded as *jivanamsam*, a 'life-share', that was owned by the *taravad*. It will also be recalled that the *karanavan* was responsible for dividing the property between himself and his siblings (and other *taravad* members), and that he usually took the greatest share for himself.

In table 15, I list the areas of land owned by the seven wealthiest *taravads* in Ramankara according to the Land Settlement Report of 1908.[6] It will be seen that six of these *taravads* are those for which I was able to collect the fullest genealogical data; the exception is Manimalaveedu for which I could only glean fragments of the genealogy, but this was because most descendants of this *taravad* do not live in Ramankara, but in the village of Manimala. The wealthiest of the other thirty-odd *taravads* in the village owned 58 acres.

Ideally, we would like to know precisely how much property was controlled by each of the married couples in generation two, but accurate information on this was unobtainable. However, on the basis of the figures in table 15 and other pieces of information, some estimates are feasible. Undoubtedly, the wealthiest household was that of the Tekkapuram-Vilangu *karanavan*, Raman A21, who seems to have retained the majority of his *taravad*'s property and given only relatively small shares to his siblings. According to one of his sons, the Kunnam *karanavan*, Aiyappan G21, was responsible for about half the *taravad*'s 640 acres, the other half

The Nayar Marriage System

Table 15. *Areas of land owned by the seven wealthiest taravads, 1908*

Name of *taravad*	Area in acres
1. Tekkapuram-Vilangu	1173
2. Kunnam	642
3. Vadakkil Manimalaveedu	262
4. Kizhakkil	252
5. Padinjerapuram	166
6. Vadakkil	93
7. Vadakkil Puthenveedu	93

being in the hands of a half-brother. Apparently, Aiyappan allowed each of his four siblings around 50 acres and retained the remaining 100-odd acres under his own control. I did not obtain accurate data on the division of property in the Kizhakkil *taravad,* nor do I know how much land was controlled by Narayanan Vilangu, A12, the mother's brother of A21. Nonetheless, despite these lacunae, it is possible to rank the wealthiest households according to the probable amounts of land controlled. After A21's household, the second wealthiest was certainly that of G21. The next two were probably those of G22/A23 (G22 was a brother of G21 and A23 a sister of A21) and A12/G23 (G23 was a sister of G21). The households of G24 and G25 (G21's other two sisters) would have been the least wealthy of those of the five Kunnam siblings, as both of them married into relatively poor Ramankara *taravads.* It is also reasonable to assume that the household of G21 had control over more land than those of his wife's (D29) siblings, and probable too that these latter three households were less wealthy than those of G22/A23 and A12/G23, although the Kizhakkil *karanavan*, Rama, D27 may have controlled a considerable amount of land. But as he had no children, we need not concern ourselves with him here. Finally, we may presume that G22/A23 was wealthier than the household of A24, a sister of A21 and A23, as her husband came from one of the less wealthy Ramankara *taravads.* (See charts 2, 3 and 4.)

There are no adequate land records for this period, but they would in any case be useless, as they deal only with legal ownership, then still vested in the *taravad.* This, combined with the inability of informants to remember accurately the acreages controlled, makes it virtually impossible to obtain estimates more precise than those I have worked out. It is thus impracticable to give the rank order of the wealthiest households, in generation two, more accurately than in the following list:

1. Raman Vilangu and Parvati Kizhakkil A21/D24;
2. Aiyappan Kunnam and Mani Kizhakkil G21/D29;
3. Rama Kunnam and Kodi Vilangu G22/A23; Narayanan Vilangu and Narayani Kunman A12/G23;

4. Kalyani Kunnam G24; Mani Kunnam G25; Kalyani Kizhakkil D210; Parvati Vilangu A24.

(Rama Kizhakkil and Janaki Vadakkil Puthenveedu D27/F21 is omitted as they had no children; Rama's younger brother (D28) is also omitted as none of his children married into 'big four' clans.)

Intermarriages between the children of the wealthiest couples listed above are depicted on chart 5.[7] Of the 48 children on this chart, 18 married persons also on the chart, i.e. there were intermarriages between these 9 families involving 18 of their children, although 2 of them married persons in generation 2 and 4 persons in generation 4. Seven married into other 'big four' families not shown on the chart and 23 married outside the 'big four'. The number of intermarriages between these families is the more remarkable when it is observed how many of them could not have married each other owing to exogamic rules. On grounds of status alone, marriages into other wealthy families should have been no more desirable than marriages into families belonging to Vadakkil, Puthenveedu, Padinjerapuram, the section of Vilangu descended from A13 or the section of Kizhakkil descended from D13. Such marriages, however, were contracted by only 7 children, as opposed to the 18 who married a member of another of the wealthiest families. The evidence shows that there was no lack of possible partners in the poorer sections of the 'big four' clans, and thus we can conclude that status factors alone cannot explain the marriage pattern in this generation.

It is not surprising that the number of these intermarriages is highest among the children of the very wealthy couples. The distribution of land, owned or controlled, is so heavily skewed that differences in wealth among the vast majority of families are relatively small; whereas those in generation two, on chart 5, controlled areas of land ranging from around 50 acres to several hundred in the case of Raman Vilangu, most other Nayar families, including those with members belonging to 'big four' clans, controlled much less than 50 acres. For the children of poorer families, of course, the choice of possible partners, who controlled areas of land similar to their own, would have been extensive; at the other extreme, for the children of Raman Vilangu, there were no potential partners in the village with control over so much land.

Of Raman's seven children, no less than six married into 'big four' clans (charts 3 and 5) and, of these six, two married children born of couples ranked third in wealth (plus another who married a daughter's daughter of one of these couples) and one married a daughter of one of the couples ranked fifth. Another married the son of G26, possibly a sister of Aiyappan Kunnam. Unions with the children of the second wealthiest couple, Aiyappan Kunnam and Mani Kizhakkil, would have broken the rules of exogamy. In any marriage arrangement, personal factors such as relative age or individual characteristics cannot be ignored, and thus it is impossible to be certain that Raman's children did, in fact, marry in each instance the wealthiest possible partner in Ramankara. Nonetheless, the number of intermarriages between wealthy families is surely high enough for us to be able to conclude that this pattern could not have arisen randomly, and cannot be explained solely in terms of status. The economic factor, the desire to maximise conjugal landowning, was clearly in evidence. But at the same time, these marriages demonstrate that the economic factor was operating within the constraints of status considerations. Except for the youngest, Raman's children did not marry outside the village; this would have been necessary were they to find partners with landownings equivalent to their own. The remarks made about the marriages of Raman Vilangu's children also apply, I think, to those of the children of other wealthy couples. But identifying the effect of the economic factor becomes progressively more difficult as a household's landowning approaches the statistical norm, for then the range of possible marriage partners, who are suitable on economic grounds, increases rapidly.

I have tried to show that the pattern of marriage in the interregnum was primarily generated by two factors: one to do with status and one which is economic. This is in no way meant to deny that other factors, such as personal preferences, also had a role, although in arranged marriages personal preferences do not always have much sway. The economic factor, specifically the desire to maximise the conjugal landowning, came to play a role in marriage arrangement as a direct consequence of the development of individual property in land, with its associated alteration in the inheritance system and the structure of the residential unit. But during the interregnum, the economic factor still operated within a set of constraints defined by status considerations, embodied in the continued preference for marriage between a 'right man' and a 'right woman', which promoted intermarriage between the 'big four' clans, and village endogamy. In the new order, as we shall see, this set of status-determined constraints loses much of its influence, allowing the economic factor to operate almost unfettered.[8]

The new order

As I have mentioned before, the overwhelming majority of marriages still takes place within the Illam subcaste. Modern Nayars like to insist that subcastes are no longer endogamous, but when asked for examples of cross-subcaste marriages, only one case from Ramankara was ever quoted: a son of D32 whose wife comes from the Itasseri subcaste. It is probable, however, that there are one or two other cases in the village, perhaps among the poorer section of the community. Nayars still insist that the ancestry (*paramparyyam*) of both spouses' descent groups should be equal, although I have already spoken of the way in which economics enters into the estimate of this. More and more marriages take place outside the village too, and an assessment of the ancestry of an unfamiliar group in an unfamiliar village is inevitably difficult; I suspect that it is increasingly taken for granted that the ancestry of a prospective spouse's group is satisfactory if his economic standing is. There is today hostility to marriage between a 'right man' and a 'right woman' although, interestingly, the terms are still employed. Similarly, there is a fairly strong objection to marriage within the village. This indicates a lessening of concern about the risks to subcaste purity attending marriage outside the village. One reason for these objections, informants said, was the fear that repeated intermarriage between families within the village might lead to genetic deformities. Nakane (1962: 25) reports that the same fear prevailed among some Cochin Nayars. How real this fear is is difficult to judge; however, it is certainly true that intermarriages between Ramankara clans are now extremely rare.

Economics, say informants, provides the other main reason why the previous marriage preference has been reversed. They state that nowadays the most important single criterion in marriage choice is the desire to make what will, in material terms, be the best marriage. The argument runs in two directions. Firstly, those who are well-off, and particularly those with good jobs, need to look far afield to find spouses of similar standing. This argument is undoubtedly correct; for such people, the chances of finding a suitable spouse within the village and its immediate vicinity are slight. Secondly, repeated partition of land has resulted in a serious economic decline for more and more families. It has thus become increasingly desirable that the best possible 'bargain' be sought when arranging a marriage. This argument, so far as it goes, also seems correct, but it is not clear why it should mean that marriage partners are searched for further afield, given that for the poor majority there exist plenty of families in similar economic circumstances nearby. I am uncertain as to how this apparent paradox can be resolved, although there does seem to be a sentiment current that the chances of an economically advantageous match are raised simply by casting the net wider, and this obviously does permit the building-up of an extensive affinal network, which could be advantageous, for example, in obtaining employment.

There can, though, be no doubt that the proportion of Ramankara Nayars marrying outside the village has greatly increased (table 13). In table 16, the villages, from which the spouses of the 98 Nayars appearing in table 13 came, are analysed according to their distance from Ramankara. (No information was available for six cases in generation four, and they have been omitted.) There is a marked peak at the 4–8 mile range. There is no apparent correlation between wealth and distance from Ramankara of spouses' villages, although this cannot be deduced from the genealogical data as I do not have relevant accurate landowning figures for these, nor do I know which of the marriages were virilocal and which uxorilocal. Data are available, however, from my census material and are summarised in tables 17 and 18.

The conclusions to be drawn from tables 17 and 18 are mostly negative.

Table 16. *Genealogical data (cf. table 13): spouses' villages*

Gen.	Distance from Ramankara in miles									All cases
	≤ 2		> 2–4		> 4–8		> 8–16		> 16	
	No.	%	No.	%	No.	%	No.	%	No.	%	
2	—	—	—	—	1	50.0	1	50.0	—	—	2
3	4	12.9	1	3.2	21	67.8	4	12.9	1	3.2	31
4	10	17.0	4	6.8	26	44.1	17	28.8	2	3.4	59
All	14	15.2	5	5.4	48	52.2	22	23.9	3	3.3	92

This may be due to the small size of the sample; a larger sample might have revealed a tendency for the wealthiest Nayars to find their spouses from further afield. No correlation between husband's age and distance emerges, and this may imply that the range over which marriages are contracted has remained fairly stable. Table 17 indicates that the proportion of virilocal marriages has increased, though not in a very striking manner. I have mentioned above the absence of a strong trend towards virilocality, although some signs of a weak one are present.

Parents search for marriage partners for their children through a network of informal contacts with relatives and friends, and these contacts are distributed fairly randomly throughout surrounding localities in which there are Illam Nayar communities. That so few marriages take place with persons from more than 16 miles away is simply explained by the problems of communication. To travel more than 16 or so miles on local buses is time-consuming and, at least for the poor, the fares represent a considerable expenditure, meaning that regular visits between families would have to be curtailed. This is something which Nayars, like other Malayalis, would loathe having to do.

In understanding modern Ramankara Nayar marriage, we are forced to rely heavily on informants' statements. They continually assert that economic considerations now predominate in marriage arrangements and often point out that these are now very similar to those of the neighbouring Syrian Christians, although unlike the latter Nayars, of course, do not pay dowry. (A father will give his daughter some gold or jewellery on marriage, but this does not represent her share of the parental estate, which she actually receives in the form of land.) There is no means of checking informants' statements on this matter nor of discovering, for instance, what exactly is the nature of the 'bargains' struck at marriage. To do this, one would need data on the landowning and income of all the families into which Ramankara Nayars have married. To collect this information would be virtually impossible, given the complexity of the inheritance system and the fact that both men and women own property.

Table 17. *Census data: extant marriages only. Classified by age of husband (excluding 13 marriages in which both H and W from outside Ramankara)*

Age of husband	H and W both from Ramankara	H from Ramankara Distance from W's village in miles							W from Ramankara Distance from H's village in miles						Total cases
		?	≤2	>2-4	>4-8	>8-16	>16	All cases	≤2	>2-4	>4-8	>8-16	>16	All cases	
20-29	–	–	–	–	1	1	–	2	–	–	–	–	–	–	2
30-39	3	–	1	1	4	1	2	9	–	–	2	–	1	3	15
40-49	11	1	1	–	–	1	4	7	–	3	2	–	–	5	23
50-59	6	–	–	–	1	1	1	3	–	–	3	1	–	4	13
61-69	3	–	–	–	1	1	1	3	–	–	1	–	2	3	9
≥70	2	–	–	–	–	–	–	–	–	–	1	–	–	1	3
All cases	25	1	2	1	7	5	8	24	–	3	9	1	3	16	65

Table 18. *Census data: extant marriages only. Classified by landowning of household (excluding 13 marriages in which both H and W from outside Ramankara)*

Landowning of household in acres/cents	H and W both from Ramankara	H from Ramankara — Distance from Ramankara of W's village in miles							W from Ramankara — Distance from Ramankara of H's village in miles						Total cases
		?	≤2	>2-4	>4-8	>8-16	>16	All cases	≤2	>2-4	>4-8	>8-16	>16	All cases	
Zero	–	–	–	–	–	–	–	–	–	–	–	–	–	–	–
1-50 cents	3	–	–	1	–	–	2	3	–	–	1	–	–	1	7
51-100 cents	1	–	1	–	1	1	–	3	–	–	1	–	–	1	5
1.01-2.50 acres	1	–	–	–	3	2	2	7	–	–	2	–	1	3	11
2.51-5.00 acres	6	1	–	–	2	–	–	3	–	2	–	–	2	4	13
5.01-10.00 acres	3	–	–	–	–	2	2	4	–	1	3	1	–	5	12
10.01-15.00 acres	4	–	1	–	–	–	1	2	–	–	1	–	–	1	7
>15.00 acres	6	–	–	1	–	–	1	2	–	–	1	–	–	1	9
?	1	–	–	–	–	–	–	–	–	–	–	–	–	–	1
All cases	25	1	2	1	7	5	8	24	–	3	9	1	3	16	65

The Nayars Today

In other words, in insisting on the significance of economic criteria in modern Nayar marriage arrangements, I am, to some degree at least, only repeating what my informants told me. I cannot provide all the objective evidence I would like, to substantiate (or modify) their statements.

Finally, the manner in which status considerations have declined in importance may be illustrated by the marriages contracted by the daughters' children of Raman Vilangu. These are depicted on chart 6. The eldest son of D31 married in the mid-1940s, and the daughter of D36 married around 1970. Each sibling group is arranged in order of age, and although I do not, unfortunately, know when each marriage took place, it is clear that on reading from left to right, i.e. in declining age order, the number of marriages within Ramankara also declines. This is more apparent if men and women are considered separately. The last marriage between two members of the 'big four' clans occurred in the mid-1950s, some ten years after the modern inheritance system and residential pattern had stablised. The same pattern as that revealed in chart 6 is apparent in other 'big four' families, and in none of them has a marriage into another 'big four' family taken place for many years. Marriages into other Ramankara clans are almost equally rare. Comparing the marriages of Raman's children with those of his daughters' children, it can be seen how the status factor has ceased to be an 'active' principle in determining marriage choice; whereas his children were attempting to maximise their conjugal landowning within the constraints of the preferential marriage rule, his grandchildren were mostly free from such restrictions.

Conclusion

I have sought to show that in the old order, status – as expressed by the rule preferring a 'right man' to marry a 'right woman' – was the most critical single factor in marriage arrangement and that during the interregnum, as a consequence of the development of individual property in land along with the emergence of the modern inheritance system and the formation of residential units based on the conjugal pair, an economic factor – the desire to maximise the conjugal landowning – became increasingly significant. In the interregnum, this economic factor operated within a set of constraints defined by the continued persistence of status preferences, but in the new order, that is today, these status considerations have declined in significance so far, that they remain little more than a 'passive' principle delimiting the boundaries within which marriage choices are made. Within these limits, the 'active' principle is economic. The subcaste is still mainly endogamous; its boundaries are those of marriage choice in most cases. There is some slight evidence that these boundaries may be crumbling, but this is far from definite, and it is hazardous to predict whether or when subcastes will cease to be generally endogamous.

The changes which have occurred in the Nayar marriage system evidently cannot be understood except in the light of the changes in the kinship system discussed in the previous chapter. There I contended that the development of individual property in land was the most significant change. I think the evidence on marriage confirms this, for it is this development which introduced into marriage arrangement the economic factor, and it is the existence of individual property in land - owned by both men and women - which underlies the modern marriage pattern.[9]

Each individual has a code number. The letter indicates clan or sub-clan. The first figure indicates generations (1 – 4). The second (or second and third) figure is an individual serial number.

A. Vilangu ——— B. Tekkapuram ─ ─ ─ C. Padinjerapuram ─ ─ ─ ─ D. Kizhakkil ─ · ─ E. Vadakkil F. Puthenveedu ········· G. Kunnam ———

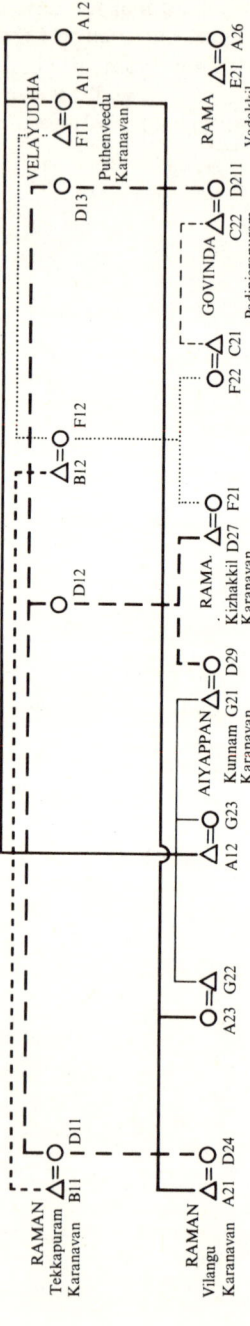

Chart 1. Marriages of the *karanavans* of the 7 principal *taravads* and their siblings who made 'big four' marriages (generations 1 and 2 only)

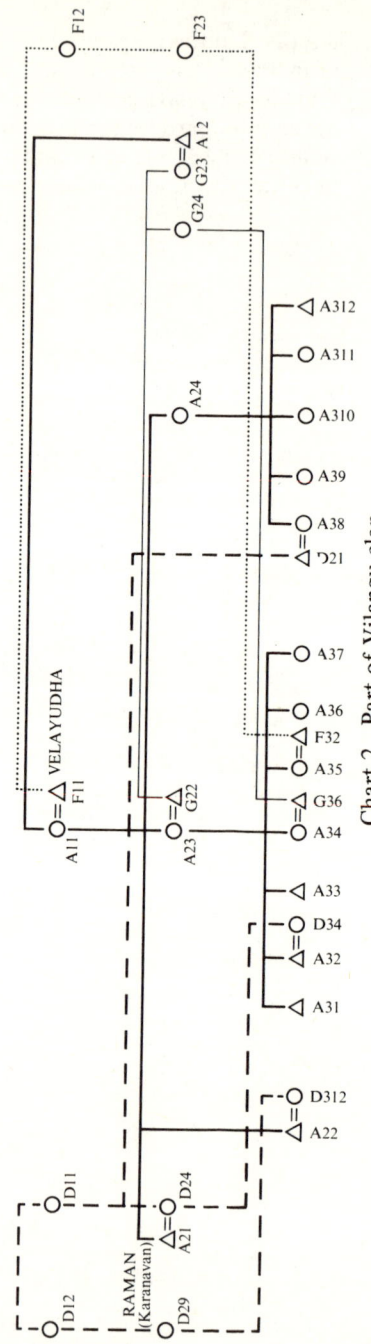

Chart 2. Part of Vilangu clan

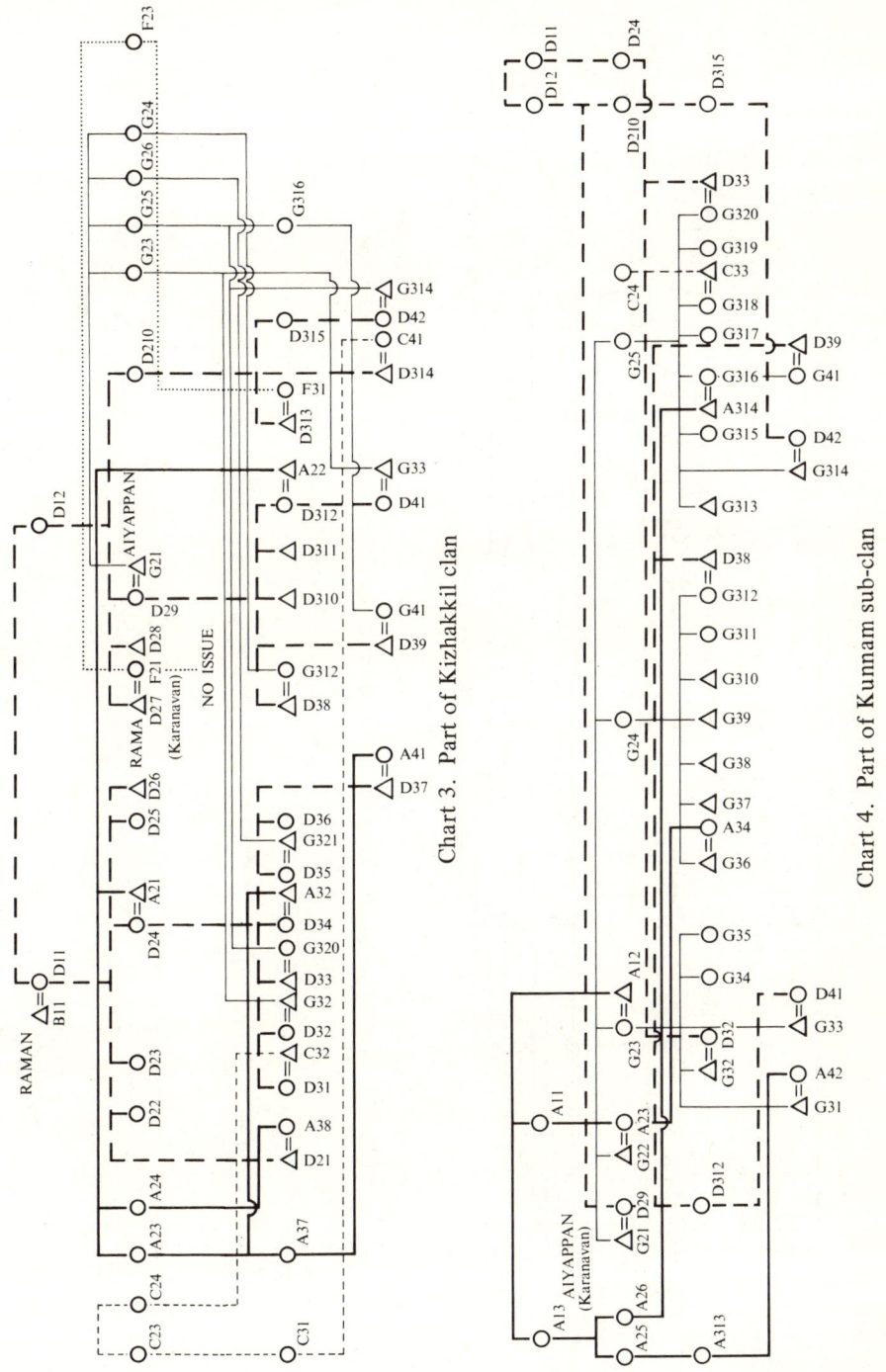

Chart 3. Part of Kizhakkil clan

Chart 4. Part of Kunnam sub-clan

KEY

■ Married into Vilangu clan   ◻ Married into Puthenveedu sub-clan   □ Married into Padinjerapuram clan

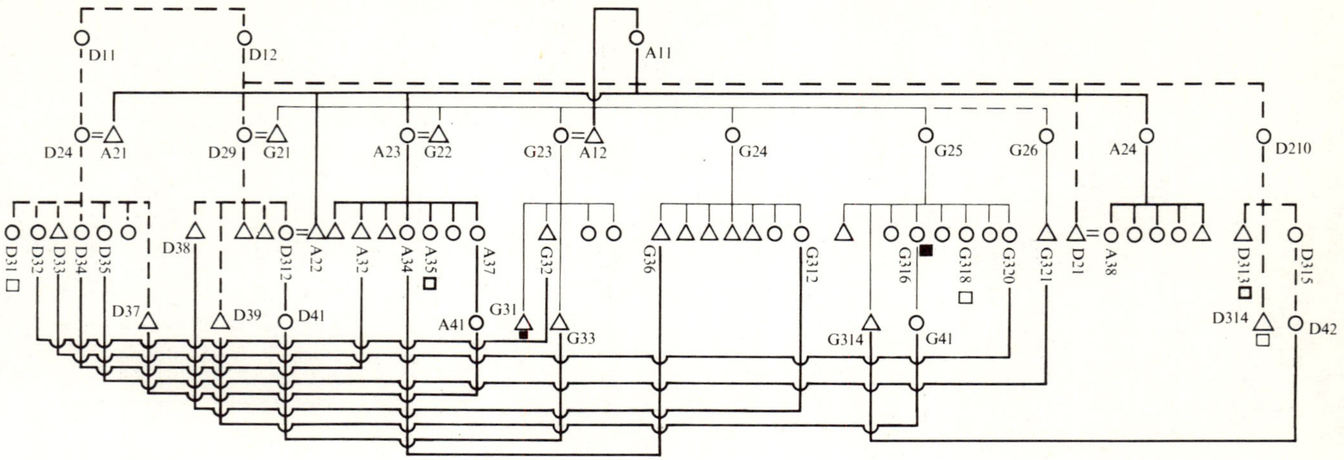

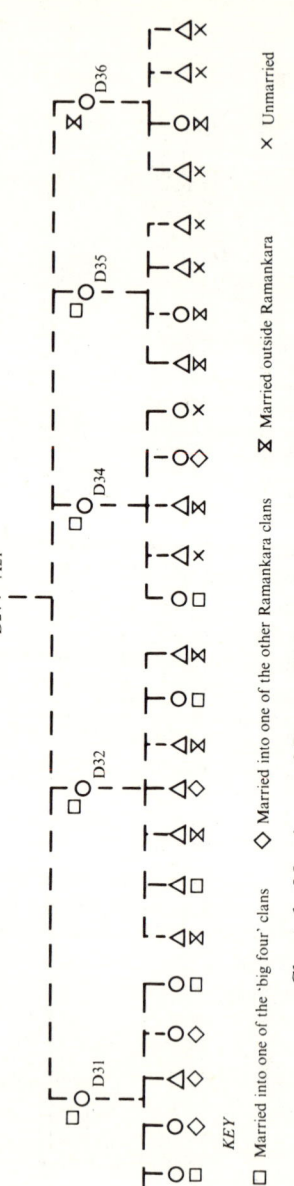

Chart 5. Inter-marriages between the children of the wealthiest households in generation 2

KEY

□ Married into one of the 'big four' clans   ◇ Married into one of the other Ramankara clans   ⧗ Married outside Ramankara   × Unmarried

Chart 6. Marriages of Raman Vilangu's daughters' children

5　The 'traditional' Nayar marriage system

In the last two chapters of this book, I move from the ethnography of Nayars in one part of Central Travancore to adopt a broader focus. In the final chapter, I shall be discussing changes in the kinship and marriage system which have taken place during the nineteenth and twentieth centuries. In this chapter, I want to look at the highly exotic 'traditional' marriage system of the Nayars. Ideally I would like to present to the reader a picture of the whole Nayar community, which would incorporate a thorough description of regional differences. But unfortunately this is not possible. For Travancore, especially, there is a paucity of historical data compared with the more northerly areas. The best information is on the Nayars in Central Kerala, and this is one of the principal reasons for devoting so much of this chapter to them. But there is another reason; only among the Central Kerala Nayars did this exotic marriage system attain its full efflorescence. Exoticism is not only a challenge to our received categories; it is also a challenge to anthropological generalisation, and the Nayars have indeed long been taken as a 'test-case' for theorists of kinship, marriage and the family.

Inevitably, this has meant that anthropologists and sociologists have spilt a prodigious quantity of ink in attempting to restore the Nayars to the fold of conventional, general theory. In my opinion, much of this effort, including some by recent writers, has been wasted, although other anthropologists – especially Gough and Dumont – have significantly aided our understanding of Nayar marriage. It is tempting for me to rush headlong into this, at times extremely esoteric debate, as I have my disagreements with most of those who have ever contributed to it. However, I shall try to restrain myself from this course, for it is probably undesirable in a book whose principal protagonists should be the Nayars themselves, rather than quarrelling anthropologists armed with their contentious theories.

Nayar kinship and marriage: a brief recapitulation

Some mention has already been made of the *tali*-rite and the *sambandham* union, the two principal features of the traditional Nayar marriage system. Argument has raged as to whether the *tali*-rite, the *sambandham* union or the two taken together, constituted the 'marriage'. At this point, it is a question of terminology and for various reasons, including a wish not to prejudge the issue, I shall not refer to the *tali*-rite or the *sambandham* union as 'marriage', but use the Malayalam terms. However, in order to avoid periphrases, I shall use the descriptive phrase 'marriage system', as I have done throughout the book.

At the risk of excessive repetition, let me begin by very briefly outlining the distinctive features of the Nayar kinship and marriage system, in order to set the scene for a more detailed examination of the *tali*-rite and the *sambandham* union. With a handful of problematic exceptions, all sections of the Nayar community had a matrilineal descent system. In South Malabar, Cochin and the northern half of Travancore, Nayars lived in matrilineal joint families (*taravads*) which constituted corporate, property-owning groups. Before puberty, each Nayar girl underwent the *talikettu-kalyanam* (lit. '*tali*-tying ceremony'), or *tali*-rite, and on reaching sexual maturity began to receive 'lovers' in the relationship known as *sambandham*. Her *sambandham* partners only visited a woman at night; they did not live with her in her *taravad*. Both men and women were permitted several *sambandham* partners, and relationships could be broken by either party at will. A woman's children belonged, of course, to her own *taravad*. The system continued in this form until the closing years of the eighteenth century. During the nineteenth century, it began to change until by around 1900 in Travancore, slightly later in South Malabar and Cochin, it had more or less completely vanished, to be replaced by a marriage system differing in detail only from that prevailing elsewhere in India.

In North Malabar, which I shall not discuss in any depth, the *taravad* had a different constitution. There the adult male members of a matrilineal segment resided together, cultivating the land held by the segment. With them lived their wives, their dependent children and elderly female kinsfolk who were widowed or divorced. Although North Malabar Nayar girls underwent the *tali*-rite like their sisters to the south, it always seems to have been a much less important rite. Later they began *sambandham* unions, but most of these were really equivalent to ordinary marriage; the union was with one man and intended to be stable, and the woman, as we have just seen, lived with her partner. In some ways, it was a curious system, because a woman, as a member of her own matrilineage, had rights to property cultivated by her kinsmen, although she was born and raised in her father's *taravad,* and later moved to her *sambandham* partner's. Only if she were divorced or widowed, was she ever likely to reside in the *taravad* wherein she possessed property rights. In southern Travancore, the residence pattern resembled that in North Malabar, for there too women lived with their *sambandham* partners. But data on this region are so scanty that I do not know whether other features of the North Malabar system were also found in southern Travancore.

The tali-rite

Let us now return to the Nayars in the central part of Kerala, especially those in South Malabar and Cochin, in order to look at their *tali*-rite more closely. It should be noted that the first part of this chapter is concerned with commoner Nayars only; the aristocratic Nayars are considered separately towards the end of the chapter. Not all of what is said about commoner Nayars is equally applicable to aristocrats. Most works on the Nayars include a description of this rite, but I have decided to draw upon two main sources: Gough's account (1955: 49-54) which is based on information she collected in a Cochin village, and Innes's (1908: 173-5), which incorporates a description furnished by a Calicut Nayar. (Thurston (1909: V, 313-28) reprints various accounts, including Innes's.) In the village studied by Gough, the full *tali*-rite had ceased to be performed in the 1920s, and she herself never observed it. However, her description has the merit of being rather more systematic than those in most older sources.

The only indispensable and invariable element in the *tali*-rite was the tying of the actual *tali* itself (Menon 1911: 192-3). The *tali* is a leaf-shaped emblem, made of gold or silver, which is worn on a string around the neck. For most South Indian women, it indicates their married status and is thus equivalent to a wedding ring in the West. As I have said, every Nayar girl had to undergo the *tali*-rite before puberty; in theory, were she to reach menarche before it had been performed, she would have been ejected from her family and outcasted. In practice, though, it appears that her family would have kept quiet and held a *tali*-rite as soon as possible (Gough 1955: 48). Iyer (1912: 22), however, states that a girl was merely polluted until after the ceremony if menstruation started beforehand.
In order to avoid any confusion, I should point out that the *tali*-rite was in no way a recognition of physiological puberty. A separate rite (*tirantukuli*) marked a girl's first menstrual flow (see, e.g. Iyer 1912: 29-30).

In the village studied by Gough, the *tali*-rite involved the whole village and was held in the oldest house owned by the lineage to which the girls belonged. In front of the house, a temporary loggia (*pantal*) made of bamboo and palm leaves was erected, and on the floor of the loggia a picture of the goddess Bhagavati was drawn. Bhagavati is the principal goddess of the Nayars and like other South Indian 'mother goddesses' – a somewhat misleading though commonly employed appellation – she is associated with war, smallpox and the earth. Her attributes are similar to those of Durga, the favourite goddess of the Bengalis, and like Durga she can also be regarded as an aspect of Parvati, the consort of the high-god Siva. Although Bhagavati is believed to protect Nayar villages and *taravads,* she is also fierce and destructive and can inflict smallpox on her subjects. A branch of a certain type of tree, connected with Bhagavati, was cut by Nayar men of the village and positioned in the loggia in order, so Gough's informants explained, 'to bring Bhagavati to the *taravad* and set up a temple in the house'.

The Nayars Today

Each Nayar lineage, consisting of one or more closely-related *taravads*, was linked to other local lineages, known as *enangan* lineages. I shall discuss the significance of the *enangan* institution in greater detail below. Briefly, however, *enangan* lineages had certain ritual and ceremonial duties towards each other, of which the most important occurred at the *tali*-rite: a girl's *tali* was tied by a male member of one of her lineage's *enangan* lineages. The tier was known as the *manavalan*. The *tali*-rite was attended by every member of the *enangan* lineages, and also by representatives of all other Nayar households in the village.

The *tali*-rite lasted four days. On the first morning, the girls went in procession to the lineage shrine, where Bhagavati was propitiated with offerings of cooked food. After they had returned from the shrine, young male members of the *taravad* set off to meet the *tali*-tiers, who arrived on elephants to the sound of music. At the gate of the house, the approaching men were met by older women from the *taravad*, carrying brass trays on which were set a burning wick, rice and coconut flowers. The *tali*-tiers' feet were bathed by brothers of the girls, and they were then given seats in the loggia. By the picture of Bhagavati were placed rice and paddy, coconut flowers, the sacred brass lamp of the household, and a tray containing eight auspicious objects – a woman's loin-cloth, a rouge-box, a mirror, an arrow, coconut flowers, rice, paddy and a burning wick. Then, at a time determined by the astrologer to be propitious, each girl in turn was taken by her brother to the loggia and seated on a plank. The astrologer indicated to the priest (a member of one of the lower-ranking Nambudiri subdivisions) that he should hand the *tali* to the tier, who then fastened it around the girl's neck. The girls, together with their respective *tali*-tiers, remained secluded in the house for the subsequent three days of the ceremony.

On the following morning, the party – without the secluded couples – gathered together. Offerings were made to Bhagavati by a Nayar oracle, or diviner, a Nayar priest and a Nayar boy who accompanied the oracle. A variety of offerings (including toddy) was put before the tree branch in the loggia. Then the priest sacrificed a cock and emptied a vessel of bloodlike liquid. The oracle donned a waist-band and anklets of bells, and picked up a sickle; by performing these actions, it is thought, he became possessed by Bhagavati. To loud music, the oracle then danced frantically, slashing his own head with the sickle. While dancing, he called out that Bhagavati was appeased by the offerings, after which his state reverted to normality.

The rest of the second and the whole of the third day were given over to feasting and music. On the morning of the fourth day, each of the couples walked to the village bathing-tank. There, the girls and their *tali*-tiers took a purifying bath. In new and fine clothes, they returned to the *taravad* house where they partook of a meal together. The others attending the ceremony were also fed but, unique to this occasion, the women received their food before the men. The *tali*-tiers were then presented with clothing and food by the head of the girls' *taravad*, after which they returned to their homes. This marked the end of the *tali*-rite.

The 'Traditional' Nayar Marriage System

Other accounts of the *tali*-rite are broadly in accordance with Gough's, although there are many differences of detail. For instance, in the ceremony described by Innes, the *tali* was tied on the third, rather than the first day. On the first morning, the girl visited the temple, where the Brahman poured over her head water, which had been sanctified by the recitation of religious formulae (*mantrams*). On her return to the house, she was elaborately adorned. In her right hand, she clasped a mirror and in her left, an arrow; in front of her were placed a lamp, a plate of rice and the tray of eight auspicious objects. A woman from one of the Ambalavasi castes then came and sang before the girl, before showering rice over her. A feast was held at midday, and the songs sung again in the evening. On the following morning, these ceremonies were repeated, and then the girl left the house, with the singer, for the nearest tank. After being bathed and decorated by the singer, she next had to perform a rite which involved jumping three times over a vessel of water, with a coconut husk floating on top. The party finally returned to the loggia, with the girl under a scarlet canopy held by two men. She also put on two cloths brought to her by a weaver. In the evening, the singing ceremonies were repeated once more.

On the third day, the girl sat in the inner part of the loggia, surrounded by auspicious objects. The *tali*-tier arrived, richly attired, and often preceded by a kind of armed bodyguard. His party was met at the gate by women of the girl's family. A man of the family washed the *tali*-tier's feet, and he then sat down by the girl. The girl's father next took the *tali* from the attendant goldsmith – paying him for it – and handed it to the tier who, at an indication from the astrologer that the time was auspicious, fastened it around the girl's neck. He carried the girl into the house, and a feast with musical accompaniment closed the day's proceedings.

On the fourth day, the girl and the tier visited the temple – mounted on elephants, if her family was wealthy. Offerings were made to the goddess and presents given to the Brahmans. The party returned home and, as it entered the house, the *tali*-tier, who brought up the rear, was pelted by plantain fruits thrown by boys in the party. Sometimes he had to pretend to force his way into the house. After all had regained the house, the girl and the tier took a meal together in the inner loggia. The rite was closed with an elaborate feast for everyone present.

There would be little advantage, I think, in summarising additional descriptions of the *tali*-rite, merely in order to reveal the diversity which existed. Two points are worth briefly mentioning however. Firstly, in some areas (of South Malabar) the last element in the rite was the tearing of a cloth, one part being given to the girl and the other to the *tali*-tier (Fawcett 1901: 231; Gough 1955: 51). Secondly, it does not seem to have been at all important that the girl continued to wear her *tali*, and in some areas she removed it shortly after the ceremony (Census 1901, Cochin: 158; Innes 1908: 177).

Some attempt must now be made to explain the 'meaning' of the *tali*-rite. Even in the truncated accounts given above, the reader will have noted many references to what are clearly ritual objects and actions, such as the auspicious items carried by the women or the offerings made to Bhagavati. For readers acquainted with South Asia, these references may ring many bells, but to others they may mean very little. Each of these ritual elements could be the starting-point of an extended essay on symbolism and iconography, but this is not the place for such a dissertation. However, a very short sketch of some of the symbolic referents of the *tali* emblem itself may offer just a little insight into the complexity of the symbolism in the *tali*-rite.

The *tali* is shaped like a leaf of the pipal tree (*Ficus religiosa*). The pipal is sacred to the high-god Vishnu, who is thought to be embodied in it, and it 'is supposed to represent fertility, to give children, and to avert disasters' (Gonda 1970: 113) – clearly appropriate in the context. In this aspect, the pipal is contrasted with the banyan tree (*Ficus indica*), which is said to be a form of Siva. Like Siva himself, the banyan has phallic associations. The pipal, however, can also symbolise male generative power and as such, is linked to the margosa tree (*Melia Azadirachta*), dedicated to Siva. In the Tamil country, the pipal and the margosa were sometimes planted together in a 'marriage' ceremony; the creeping branches of the margosa twining round the pipal like a faithful wife embracing her husband (Dubois 1906: 653; Gough 1955: 52). The *tali* may also have phallic associations of a more direct nature for, at least in Tamilnadu, it often has a *lingam* (the phallic emblem of Siva) engraved upon it (idem; Dumont 1957b: 227). This paragraph does not, of course, take into account the symbolic relations of complementarity and opposition between the *tali* and other ritual elements, which may be amenable to structuralist analysis; however, brief though it is, it may offer some hint of the kind of symbolism involved and especially of the multiple, pan-Hindu referents of the ritual objects.

Now to the more obvious question: what was the point in Nayar girls undergoing the *tali*-rite? Argument has long raged, amongst those interested in the Nayars, about whether the *tali*-rite was, or was not, a marriage. For example, the tearing of a cloth at the end of the ceremony, to which I referred above, has been interpreted as a 'divorce', from which it evidently follows that the rite itself must have been a marriage. But as we have seen, a cloth was not torn at the close of the ceremony throughout Kerala. Conversely, the fact that a girl often removed the *tali* shortly after the ceremony has been taken as evidence that the *tali*-rite was not a marriage, for this behaviour contrasts strikingly with that of most married women in South India, who conscientiously wear the *tali* until their husbands' deaths. On the other hand, the fact remains that the *tali* is generally an emblem of marriage.

My own view is that discussions of this nature are essentially misguided. In this, I follow Leach (1961a: 107–8) who has argued, to my mind convincingly, that there cannot be a definition of marriage which has universal, cross-cultural validity. What is embodied in the institution called by us 'marriage', or by others by a term translated as 'marriage', is not identical in all cultures. The problem, therefore, is not to decide whether the *tali*-rite was a marriage; it is rather to determine what was 'stated' in the rite, and then to compare these 'statements' with similar or identical ones made in other communities in order, hopefully, to grasp what the *tali*-rite indicated and symbolised.

A detailed critique of other writers' interpretations of the *tali*-rite is probably undesirable in a book of this kind. I shall thus cut a swathe through the controversy and put forward my own view on the matter, returning to alternative theories later. The most perceptive remark of those who argued about whether the Nayars had marriage was, I think, made by Iyer (1912: 27-8) who noted that, among many other Hindus, marriage had two separate components – the 'betrothal' and the 'consummation'. He proposed that the *tali*-rite was equivalent to the betrothal and the *sambandham* to the consummation, and that the two taken together therefore constituted marriage. Basing myself partly on Iyer's suggestion and partly on the remarks made by Dube (1953) on pre-puberty 'token' marriages, I think it is perhaps most sensible to consider Hindu marriage, for a woman at least, as being divisible into two basic parts. The terms 'betrothal' and 'consummation', however, are not strictly accurate in the Nayar context, so I shall adopt the simple labels 'first marriage' and 'second marriage'. (My terms imply an amphibology, but other new terms might cause still more confusion. I should make it clear, too, that my distinction is not the same as Dumont's between 'primary marriage' and 'secondary marriage' (1970: 114).) The first marriage is primarily a rite of passage for the girl, marking her progress from the social category of girl to that of woman; it mainly centres on her own personal status and is broadly comparable with female initiation rites elsewhere. In the second marriage, a woman is linked as a sexual partner to one or more men, by whom she is expected to bear children; this second marriage is principally concerned with the continuation of her or her husband's line through the birth of legitimate children. In the majority of Indian communities, first and second marriages are not actually separated. They are both included within one 'ordinary' marriage, which is thus a rite of passage for the bride, as well as a ritual concerned with sexual relations and the progeniture of children. Among the Nayars though, so my argument goes, the two types of marriage were kept apart; the *tali*-rite was a first marriage and the *sambandham* a second marriage. Hence if we were to continue our search for the (chimerical) marriage of the Nayars, it would be best to follow Iyer's lead and take the *tali*-rite and the *sambandham* union together as constituting Nayar marriage.

The division into first and second marriages is not, however, quite as simple as I have portrayed it; in particular, the *tali*-rite was not solely a rite of passage for the girl. In most cases – there were exceptions – a man always acted as the *tali*-tier, and the relation between this man's family and that of the girl cannot be ignored; indeed, it was of fundamental significance. Whether it was equivalent to an affinal relationship is a topic taken up below. Clearly, though, were the *tali*-rite no more than a female rite of passage, there would be no ostensible need for a specific man of a specific status to act as a tier, and the whole issue of affinity would be irrelevant.

I should perhaps discuss in a little more detail what the progress from girlhood to womanhood meant for a Nayar. Dumont (1961: 18) stressed the strict separation of men and women within the *taravad* house, in contrast to the free intermingling permitted to children of both sexes. Though his point is important, what is surely more crucial is the ritual validation afforded by the *tali*-rite, of a woman's right to receive men of appropriate status as sexual partners and to bear by such men legitimate children. In other words, the *tali*-rite recognised a woman's right to enter a *sambandham* union. Now this interpretation differs somewhat from Gough's, for she has insisted that the *tali*-rite was clearly 'ritually if not actually a defloration ceremony' (1955: 50). The fact that the girl and her *tali*-tier took a purifying bath at the end of their seclusion might be taken as evidence for Gough's view. The question of actual defloration, though, is highly problematic. Among most Nayars, *talis* were often tied on young children and so defloration can hardly have been possible. But in royal and chiefly families, girls usually seem to have been approaching puberty when their *talis* were tied, and it is these princesses who feature in most of the early travellers' accounts, cited by Gough as evidence that actual defloration used to occur. To quibble about these accounts is pointless; I shall merely state that my own reading of them (see chapter 1, note 1) has led me to the conclusion that Nayar girls rarely, if ever, lost their virginity in the *tali*-rite.[1] In any case, though, I am in agreement with Dumont (1961: 18) in seeing a fundamental parallel between the *tali*-rite and pre-puberty marriage elsewhere in India; in the latter, of course, there is no defloration of a young girl by her husband. The parallel is fundamental because in both cases there is a focus on the purity of the woman, and hence the purity of the caste; Yalman (1963) in particular has made this clear. In Hindu society, there is a preoccupation with the purity of women, and in particular with the status of their sexual partners, because it is held that if a woman were polluted through intercourse with a man of lower status, not only would she herself be polluted, but she might also bear polluted children who could destroy the purity of her caste. The question of the status of sexual partners will be considered in more detail when I turn to the *sambandham* relationship. The relevance of all this to the *tali*-rite is that this rite was, in effect, a kind of ritual guarantee that a Nayar woman was eligible to enter appropriate sexual relationships. For this guarantee to be effective, it had to be conferred before menarche, not only so that one could be fairly sure that the girl had no sexual experience, but also – and more crucially, I think – because menstruation is, in itself, polluting.[2] This latter point is somewhat contentious; there is, however, considerable evidence to suggest that, because Hindu women suffer monthly pollution during their menstrual periods, they are by this not only distinguished from men – their monthly pollution being a part of both the rationalisation and explanation of their lower status – but also from pre-pubescent girls. In other words, pre-pubescent girls are, in certain respects anyway, intrinsically purer than mature women. In a sense, therefore, the *tali*-rite, like pre-puberty marriage, was a more effective guarantee of a girl's purity – and hence of her eligibility to bear children – simply because it was conducted before she began to suffer menstrual pollution.

I have to admit that much of the above paragraph is assertion rather than demonstration, and that my argument leaves a multitude of loose ends which cannot be tied here. The most elaborate analysis of the *tali*-rite to date has been Gough's (1955), which adopts a psychoanalytical perspective. I have no dogmatic objection to such a perspective; I do, however, think that Gough has failed to exhaust the possibilities of a more conventional anthropological approach, as Yalman has pointed out (1963), and that such an approach should be broadly along the lines indicated in the preceding paragraph.

One major aspect of the *tali*-rite remains undiscussed: the question of who tied the *tali* and the related issue of affinity. However, this topic cannot meaningfully be tackled until we have seen who acted as *sambandham* partners as well. So let us now look at the *sambandham* relationship.

The sambandham relationship

Traditionally, the *sambandham* relationship was inaugurated with relatively little ceremony and without religious rites (Gough 1955: 48). In this, it was in marked contrast to the *tali*-rite. Chandu Menon provided a lengthy description of the ceremonies surrounding the inauguration of the *sambandham* relationship (G.O.M. 1891, Encl. C; qu. in Thurston 1909: V, 328–32), but it should be noted that, firstly, Menon was writing about the situation as it existed at the end of the nineteenth century, by which time the *sambandham* union had become more important than the *tali*-rite, and secondly, that he was compaigning strongly for legal recognition of the *sambandham* union as marriage.

The main features of the ceremony held at the beginning of a *sambandham* relationship have been described by a number of writers; I draw particularly on Iyer (1912: 30–31). He states that the ceremony was, in essentials, identical throughout the region. The proposal could come from the parents or friends of either of the prospective partners, but the *karanavans* of their *taravads* were invariably consulted immediately. If there was general agreement on the desirability of the match, the astrologers were asked to fix an auspicious day for the ceremony. On this day, a few caste-fellows and friends of the male partner met in his house, from where they went in procession to the woman's home. There, the party was welcomed and given seats. A sumptuous meal was provided for the guests, and at the auspicious hour the male partner and his party were led to a conspicuous part of the house. He was seated, and two lit lamps were placed by his chair. The two partners then paid their respects to the *kara-*

navans and their elders, and gave money to the attending Brahmans, who conferred their blessings on the couple. After a while, the couple were left alone and the next morning the man departed, leaving some money under his pillow. His departure marked the end of the *sambandham*'s inauguration, although it was usual for the man's family to send a gift of clothes to the woman a few days later.

The nature of the *sambandham* relationship itself has also been described many times; the following account is mainly based on Gough (1959a: 26–7; 1961: 357–70). In the past, a woman could, of course, receive several men as *sambandham* partners. (I am not sure whether the ceremony described above was held for each new partner.) Her *tali*-tier might be one of these men, but he was not preferred over others. Her *sambandham* partners visited a woman in her private room in the *taravad* house at night, and normally they took no food there. Nor, of course, did they have any economic rights in or obligations towards their partner's *taravad*. Both the woman herself, and her *karanavan*, had to give their consent before a man could become one of her partners, and either party could break off the relationship at will. At each of the three principal Malayali festivals (Onam, Vishu, and Tiruvadira), a man was expected to present his partner with a few token gifts such as a cloth, betel-nut, hair- and bathing-oil, etc. These are all gifts considered appropriate between lovers, and they do not amount to significant economic transactions. If a man failed to give these tokens, it was interpreted as a sign of his intention to sever the relationship.

When a woman became pregnant, one or more of her *sambandham* partners had to claim paternity. He did this by giving a piece of cloth and some vegetables to the low-caste woman who acted as midwife. If no-one would acknowledge paternity, then it was presumed that the mother-to-be had had sexual relations with a man of lower caste or a non-Hindu, both of which were prohibited. The punishment for this crime, applying to both the mother and her baby, was outcasteing followed by execution or sale into slavery. (How often this retribution was actually inflicted is impossible to say, for there is little relevant evidence, although Gough (1959a: 27) did hear about cases of outcasteing.) Legitimate children, as we know, were members of their mother's *taravad* and their fathers, whether putative or certain, had no responsibility for them at all. In fact, of course, they often had little contact with them during their nocturnal sojourns.

I have previously mentioned restrictions on a woman's choice of *sambandham* partner. First of all, there were exogamic rules barring a woman from taking as a partner a member of her own matrilineal descent group. Close patrilateral relatives were also rarely, if ever, partners, but it is unclear whether they were absolutely prohibited like matrilineal kin. Neither was a man allowed a *sambandham* relationship with two women of the same household, nor a woman with two men of the same household. More interesting, however, were the status-based restrictions, which in sum stated that a woman was only permitted a partner whose caste, or caste subdivision, was of a status equal or superior to her own; she was forbidden sexual relations with a man whose caste status was inferior to her own. The majority of commoner Nayars took *sambandham* partners of equal status, but a few commoner and most aristocratic Nayar women had *sambandham* partners of higher status, including on occasion Nambudiri Brahmans.

Some of the wider implications of these status differences between *sambandham* partners will be looked at in more detail shortly. But first of all, I must explain why there was any status-based restriction at all. The answer partly has to do with the serious pollution a woman would suffer, were she to have sexual relations with a lower-caste man. But much more importantly, I think, it has to do with the status of children. A caste is a bilateral grouping, and a child's membership of a caste, in contrast to a descent group such as the *taravad,* cannot be determined by only one parent. A caste in which the question of paternity was totally ignored would be a contradiction in terms. Much of the earlier work on the Nayars went astray because, in attempting to deny that the Nayars had any notion of fatherhood, it failed to appreciate this crucial point. In Hindu society, a child born of a high-status mother and a low-status father would be polluted and 'anomalous'; it certainly could not become a member of its mother's caste, and probably not of its father's either, though the latter point is somewhat theoretical. Consequently, some guarantee that a Nayar woman's partners were of equal or higher status, and an assurance when she became pregnant that one of them was the father, were absolutely imperative.

As we saw in the first chapter, the *sambandham* institution provoked much comment from foreign visitors to Kerala. To most nineteenth- and early twentieth-century anthropologists, the *sambandham* union was a patent case of polyandry – a topic which seems to have been an endless source of fascination and speculation. A few writers, though, regarded the *sambandham* as a case of cicisbeism, i.e. the taking of several lovers, rather than husbands, by a woman (e.g. Gait, in Census 1911, India: 239). When Nayars themselves became involved in the debate, it grew much more heated. Many modern-minded Nayars considered the label 'polyandrous' a gross insult. Chandu Menon was one such; he insisted that polyandry was not found among the Nayars, at least in the late nineteenth century, and that if it had existed previously, then it was 'a monstrous innovation due to the baneful Nambudiri influence' (G.O.M. 1891, Encl. C: 10). Panikkar (1918: 293), a leading member of the Nayar community, went so far as virtually to deny that any form of polyandry had ever obtained among the Nayars. Now there are two distinct issues here. The first is whether Nayars were permitted more than one *sambandham* partner at once; here the evidence is overwhelming that they were. To that extent, they were polyandrous, and Chandu Menon and Panikkar were quite plainly wrong. (Aiyappan – an Izhava – accused Panikkar of letting 'caste-pride ... cloud his vision' (1932: 78) on the subject.) The second issue – polyandry versus cicisbeism – is merely a reformulation of the old debate as to whether *sambandham* was a marriage or not. On this point, I have already made clear my view; namely, that it is best seen as a second marriage, concerned as it was with the status of sexual partners and the birth of legitimate children. During the nineteenth century, though, as I shall try to show in the subsequent chapter, the *sambandham* did develop into a more or less 'ordinary' Indian marriage.

Affinal relations in the tali-rite and sambandham union

It is now time to consider in greater detail the question of who tied the *tali* and who were the *sambandham* partners. I have left this problem until now because it raises a series of rather complicated theoretical questions; to put it in a nutshell, modern writers on the Nayars have concentrated their attention on the relations between the *tali*-tier's and the girl's families, and between *sambandham* partners' families, and have asked whether these were affinal relations. Of course, in so doing, these writers are only repeating the riddle about whether the Nayars had marriage or not. However, they are doing so at a 'deeper' level, in an attempt to isolate the structural principles of the Nayar marriage system, so as to be able to make systematic comparisons with marriage in other communities.

I shall begin looking at the *enangan* institution a little more closely. As stated earlier, each commoner Nayar lineage in Central Kerala was linked to one or more other lineages by 'hereditary ties of ceremonial co-operation', as Gough (1959a: 25) expresses it. These ties were reciprocal, but because each lineage could have more than one *enangan* lineage, a chain of such ties indirectly linked all the lineages in a locality. All *enangan* lineages were of equal status. The *tali*-tier, as we have seen, belonged to one of the girl's *enangan* lineages.[3]

The role of the *tali*-tier from the *enangan* lineage is central to the argument put forward by Gough in her paper 'The Nayars and the definition of marriage' (1959a), the most important of her theoretical analyses of Nayar marriage. She contended that the *sambandham* union was a marriage for two reasons: firstly, 'although plural unions were customary, mating was not promiscuous' – the polyandry versus cicisbeism argument again; secondly and more crucially, 'the concept of legally established paternity *was* of fundamental significance in establishing a child as a member of his lineage and caste' (ibid. 31; its. orig.). The concept of legal paternity is, for Gough, the critical attribute of marriage. Now the objections to this style of argument have already been mentioned; they are those of Leach, and centre upon the analytical futility of searching for a universally valid definition of marriage. As I have said, I agree with Leach, but I do not wish to pursue this controversy here. Let me, for the moment, suspend my objections to this part of Gough's argument, in order to look at the rest of her discussion. She suggests that what existed among the Nayars was a 'clear case of group-marriage'; the *tali*-rite 'initiated for each individual Nayar girl a state of marriage to a collectivity of men of appropriate caste'. It did this, firstly, by ritually endowing the girl with sexual and procreative functions; secondly, by transferring rights in her sexuality from kinsmen to others; thirdly, by the acceptance of these rights by the *enangan tali*-tier as a representative of his own (and higher status) castes; and fourthly, by providing the girl with a 'ritual husband' who symbolised the category of men with whom she might subsequently have sexual relations. (It also provided her children with a 'ritual father'.) In *sambandham* unions, a woman's partners claimed their sexual privileges and all of them were, as members of appropriate castes, 'potential husbands', whose duties were to 'provide the woman and her lineage with children and to acknowledge their potential biological paternity through birth-payments which legitimized the woman's child' (ibid.: 31–2).

There are, I think, two fundamental objections to Gough's argument about 'group-marriage', arising out of her third and fourth points. The first of these is that the *tali*-tier, among commoner Nayars an *enangan* and therefore a member of a lineage whose status is *equal* to that of the girl's, cannot represent or symbolise a collectivity of men (her potential *sambandham* partners), many of whom were of *higher* status or even of *higher* caste. For were he to do so, it would run directly counter to the principles of Indian status attribution in which, to use Dumont's term, the higher 'encompasses' the lower. The low cannot represent or symbolise an aristocratic Nayar, let alone a Nambudiri Brahman.

The second objection concerns the concept of the 'ritual husband'. In the area in which Gough collected her data, a woman and her children suffered pollution on the death of her *tali*-tier; otherwise, death pollution was observed only for matrilineal kin. Gough takes this as evidence that the *tali*-tier was, in some sense, a husband; the observation of death pollution for him was 'a mark of proof that she had once been married in the correct manner' (ibid.: 30). Similarly, the children, by observing death pollution, acknowledged their 'ritual father' (ibid.: 32). Leach (1961a: 107) also emphasised a woman's obligation to observe death pollution for her *tali*-tier, arguing that it demonstrated the presence of a notion of affinity. Dumont, too, came to a similar conclusion, namely that the observation of death pollution showed that 'the *tali*-tier (mari-de-tali) well and truly remains the ritual husband of the woman and the ritual father of her children' (1961: 19; also, 1970: 119). However, the ethnographic evidence does not permit such definite conclusions. Certainly, Nayar children did not suffer death pollution for their mother's *tali*-tier throughout Central Kerala, as is demonstrated by Mencher's unequivocal report (1965:172). Innes (1908: 177) implies that a woman observed death pollution among only some Nayars, and Iyer (1912: 27) states that in certain areas, a woman did not observe pollution but merely bathed – though admittedly this indicates some special connection.

The evidence from Travancore is also pertinent. There, *enangans* could sometimes tie the *tali*, but, except in the extreme north of the state, it was more usually done by a member of a *macchampikkar* family. In each village, there were three or four *macchampikkar* families: ancient Nayar families appointed as *tali*-tiers by royal writ. Like *tali*-tiers from *enangan* lineages, those belonging to *macchampikkar* families were apparently of equal status to the girls' families (Aiya 1906: II, 353; Thurston 1909: V, 319). Unfortunately, there appear to be very little data available on the *macchampikkar* families. However, it seems to be plain that, in all major respects, the *tali*-rite in the northern half of Travancore closely resembled the rite in Central Kerala and, what is relevant here, it also appears to have been normal for a woman *not* to observe death pollution for her *tali*-tier. According to Aiya (ibid.: 356), only Nayars belonging to the Illam and Svarupam subdivisions, living in certain parts of the country, observed this pollution.

No doubt, the evidence on death pollution observation is uncertain. However, precisely because of this, it seems unwise to take it as proof that the *tali*-tier was some kind of husband. This, though, does not dispose of the problem of affinal relations altogether, as we shall see by looking at Dumont's contribution to the understanding of Nayar marriage.

Dumont's paper 'Les mariages Nayar comme faits indiens' (1961) is both dense and complex, and a thorough critical review is impossible in a book of this kind. I shall therefore concentrate only on what is, in my judgment, his most important point; as the title implies, this is to show that the Indian context itself supplies an adequate conceptual framework for understanding the Nayars. In other words, the Nayars are not ethnographic curiosities but are, first and foremost, Hindus living in the caste society. The crucial concept here is the distinction between 'primary marriage' and 'secondary marriage'. By 'primary marriage', Dumont means a woman's first marriage, which is either indissoluble or, if it is not, can be followed by other 'secondary marriages'. Primary marriages are inaugurated with greater ceremony than secondary marriages and greater prestige attaches to them; consequently they are normally much less free – in terms of choice of partner and post-marital behaviour – than are secondary marriages (1970: 114). Among the Central Kerala Nayars, suggests Dumont, the *tali*-rite was a woman's primary marriage, and the *sambandham* unions were secondary marriages (1961: 19). (Gough (1965: 11) later modified her argument about 'group-marriage' and endorsed Dumont's suggestion.)

Is this suggestion fruitful? To some extent I think it is, as it raises a number of interesting new questions. But it is open to objections similar to those levelled against Gough. Firstly, if we follow Dumont, we are still on a chase to force Nayar marriage into a cross-cultural definition, for it is scarcely easier to formulate a definition of marriage applicable to all Indian communities, than it is to find one for the entire world. Secondly, there is again the problem of death pollution, which has already been discussed; Dumont (idem.) takes the observation of this pollution for the *tali*-tier as a crucial piece of evidence supporting his argument that the *tali*-rite could be regarded as a primary marriage.

But it may be more profitable to continue to the next stage of his argument, which focuses on the nature of relations between *enangan* lineages.

Here he makes comparisons with affinity as it is manifested elsewhere in southern India. At this point, I shall have to simplify grossly, so that readers uninitiated into the esoteric field of South Asian kinship theory can follow the thread of the argument and, more pertinently, can see some relevance in it. Among many South Indian communities, for example the Tamil Kallar caste who were studied by Dumont (1957b) and figure prominently in his theoretical writings, there is a preferential rule of cross-cousin marriage; i.e. there exists an explicit rule which states that a man should marry a woman who is either his true cross-cousin or is placed in the same category as his true cross-cousins by the kinship terminology. According to Dumont (though it is debatable),[4] this rule is expressed in the terminology itself, which simultaneously embodies an ideology of 'balance' between consanguinity and affinity (1953; 1957a). What this means, to put it extremely naively, is that ties with affines are socially as important as ties with consanguines – the implicit contrast is with societies organised around a principle of unilineal descent. The stress on affinal connections is both created and maintained by the institution of cross-cousin marriage, which itself gives rise to an 'alliance relation' between the groups marrying in accordance with the cross-cousin rule. To explicate fully the meaning of 'alliance' would be an extended essay in itself; briefly and generally, however, Dumont defines 'alliance' as 'extended and permanent affinity' (1970: 112). Earlier though, he presented a more detailed definition, when he argued that a rule of cross-cousin marriage ' causes marriage to be transmitted much as membership in the descent group is transmitted. With it, marriage acquires a diachronic dimension, it becomes an institution enduring from generation to generation, which I therefore call "marriage alliance", or simply "alliance"' (1957a: 24). Between groups linked to each other by repeated marriages, contracted in accordance with the cross-cousin rule, there is thus said to be an alliance relation.

It is an important point in Dumont's argument that when there is a rule of cross-cousin marriage, the rule applies first and foremost to the principal marriages (of a man) and not to subsidiary marriages;[5] a man should marry a cross-cousin in his principal marriage, but if he marries again he has a free choice of partner. In parallel fashion, what may be described as the affinal implications of the South Indian cross-cousin system, should be present among the Nayars in their primary marriage, the *tali*-rite, and thus in the relations between *enangan* lineages. Dumont suggests that the role of the *enangan* lineages closely resembled that of allies elsewhere, and he therefore postulates that: 'the content of affinity of the *enangan* institution is the same as that of [cross-]cousin marriage' (1961: 21). Among commoner Nayars, where *enangan* lineages were of equal status, there existed between them a relation of 'perpetual affinity', equivalent to that defined by the cross-cousin rule in other areas (ibid.: 22). To sum up: what Dumont tries to demonstrate is that there was, among commoner Nayars in Central Kerala, a concept of affinal relations strictly comparable to that found in other South Indian communities.

Certainly, this argument makes some sense. Just as there are parallels between the *tali*-rite and ordinary Indian marriage ceremonies, so there are parallels between the roles of affines among, say, the Kallar and the roles of *enangans*. In particular, there are striking resemblances between the duties performed by *enangans* at funerals, and those carried out by Pramalai Kallar affines on the same occasion (Gough 1961: 327-8; Dumont 1975b: 251-6). It is also true, of course, that *enangan* ties were hereditary and persisted across the generations like an alliance relation. To this extent, therefore, one can agree that the relations between *enangan* lineages were of an affinal nature and resembled alliance relations. But I do not find it logical to follow Dumont, when he claims that the 'content' of affinity of the *enangan* institution was *identical* to that of cross-cousin marriage. Many of the important rights allocated at marriage in most of India (e.g. a husband's rights over his wife) were not, of course, allocated in the *tali*-rite; nor was the rite accompanied by the series of gift exchanges between affines, which is such an important feature of most Indian marriages. The relation between *enangan* lineages thus incorporated only some of the elements present in affinal relations elsewhere in southern India. The problem with Dumont's approach is its black-and-white nature; he does not seem prepared to admit the existence of variation in the strength of affinal and alliance relations. To me, it makes much more sense to say that the *tali*-rite did create and maintain affinal and alliance relations between *enangan* lineages, but that these relations were relatively weak in comparison with their counterparts in other South Indian communities.[6]

I fear that some readers, having followed the above argument without too much difficulty, may still feel that they are not much enlightened. Let me briefly recapitulate on the argument about affinity. Nayar marriage, though unique, was not a wholly aberrant phenomenon. Some of the parallels between the *tali*-rite and the *sambandham* union, and 'ordinary' Indian marriage have already been explored, and we have seen that the Nayar marriage system embodied some typical pan-Indian concerns about, for instance, purity and legitimacy. The argument about affinity is at a more 'structural' level. Not only do the Nayars share certain cultural features with their fellow Hindus; they also had a structure of inter-group relations, exemplified in this context by the *enangan* institution, which closely paralleled the structure of affinal relations elsewhere in South India. This does not imply that the structure underlying the Nayar marriage system was identical to that underlying, say, the Kallar marriage system; but what it does mean is that the two structures are logically comparable, and therefore that the structure of Nayar society can be understood within the context of the wider Indian society. The importance of Dumont's contribution to the analysis of the Nayars is that, in spite of its many problems, it helps us to restore the Nayars definitively to a place in Indian society.

The question of affinal relations in the *sambandham* union obviously arises now. Here the issue is much simpler, for there was practically no affinal content to the *sambandham*. In particular, *sambandham* relationships were transient and generated no long-standing, let alone hereditary, relations between the partners' families, nor did these families have any reciprocal duties to perform for each other. In other words, the most important characteristics of affinity were not present in the *sambandham* relationship.

Hypergamous marriage among the Nayars

So far, I have concentrated attention on the commoners and have made little allusion to the aristocratic Nayars. But the marriage system of the aristocrats has long been one of the most noted features of Nayar society, involving as it did cross-caste hypergamous relations with Brahmans, Kshatriyas and Samantans.[7] As we have seen, although commoner Nayar women could, and sometimes did, take higher-status men as *sambandham* partners – i.e. in a hypergamous relationship – their partners were mostly of equal rank, and *talis* were almost invariably tied by *enangans* of equal status – both isogamous relationships. But among the Kshatriyas, Samantans and aristocratic Nayars, *talis* were always tied by men of higher status, and women always took *sambandham* partners of superior status; relationships set up by both the *tali*-rite and the *sambandham* union were therefore hypergamous. As Gough (1959a: 28) put it, each high-status family acknowledged ritual superiors and inferiors, but no peers.

Like the Nayars, the Kshatriyas and Samantans were matrilineal, and they shared the same marriage system. Their *tali*-rite had the same functions as the Nayar rite, although it differed somewhat in form; in the highest-status families anyway, it was performed for each girl separately shortly before she attained puberty, and was accompanied by various Brahmanical religious rites. The *sambandham* union differed little from that of the commoners, although in some cases it was inaugurated with no ceremony at all.

As I suggested in chapter 2, the Kshatriya and Samantan subdivisions are best regarded as supereminent Nayar subdivisions; all of them were involved in a 'status game', played to maintain or raise their rank. All these subdivisions had very small populations, and many of them were equivalent to single *taravads,* or even sections of *taravads*. One of the most important criteria for the attribution of status to a particular family (or subdivision) was the status of the man who tied the *tali* for that family's girls. Conversely, for whom a man tied a *tali* could influence the status of his family. The status of *sambandham* partners also had some relevance in the status game, very much more so for a woman and her family than for a man and his. One way of looking at this is to consider the statuses of *tali*-tiers and *sambandham* partners as diacritical markers of a family's (or subdivision's) status. The entire process can also be understood as one of 'inclusion' and 'exclusion' (Pocock 1957: 28); a girl's family tries to include itself with

The Nayars Today

the higher-ranking *tali*-tier's or *sambandham* partner's family, while excluding itself from those ascribed lower status because they are refused as *tali*-tiers or *sambandham* partners.

Some examples should make clearer what I mean. (Complete data on the statuses of *tali*-tiers and *sambandham* partners are not available for all high-ranking subdivisions; in any case, though, I shall not attempt a complete description here.)[8] The families with highest status were those in which only Nambudiri Brahmans acted as *tali*-tiers and only Nambudiris were accepted as *sambandham* partners. In Central Kerala, the only family definitely practising Nambudiri exclusivism was the Kshatriya Cochin royal house. A Nambudiri tied the *tali* for one princess at a time, and he was paid for his services. It is possible that the Cranganore chiefly family also employed Nambudiris to tie their daughters' *talis* (Census 1901, Cochin: 145-6; Iyer 1912: 152). Gough (1955: 49, 53; 1959a: 29; 1961: 377) implies that they often tied *talis* for aristocratic families, but Mencher and Goldberg (1967: 93-4), who have carried out field-work among the Nambudiris, state flatly that in Central Kerala, except for the Cochin princesses, Nambudiris never tied the *tali* for any girl of another caste. For various reasons, I am inclined to believe that Mencher and Goldberg are correct – principally because their assertion makes the most logical sense in the context of what happened in other aristocratic families.

In other Central Kerala Kshatriya families, the *tali*-tier was an Aryapattar – a Tamil Brahman whose customs closely resemble those of the Malayali Brahmans – and the women took as *sambandham* partners either Nambudiris, other Brahmans or Kshatriyas (Census 1901, Cochin: 145-6; Iyer 1912: 152). In Travancore Kshatriya families, girls' *talis* were tied by Nambudiris or Aryapattars (Pillai 1940: I, 851). However, these Nambudiris were probably relatively low-ranking, as none of the highest-status members of the community lived in Travancore (Mencher and Goldberg 1967: 90). Travancore Kshatriya women took only Nambudiris as *sambandham* partners.

In the Zamorin of Calicut's family, i.e. the Eradi subdivision of Samantans, *talis* were tied by Kshatriyas from the Cranganore chief's family, which the Zamorin recognised as more ancient and therefore of higher rank; while in the Walluvanad raja's family, equivalent to the Vallodi subdivision, *talis* were tied by men from the higher-ranking Beypore chiefly family (Iyer 1912: 147; Gough 1955: 49). The *talis* of other Samantan girls were usually, but not invariably, tied by Kshatriyas. In the Zamorin's and other chiefly families, the majority of the women's *sambandham* partners were Nambudiris, although Kshatriya men from ancient royal families were sometimes accepted (Census 1891, Madras: XIII, 231; Iyer 1912: 147; Gough 1955: 47).

In Travancore, the *talis* of girls in the higher-ranking Samantan subdivision – which included the Travancore royal family – were tied by Kshatriyas, while in the lower-ranking subdivision, the *tali*-tiers were

Aryapattars (Pillai 1940: I, 852-3). Data on Travancore Samantan *sambandham* partners are unavailable, so far as I know, although Mateer (1871: 118; 171-2) stated that Travancore princesses accepted only Kshatriya men as partners.

The information on aristocratic Nayars is very incomplete, and a great deal of diversity clearly existed. In general, according to Gough (1955: 49), girls' *tali* were usually tied by men of the appropriate higher subdivision; for instance, the daughters of a village headman had their *talis* tied by men of the district headman's family. In Cochin, records Iyer (1912: 24-5), it is probable that the tier was normally a member of one of the Samantan subdivisions.

Despite many lacunae, something of the logic of this hypergamous system has, I hope, emerged. For instance, one family (or subdivision) might have asserted its superiority over another by, say, having Kshatriya rather than Samantan *tali*-tiers, or by accepting only Nambudiris, rather than any Brahmans, as *sambandham* partners for its womenfolk. Who the men took as *sambandham* partners was much less critical because, it appears, their choice of partners carried little, if any, risk to their status. Although it is not clear, it might also have been the case that one family could claim superiority, by refusing to supply *tali*-tiers to an alleged inferior. Obviously such a refusal necessarily implies a claim to superiority, but what I am unsure about is strategy: whether or not a family would have actually tried to raise its status by this method. (Loss of status through acting as the *tali*-tier or *sambandham* partner to a lower-ranking family will be considered further below.)

I should like to emphasise that this hypergamous system was in no way static; on the contrary, the status game had considerable built-in dynamism. If a commoner *taravad*, probably after it had grown wealthy or otherwise powerful, wished to raise its status, it had to start contracting hypergamous relations, severing its previously isogamous ones (cf. Mencher 1966a: 159). It might have begun by permitting only higher-status *sambandham* partners to its womenfolk. Cutting *enangan* ties was almost certainly harder owing to their hereditary nature; however, it would have been an essential part of the status-raising process for, as we have seen, the *tali*-tier was invariably of higher rank in aristocratic families. An aristocratic *taravad*, whose relations were already hypergamous, could try to ascend still further by finding men of yet higher status to act as *tali*-tiers and *sambandham* partners. Gough (1955: 47) says that in the eighteenth century the Zamorin's family chose to accept only Nambudiri *sambandham* partners for its women, whereas previously certain Kshatriya men had been acceptable as well — presumably as part of such an attempt to raise status still further. But just as *taravads* could rise, so they could also fall if those who acted as *tali*-tiers and *sambandham* partners refused to continue, thus forcing the *taravad* to look to men of lower status. It is to be regretted that we have no detailed account of these processes as they actually occurred

The Nayars Today

in the past, but my description has, perhaps, given some impression of the nature of the dynamic process and of the central importance of the marriage system to it.

Status exchange in hypergamous relations

In Central Kerala, as I noted above, probably the Cochin princesses alone enjoyed the privilege of having their *tali* tied by Nambudiris. It is interesting to note that among the Nambudiris themselves, the man who fastened the *tali* for these princesses was considered degraded and polluted. For his trouble, he was paid a considerable sum (Mencher and Goldberg 1967: 93-4). Clearly, a kind of status exchange operated here — the Nambudiri tier losing status as the Cochin royal family gained it, the loss being compensated by payment. I have been unable to find concrete evidence that such a status exchange was present in all *tali*-rites, so that the tier always lost status when a lower-ranking family had him tie their girls' *talis*. But payments to higher-ranking tiers do appear to have been common — whether or not they were universal, I am unsure — and this might be taken as evidence that a status exchange always existed. In this respect, the *tali*-rite certainly does seem to be in marked contrast with the *sambandham* relationship in which, so far as I can understand, a status exchange either never operated at all or was of only minimal significance. In other words, although a Nayar woman's status, and that of her *taravad,* was raised if she took a Nambudiri as a *sambandham* partner, the Nambudiri himself lost nothing or very little.[9] A contrast of this sort would clearly correlate with the undoubted fact that, whereas men from the highest castes seem to have been very selective about the girls for whom they would tie *talis,* all of them appear to have been willing enough to take even commoner Nayar women as *sambandham* partners.

Now obviously there is a very straightforward, albeit cynical, explanation for this. The pleasure to be derived from taking a Nayar woman as a *sambandham* partner — even if she were of lower status — no doubt exceeded that produced by attending a *tali*-rite, which was frequently, I suspect, a rather boring and stuffy affair. Indeed, lower-status *sambandham* partners may have been preferred, for the notion is widespread in India as it is in many stratified societies, that lower-ranking women are more voluptuous lovers. But even if this explanation were granted, behaviour of this sort had to be justified, or at least rationalised, and it is the nature of the justification, and its implications, with which I am concerned here.

Gough (1959a: 29) has pointed out that Nambudiris did not regard *sambandham* unions as true marriages — which could only be to Nambudiri women — but as a kind of concubinage. Dumont (1961: 26-7; cf. 1970: 119), reiterating Gough, extends the argument further and contends that *tali*-rites in which Nambudiris acted as tiers — which he thought much commoner than in fact they were — were also not marriages for Nambudiris, as they did not take the shape of correct Brahman ritual. In my opinion, these arguments are somewhat truistic. They are, too, slightly beside the point: firstly, because we are dealing with a situation general to Kshatriyas, Samantans and Nayars and not one confined to Nambudiris; and secondly, because the mere insistence that it was not true marriage does not really explain or justify Nambudiri conduct.

In his paper (1961: 23-9), Dumont devoted considerable space to an analysis of affinity and status in hypergamous relations. I have not found these arguments very enlightening and propose to omit them here.[10] But a further reconsideration of his arguments about affinity and the *enangan* institution, which I discussed above, may help to shed some light on our present problem. I suggested before that the *enangan* relation among the commoners was a kind of weak affinal and alliance relation, whereas the *sambandham* union had practically no affinal characteristics. I would suggest that the same is true of *enangan* relations among aristocratic Nayars, Kshatriyas and Samantans, and those Nambudiris involved with them. Here, of course, *enangan* relations were asymmetrical, rather than reciprocal, i.e. a family would receive *enangan* services from one ranked above them but provide them for one ranked below them. However, the ritual duties of aristocratic *enangans* seem to have differed little from those of commoner *enangans* (Gough 1961: 377), and, like relations between commoner *enangans*, those between aristocratic *enangans* also persisted across the generations. As among commoners, *sambandham* relations among aristocrats were transient and could not normally become the basis of a continuing connection between two families. Throughout India, there are important status implications involved in affinal relations, and an actual or potential status exchange (frequently accompanied by an exchange of goods) is always present. The fact that the status of the *tali*-tier, and the status of the families for whom a man would act as a *tali*-tier, were so closely circumscribed correlates, I suggest, with the affinal nature of relations established and maintained by the *tali*-rite. Conversely, the choice of *sambandham* partners was so free because the *sambandham* union lacked affinal content.

In the final analysis, though, it surely has to be admitted that there was a certain amount of hypocrisy - not to put too fine a point on it - about the status connotations of the *sambandham* relationship. That Nambudiris and other high-ranking aristocrats did not risk their rank, when sleeping with lower-status Nayar women, may accord with the non-affinal nature of the *sambandham,* but such sexual activity should surely have been highly polluting. In hypergamous *sambandham* unions, men refused to eat in the homes of their partners, and had as little contact as possible with them and their children, especially after the morning bath, when they would not touch them at all. These restrictions were all in the name of preserving purity. One cannot help but have some sympathy for those reformers who railed against Nambudiri exploitation of Nayar women, asking why, if they were so concerned for their purity, were they so willing to couple with lower-caste women. In fact, Hindu pollution theory does allow a possible explanation, or rationalisation, of this conduct through its

The Nayars Today

sharp distinction between 'internal' and 'external' pollution (Stevenson 1954: 56). Internal pollution results from absorbing polluting substances into the body and is much harder to remove than external pollution, which is a consequence of mere contact with polluting substances. The physiology of sexual intercourse inevitably means internal pollution for the woman, but only external pollution for the man. His purity is therefore more at risk in eating food cooked by a low-caste person, than it is by indulging in sexual relations with a low-caste woman. Nonetheless, to my mind anyway, there still remains a certain amount of rule-bending here, for coition with a low-caste woman is indisputably a highly polluting activity, and in most of India it was never overtly tolerated on the scale found in Kerala.

Conclusion

The study of South Asian kinship has now become a highly technical subject, and measured by the standards of modern specialist work, this chapter, as I have implied more than once, contains many simplifications and lacunae. The explanations of Nayar marriage presented by certain writers have been ignored altogether, and many of the issues raised by Gough and Dumont have not been tackled. In particular, to produce a genuinely satisfactory analysis, we need, I think, some sort of fusion between Gough's perspective, which derives predominantly from functionalism and descent-theory, and Dumont's, which stems mainly from structuralism and alliance-theory. But this is a much wider issue of kinship theory and will take us too far from the Nayars. What I have tried to do is focus on the main elements of the *tali*-rite and the *sambandham* relationship and, avoiding the (to my mind) futile controversy over whether the Nayars had marriage as such, show how these elements make sense in the specific Nayar and general Indian contexts. How, for example, the *tali*-rite can be seen as a girl's rite of passage and how it resembles pre-puberty marriage elsewhere in India; why the restriction on the *sambandham* partner's status accords well with the bilateral definition of the caste; in what ways the *enangan* relation resembles affinal and alliance relations in other parts of South India; how the statuses of the *tali*-tier and *sambandham* partners fit in with the status game as played among the high-ranking castes and subdivisions. The aim was to make sense of the Nayar marriage system by demonstrating that it was not uniquely bizarre, without at the same time denying its uniqueness as a totality and without forcing it into the framework of some constrictive paradigm of Indian kinship. Although I do not find it hard to criticise the arguments of other writers, I have to admit that there are many aspects of Nayar marriage which continue to baffle me. I have little doubt that, even though the Nayars' traditional marriage system has now vanished, it will continue to fascinate and remain the object of many a new investigation.

The 'Traditional' Nayar Marriage System

Postscript on the origin of the system

Speculative history remains unfashionable among modern anthropologists. Personally, I think it can be justified on occasion, for it can raise issues that might have otherwise gone unremarked, and problems so raised may sometimes be tackled in a sociologically acceptable manner. Justification apart, however, I know from talking to people other than professional anthropologists that I am not alone in thinking that one of the most fascinating questions of all is how did the Nayar marriage system begin and why was it introduced.

Gough has devoted a couple of pages of very general remarks to this problem (1961: 370-1), but most early writers were prone to consider the issue at length – not, admittedly, to much profit in most instances. However, the most serious attempt by a historian to confront the problem is by E.K. Pillai (1970: ch. 19). Pillai has argued (ibid.: ch. 20) that Nambudiri power and influence only began to rise significantly from the twelfth century, and that the matrilineal, polyandrous system was at that time imposed on the higher castes by the Nambudiris. Previously, these castes had had a patrilineal kinship system. He suggests that the matrilineal system first emerged in the Central Kerala region where Nambudiri power was greatest, and that it spread over the rest of Kerala during the thirteenth and fourteenth centuries. Nambudiri power was such that both royalty and commoners had to switch over to a matrilineal system.

The traditional explanation holds that Parasurama, the sixth incarnation of Vishnu and the creator of Kerala, commanded the Nayar women to satisfy the sexual desires of Nambudiri men, pronouncing that chastity was no virtue and promiscuity no vice for Nayars (see, e.g. Iyer 1912: 39). Mythical explanations apart, the crux of the problem lies in the size of the Nambudiri community. In Cochin, where their proportion in the population was probably as high as anywhere in Kerala, only 0.5% of the population was Nambudiri in 1931, whereas the Nayars formed around 15% of the total Kerala population. How could such a tiny number enforce their desires on a much larger community? Pillai (1970: ch. 13) has suggested that Nambudiris formed as much as 25% of the population in certain areas of Kerala in the twelfth century. But his conclusion is far from indisputable, and in any case it fails to explain how the Nambudiris' will was imposed.

Granted that – if the Nayars did once have a patrilineal system – some resistance to change must have been inevitable, it still remains the case that all writers have assumed that the matrilineal system must have been imposed upon them. The obvious alternative is to assume that it was not imposed. Advantages there may have been for the Nambudiris, but one can see distinct advantages for the Nayars as well. There clearly existed a functional connection between the military system and the marriage system (Gough 1952a: 76-8); conceivably, as Barbosa and Montesquieu thought, the latter actually developed in response to the problems caused by their

121

The Nayars Today

military role. The sexual problems of soldiers away from home have, after all, produced some weird and often much more horrendous solutions in the history of the world. One might also argue that the Nayar marriage system did in fact solve various fundamental problems concerned with sexual relationships, which have plagued other societies. If Camoens was right – and he was not alone in his judgment – the curse of sexual jealousy hardly existed among the Nayars. And the subordination of women was undoubtedly much less than it was in most other societies. I am coming very close to making value-judgments here, but it is, I think, worth pointing out that the Nayar marriage system need not necessarily have been imposed against opposition and that, arguably at least, it provided pay-offs for all Nayars as well as Nambudiri men – though not, of course, for Nambudiri women. Inevitably, this simply leads onto a series of further questions, of which the most general and most patent is this: why, if the system was so marvellous in certain respects, was it unique? I leave the reader to formulate his own answer.

6 The disintegration of the matrilineal joint-family system

Throughout modern Kerala, to the best of our knowledge, the old Nayar matrilineal joint-family system has disintegrated. *Taravads* have split up and modern households form smaller units. Property is no longer held jointly but is owned by individual men and women, and inheritance is bilateral, although certain features of matrilineal descent persist. The *tali*-rite is no longer celebrated, nor does the *sambandham* institution still exist. Today, Nayars marry in more or less the same way as other Hindus, and their marriages are expected to be monogamous and lasting. Nambudiri men, further, can no longer take Nayar women as lovers.[1]

In this chapter, I discuss the changes which have occurred in the Nayar kinship and marriage system over the last two centuries or so and try to discern the reasons for them. As has so often been the case throughout this book, a complete survey of regional variation is prohibited by insufficient data. However, I can at least point out the principal differences between the situation in Central Kerala communities (studied by Gough, Mencher, Nakane and Unni) and those in Ramankara, and draw attention to the significant differences, on a wider scale, between the various regions of Kerala. In the conclusion to this chapter, I shall make some remarks on the wider implications of these changes.

Demobilisation of the Nayar armies

It is an anthropological commonplace that a fundamental 'problem' of matriliny centres upon the marital tie. Given that men dominate women, in a general sense, in matrilineal as well as patrilineal systems, and therefore cannot be incorporated, qua husbands, into their wives' matrilineal descent groups as women, qua wives, can be into their husbands' patrilineal descent groups, the formation and maintenance of strong matrilineal descent groups require that the marital tie be extremely weak. This condition has rarely been fulfilled and, in fact, societies with strong matrilineal descent groups are and were very rare; one such society, however, was that of the Nayars. It should be plain, from what has gone before, that the strength of the Nayar matrilineal joint family was contingent on the weakness of the 'marital' bonds, i.e. those set up at the *tali*-rite and, more importantly, those of the *sambandham* union.

It is, I think, fairly clear that there was a functional connection between the Nayars' military organisation and their kinship and marriage system,

The Nayars Today

as Barbosa, Montesquieu and other early travellers and commentators perceived. As soldiers, Nayar men were frequently away from their native villages for several months a year and often on the move. The marriage system inhibited the development of close attachments between Nayar men and women in their native villages and, at the same time, permitted them sexual access to Nayar women throughout the land. Gough (1952a: 77) correctly insists that no causal connection, in either direction, between the military organisation and the marriage system can be presumed, i.e. it would be fallacious to argue that the military organisation was the cause of the marriage system, or vice versa. Nonetheless, I trust that the reader will agree that there was a fairly evident functional 'fit' between the Nayars' military role and their marriage system.

After annexing Malabar in 1792, the British disbanded the armies, and Nayar men returned to their homes; this promoted the following developments in Central Kerala, according to Gough (ibid.: 79): ' Most important, polyandry began to die out early in the nineteenth century. ... in general marriage became monogamous ... The pre-puberty *tali*-rite lost much of its significance, and the *tali*-tier was no longer required to cohabit with his ritual "wife". Instead the post-puberty *sambandham* union was regarded as the " real " marriage; it was expected to be permanent.' By ' polyandry ' Gough refers, of course, to the fact that a woman could take several *sambandham* partners. The overall development she traces is one in which the *sambandham* union tends progressively towards a more or less permanent union between one man and one woman. This development leads, at the same time, to a decline in the significance of the *tali*-rite – leaving aside the question of whether the *tali*-tier did but rarely enjoy sexual relations with the girl. It is reasonable to postulate that the demobilisation of the Cochin armies in 1809 and of the Travancore armies, enforced by Martanda Varma in the mid-eighteenth century, had similar effects.

We must, however, guard against the temptation to exaggerate the effects of demobilisation. It is indisputable that the *tali*-rite did decline in importance throughout the nineteenth century, while the *sambandham* union moved towards stable, monogamous union during the same period, but there is not, so far as I know and as the sceptic may have suspected, any concrete evidence to demonstrate that these changes resulted from the disbandment of the Nayar armies. The argument is logically deductive, rather than empirically inductive, and must not be pushed too far. It does seem plausible that the permanent return of the Nayar men to their homes would have considerably promoted the formation of bonds with their *sambandham* partners, stronger than those existing when they were frequently away. In other words, I am postulating that in the absence of social or cultural mechanisms having the function of inhibiting the process – and no such mechanisms developed after the armies were disbanded – it is almost inevitable that sexual partners will, in general, be prone to form increasingly powerful attachments to each other if they meet regularly and, at the same time, enter into fewer sexual liaisons with others. But given that there was never any fighting during the monsoon season, and that it was not continuous during the dry season, few Nayar males can have spent more than half the year on active service, and most were probably away for less time. It would clearly be wholly incorrect to argue that demobilisation, in itself, led to the disintegration of the matrilineal joint-family system. It is rather that the changes following demobilisation constituted, so to speak, a crack in the fabric of the system. The crack may not have been very deep; nonetheless, the disbanding of the Nayar armies may well have been an important initial factor promoting the eventual collapse of the old kinship and marriage system.

As the importance of the *sambandham* union grew, its inauguration began to be celebrated with more ceremony while, conversely, the *tali*-rite became less and less of an occasion and eventually disappeared altogether. In Central Travancore, its celebration seems to have ceased by the turn of the century, and performance of the first menstruation ceremony (*tirantukuli*) stopped a few years later. The *tali*-rite died out around 1930 in Cochin (Gough 1955: 49) and a little later in parts of South Malabar, where the *tirantukuli* persisted for much longer (Mencher 1965: 178-9). The transformation of *sambandham*, into a relationship more or less identical to marriage as understood elsewhere in India, has been accompanied by the development of an inaugural ceremony, closely resembling the marriage ceremony of other high-caste South Indians (idem.). Nambudiri connections with Nayar women had become rare by the 1930s, owing not only to Nayar opposition to Nambudiri 'exploitation', but also to the reformist pressure of Nambudiris themselves, particularly younger sons who demanded the right to take Nambudiri wives. This demand was a main plank in the campaigns of the Nambudiri reform movement, which started in Central Kerala around 1917 (Mencher 1966b: 190-94).

Partition of taravads

During the nineteenth century, it appears that *taravad* property came to be divided with increased frequency in Central Kerala (Gough 1952a: 79; 1961: 343-4; Mencher 1962: 231). It is quite probable that a similar development occurred in Travancore, but I have no evidence of this. The partition of property was along the lines discussed in connection with the *taravads* in Ramankara; partition was between *tavazhis*, segments of the *taravads*. Although the household might not have divided at exactly the same time as the partition of property was effected, it is almost certain that households split in such a way that they tended to remain congruent with property groups. *Taravads* thus became shallower and narrower; i.e. they had a lesser generational depth and included fewer distantly-related kin. However, there was as yet no deviation from matrilineal principles. The household and property group remained a matrilineal segment, and ancestral property was not being transmitted to affines, men's children or other outsiders.

We can isolate three basic factors, which probably contributed towards this increase in the frequency of *taravad* partition. The first of these is population growth. It is clear that the larger a *taravad* became, the greater was its tendency to divide. That this is so is not, I think, open to dispute (cf. Gough 1961: 344; Menchet 1962: 233). Even after allowance has been made for the unreliability of population estimates for Kerala at the beginning of the nineteenth century, it is certain that the population of Malabar, Cochin and Travancore in 1901 (totalling 6.65 million) was at least three and possibly four times as great as it had been one hundred years earlier. There can be little doubt that this is a significantly higher rate of demographic growth than had obtained previously and, given that there is no reason to believe that the growth rate of the Nayar population was lower than that of the rest of the community, it seems highly probable that numbers alone were an important factor in raising the rate of *taravad* partition.

The second factor has to do with a probable rise in the men's ambition to become *karanavans*. It is an inevitable feature of a matrilineal succession system, in which the family head is the eldest male, that a man cannot expect to become the head until he is old. Indeed, the Malabar Marriage Commission asserted that most *karanavans* were actually senile by the time they succeeded to their position (G.O.M. 1891: 29). Gough (1961: 344) plausibly suggests that the return of younger men to their homes, after the end of their soldiering careers, led to a desire on the part of many of them, given that they did not have much else to do, for an increased measure of responsibility and authority at an earlier age. Such a desire could only be met by partitioning the *taravad*.[2]

The third factor is more complicated; it is the effect on the *taravad* of the changing nature of the *sambandham* union. We have already noted that the partition of the *taravad* was one between matrilineal segments. Insofar as a partition is a result of conflicting interests, a partition of this sort stems from a conflict between the interests of members, especially senior males, belonging to different segments. The fact that no partition of *taravad* property had any legal sanction, until reforms were enacted in the twentieth century, meant that partition was itself a bountiful source of litigation within *taravads* (cf. Jeffrey 1973: 222). However, it is important to note that there is no immediate nor direct reason why an increasing stress on affinal and paternal ties, consequent on the type of *sambandham* union which was emerging, should in and of itself foster conflict between matrikin. There is no clear evidence of widespread attempts by men to transfer *taravad* ancestral property to wives and children; rather, it appears that conflicts within the *taravad* tended to stem from a *karanavan*'s alleged favouring of his own *tavazhi*, to the detriment of others. This emerges strongly, for example, from the report of the Malabar Marriage Commission at the end of the century (G.O.M. 1891).

Disputes over property seem to have originated mainly in men's self-acquired property, not *taravad* property. According to legal authorities (e.g. Moore 1905: 174), self-acquired property was at its owner's absolute disposal during his lifetime, but reverted to his *taravad* on his death. However, during the nineteenth century, men started to bequeath self-acquired property to their wives and children. Transfers of this sort engendered trouble. When exactly this became a serious problem is not wholly clear. Burton, who was in Calicut around 1850, states (and I know of no earlier report in this vein) that: 'Of late years some heads of families have made a provision for their own children during lifetime, but it has been necessary to procure the assent of rightful heirs to bequests thus irregularly made' (1851: 218). I infer, though the inference is open to dispute, that Burton refers to self-acquired property. He does not specifically mention disputes over self-acquired property, and whether or not they had become prevalent by the middle of the nineteenth century is unclear. Other sources do not help to answer this question. All that we can say, I think, is that by this period the *sambandham* union had so strengthened that men did, occasionally anyway, transfer self-acquired property to women (their *sambandham* partners), now effectively wives, and that transfers of this sort could have promoted disputes between men and their matrilineal relatives, who would have wished this property to revert to the *taravad*.

Crisis in the late nineteenth century

In the last quarter of the nineteenth century, the state of the Nayar community and its matrilineal joint-family system, in particular, appears to have entered a crisis. In speaking of crisis, caution is desirable – for the impression is gleaned from statements, many of which were of an openly propagandist nature. Many of them were issued by members of the Nayar elite, most of whom were highly educated, and they cannot be taken as accurate representations of the feelings of ordinary people. There is in fact evidence that they were not. However, it is of interest to begin by surveying the situation through the eyes of these spokesmen, although there was, I should make clear, considerable disagreement among the Nayar leaders about the reforms which were needed (Jeffrey 1973: 263).

By 1875, change was definitely in the air in Cochin, and the Census Commissioner of that year, A. Sankariah (a Tamil Brahman), recorded his opposition to it (Census 1875, Cochin: 38): 'Now-a-days some unreasoning prejudice seems to be setting against it [matriliny], which is doubtless due to the influence of the adherents of the rival system; and parents too often contrive to make provision for their children at the expense of the peace and comfort of their own tarawads.' The last remark indicates plainly that the conflict between affinal/paternal and matrilineal ties was the crux of the problem. In Travancore too, hostility to the system had become explicit by this time, and in his Administration Report for Travancore in 1874–5, the Dewan, Mahdeva Rao, declared that the law must be altered so that individual partition of the *taravad* would be legally possible; he admitted though: 'Not that such a law would be generally acted upon at once: the feeling in favour of relatives living together in an undivided state of property is too strong to yield to reason in the present generation' (qu. in Mateer 1883a: 185). In 1884, the Malayali Sabha (Association) was founded in Travancore; it aimed to promote the 'welfare of the Malayali community, by aiding the diffusion of Western knowledge, by encouraging female education and by reforming the marriage system' — aims, which as Jeffrey (1973: 194) points out, are 'peculiarly Nayar'. Perhaps the most fascinating piece of propaganda to emerge during this period was the first Malayalam novel, *Indulekha,* written by a Malabar Nayar, O. Chandu Menon, in 1899. The novel recounts the story of Indulekha, the beautiful and talented Nayar heroine, and her ultimately successful attempt to marry Madhavan, a member of a Nayar *taravad* in South Malabar. The book, which strongly defends the relatively emancipated position of Nayar women, also bitterly attacks the joint-family system, in particular the arbitrary power of the *karanavan,* and mocks to great effect the pretensions of the Nambudiris who came to indulge their sensual pleasures with the Nayar women.

Before looking at the reasons for the crisis, and the measures later taken by the governments to try to cope with it, it might be desirable to itemise the various points at issue. The generalised objections which were expressed tend to disguise the fact that there were several points of contention, not all of which were equally emphasised by or relevant to all Nayars. Firstly, there were objections to the fact that the *sambandham* union was not recognised as a legal marriage, and that there was therefore no such thing as legal marriage among the Nayars. Secondly, and closely connected with the first issue, there was controversy over a man's right to give property to his legally unrecognised wife and children. Thirdly, there was hostility to the Nambudiris' sexual privileges and to their refusal to bear any economic responsibility for the children they fathered by their Nayar lovers. And fourthly, there were objections to the structure of the joint family itself — to the *karanavan's* power and his tendency to favour his own *tavazhi,* and indeed to the very matrilineal principles on which the family was based.

The principal causes of the crises in Travancore and Central Kerala were not identical. Let us look at Travancore first. Here the effects of land legislation in the 1860s were crucial. In 1865, the Travancore government conferred full ownership rights on all its tenants (*kanamdars*), i.e. those holding land from the state (see chapter 2). Immediately, many Nayars attempted to realise the value of their lands through sale; in part, this was because more and more of them were apparently falling into debt. As property was held jointly, there was a vast rise in the amount of litigation (Jeffrey 1973: 188) and also in the rate at which *taravads* were, de facto, partitioned. One of the effects of the 1865 Proclamation was, therefore, a further weakening of kin bonds within the *taravad.* For those living in Central and northern Travancore especially, the main threat to the Nayars' social and economic position, at least as perceived by Nayar leaders, was the rising prosperity of the Syrian Christians and, to a much lesser extent, of the Izhavas. The 1865 Proclamation gave a powerful boost to the developing capitalist economy of Travancore. Plantations and cash-cropping also developed rapidly, helped by the government's relinquishment of its purchasing monopolies, especially that on pepper, in the 1860s, which 'gave commercial resources... an impetus never known before' (Aiya 1906: III, 184). During the 1860s, Travancore's exports doubled in value. From this time onwards, Travancore rapidly developed as an export-crop economy, whose prosperity depended on its products (especially those derived from coconut) being purchased by the rest of India, and also Europe and North America. Seventy years later, catastrophe struck; the Great Depression dealt Travancore a severe blow from which it did not recover for many years. But long before this, serious problems were beginning to emerge. In particular, the cultivation of food crops, especially rice, failed to expand fast enough. In 1870, Travancore started to buy rice and the volume of imports rose continually from then on (Pillai 1940: III, 19). More and more families with relatively small landholdings were forced to buy rice in the market, as they could not grow enough themselves. There is evidence that many of those in this position were Nayars, some of whom were finding it harder and harder to find the requisite cash. For a high-caste Hindu in Kerala, not to be able to eat rice symbolises poverty in a disproportionately powerful manner, and this may well have been one of the factors leading to the perceived crisis of the Nayars in Travancore.

I have referred to the threat posed by the Syrian Christians in Central and northern Travancore. It is, I think, fairly clear that the Syrians' success was principally due to their position in the trading sector. Although lacking a monopoly, they did control a large proportion of local trade in the region around 1850 (Jeffrey 1973: 51), as they had indeed done for many years (Fuller 1976: 56). Their entrenched position in this sector gave them a differential advantage in the growing economy over other communities, in particular their main rivals the Nayars, not only in terms of know-how and experience, but also in access to finance, much of which was raised through the indigenous credit societies known as chitties and kuris. As the Syrians grew richer, they began to buy land – mainly from Nayars. Being the major landholding community in the country, the Nayars were bound to suffer a relative decline when a lower-ranking community, such as the Syrians, rose. The prospect of losing their land seems to have seriously frightened the Nayars: 'the most concrete and alarming manifestation of Syrian prosperity was their acquisition of land' (Jeffrey 1973: 247). In fact, there was an element of panic in the Nayars' reaction to growing Syrian wealth. Jeffrey points out that: 'Syrians had by no means completely supplanted Nayars as the economic power in the state' (ibid.: 248) and the 'Nayars were not about to be swept away' (ibid.: 250). Much Nayar propaganda, in other words, was grossly exaggerated. Nonetheless, it was certainly not without any foundation, and overall the economic outlook for the Nayar community in Travancore – especially in the centre and the north – in the

The Nayars Today

last years of the nineteenth century was poor and worsening. It was aggravated by the Tamil Brahman stranglehold on many positions in the government service, and this too was the source of much Nayar agitation, although this probably concerned southern Travancore Nayars more. Again, Nayar propaganda tended to exaggeration. In 1872, Nayars held 65% of the 16 000 jobs in the government service; on the other hand, it is true that they occupied very few of the top positions (ibid.: 182). However, this latter problem need not be discussed here. What is relevant to our discussion is the explanation, proposed by Nayar leaders, of their decline. Essentially, they attributed it to the matrilineal joint-family system.

As I have suggested, the Syrians' success was predominantly a result of their position in the trading sector, and the Nayars' failure of their position in the land system. Even as late as 1940, according to Pillai (1940: III, 79), the proportion of earners following occupations other than agriculture was, of all sizeable communities, least among the Nayars, and Jeffrey (1973: 136) refers to their 'fixed ideas about what constituted respectable employment'. I myself doubt the existence of any functional connection whatsoever between matrilineal joint families and economic failure. However, what matters here is the Nayar leaders' belief in such a connection. They became convinced that reform of their kinship system was a precondition for prosperity. Undoubtedly, their conversion to this view was partly due to the spread of Western ideas in Travancore. Ruskin, Carlyle and Samuel Smiles were all standard texts in Travancore colleges, attended by large numbers of Nayar students in the nineteenth century; as Jeffrey (ibid.: 185) says: 'It is reasonable to suggest that such studies helped to propagate an individualism incompatible with the "communality" of the old taravad'. Nayar intellectuals were prone to quote Bentham and Mill who, they thought, provided some kind of philosophical backing to their arguments.[3] The Nayars were also subject to a great deal of Christian propaganda from European missionaries, such as Mateer (1883a: 180-88; 1883b), as well as from other Hindus; cumulatively, this certainly seems to have had some effect in Travancore (ibid.: 73-5, 186-7). Gough (1952a: 83-4) denies that it had much effect in Cochin and Malabar, although some contemporary evidence contradicts her: 'the influence of English education has wrought considerable changes in the sexual relations, especially of the middle classes, and in the circles so influenced, [matriliny] has begun to assume the outward garb of [patriliny]' (Census 1891, Cochin: 78).

The picture for Nayars in Travancore at the close of the nineteenth century was, then, fairly black; as the 1901 Census Commissioner expressed it in his measured tones: 'The present economic condition of the Nayars is not free from anxiety' (Census 1901, Travancore: 333). The strength of the *taravads* had been undermined by the 1865 Proclamation and the ensuing litigation. There is a certain amount of evidence that *karanavans* had begun to abuse their power on a wide scale and that many *taravads* were being managed very poorly. Legal actions against *karanavans* seem to have grown in number markedly (G.O.T. 1908: App. I). These trends, combined with the Nayars' failure to profit from the wider economic development of the time, brought forth a comparison between their contemporary position and the one they had enjoyed in a past Golden Age, when Nayars had passed their lives in contented and prosperous *taravads* (Jeffrey 1973: 221). Needless to say, the comparison was invidious to Nayar reformist leaders.

In Central Kerala, as I have implied, the problems besetting the Nayars differed somewhat from those in Travancore. Many of the data on Cochin and South Malabar suggest that the principal problem was the rising number of men acquiring property on their own behalf, a result of Nayar success in the new, expanding employment sector, particularly in 'white-collar' jobs. This meant that more and more Nayar men were able to earn independent incomes. In Cochin: 'No class of the community is availing itself of the benefits of modern education as the Nayars, who are fast becoming conspicuous in every literate walk of life. In every department of the State and in all the learned professions, they form a respectable majority and the only people who successfully compete with them in this respect are the [Tamil Brahmans]' (Census 1891, Cochin: 110). Even as late as 1941, when their preponderance had declined, Nayar males (11% of the total male population of Cochin) represented 40% of gazetted and 24% of non-gazetted government officers, and 21% of those classified as 'lawyers, doctors, teachers, etc.', although it should also be noted that these three categories together only accounted for 6% of all independent male Nayars (Census 1941, Cochin: 109–10). With their self-acquired income, Nayar men often supported their wives and children, and this could easily become a source of conflict: 'The attitude of the Tarwad people towards an earning and married member is at times suspicious, and it is no easy task for him to adjust the claims of the relations on both sides' (Census 1901, Cochin: 155). It became common for such Nayars to buy land and houses with their self-acquired income, and bequeath these to their wives and children, although this was still done in a matrilineal 'idiom', for men attempted to found new *tavazhis* headed by their wives. Normally, of course, a man would not save enough cash to buy much land until late in his life and so most of these *tavazhis* were founded by older men. (See also Gough 1952a: 79; 1961: 646–7; Mencher 1962: 233; 1965: 177; Nakane 1962: 23.)

An initial impression would be that in Central Kerala the Nayars' problem stemmed from success, a result of their progress in the professions, etc., whereas in Travancore the problem was one of failure, a result of declining agricultural prosperity. But this is almost certainly a misleading picture, created by the Nayar reformists' propaganda. Firstly, Travancore Nayars were not at all unsuccessful in the professions (although their progress to the top of the government service was blocked), and indeed there may have been better employment opportunities in Travancore than in Central Kerala. But southern Travancore Nayars probably gained more, in this field, than did Central and northern Travancore Nayars. In the latter region, trade and industry were expanding fastest, and Syrian Christians reaped the greatest benefits; relatively, therefore, Nayars were doing badly there, and the reformist leaders tended to stress this. In southern Travancore, and also in Central Kerala, Christians were much less numerous and posed no serious threat to the Nayars. Secondly, despite Nayar successes in Central Kerala, it is almost certain that the majority of them gained nothing from the new employment opportunities. The Malabar Marriage Commission remarked that most *taravads* were poor, and estimated that nine-tenths of all *karanavans* were small farmers struggling with the nigh-impossibility of providing for all their *taravad* members (G.O.M. 1891: 32). But because the very people who were responsible for reformist pressure were themselves educated Nayars, many of them with professional occupations and self-acquired wealth, the problems of successful Nayars, who had acquired their own property, gained the most publicity, whereas those of the poor majority failed to attract the attention they received in Travancore. Further, partly because there had been no equivalent of the 1865 Travancore Proclamation in either Cochin or Malabar, and partly because there was no significant economic threat from a lower community like the Syrians in Central Travancore, the poverty of many landholding Nayars in Central Kerala could be attributed neither to the rise of a lower community, nor to a fall in the Nayars' relative position. So although there were objective differences between the problems confronting Nayars in the various regions of Kerala, reformist propaganda does not always accurately reflect the situation.

These qualifications apart, however, it is plain that the issue of self-acquired property was significant in Central Kerala. According to traditional law, as we have seen, self-acquired property was meant to revert after death to the owner's *taravad*; the ostensible justification for this was that no man would ever have had any success had he not been able to rely on his *taravad* when a child. But in spite of the law, self-acquired property was being regularly bequeathed to wives and children. This was the nub of the controversy. According to Gough (1961: 647):

These circumstances greatly exacerbated the traditional tensions between conjugal and paternal ties on the one hand and matrilineal ties on the other. Litigation over property between men of the same taravad and bitter quarrels between the children and matrilineal heirs of men who died intestate thus became regular features of family life in the higher matrilineal castes.

The category of property referred to by Gough is clearly self-acquired property, and the quarrels and litigation she mentions were evidently due to the growing importance of affinal ties. But acrimony of this nature provides no explanation for the apparent increase in disputes between *matrikin* over *taravad* property, and in accusations of favouritism towards their own *tavazhis* hurled at *karanavans*. The latter, it may be plausibly suggested, was mainly caused by declining attachment to those values upholding *taravad* solidarity. In part at least these values must have been undermined by the accrescent rate of *taravad* partition throughout the

The Disintegration of the Matrilineal Joint-family System

nineteenth century. As we have seen, matrilineal principles themselves had not vanished, for men continued to found new *tavazhis* through their wives. What had died was the old value placed on the *taravad* as a joint property-holding and residential grouping. The passing of traditional *taravad* life seems to have been welcomed only ambiguously; I referred earlier to the idealisation of the past by Travancore Nayars, and Gough (1952a: 84) notes a similar sentiment in Central Kerala.[4]

Response to the crisis

In 1891, the Malabar Marriage Commission, set up by the Madras Government, reported. Few publications can ever have been more hostile to the matrilineal joint-family system. The Commission concluded that the laws relating to matriliny did not 'recognize the institution of marriage' (G.O.M. 1891: 26) and condemned wholeheartedly Nambudiri-Nayar *sambandham* relationships: 'An institution which by debauching the the women of one class, condemns the women of another to life-long and enforced celibacy, is not one which justice need hesitate to condemn' (ibid.: 26). The Nambudiris were damned by Chandu Menon, a member of the Commission, who argued that their unscrupulous sexual exploitation of Nayar women was no justification, any more than was the existence of the matrilineal system, for Nayars to be deprived of the right to the institution of legal marriage (ibid., Encl. C:10). The joint-family system came in for heavy attack too, and the Commission concluded that *karanavans* normally abused their power: 'it is indeed wonderful that any karanavan should be honest' (ibid.: 29). According to the witnesses examined, conflict between the *karanavan* and his junior members was endemic (ibid.: 31). The principles on which the matrilineal joint family was based drew the Commission's scathing contempt: the system 'offends against every principle of political economy, and of healthy family life', and rests on the doctrine that there is 'no merit in female virtue, and no sin in unchastity'; it 'sanctions the reckless propagation of the species' and 'destroys all motive for prudence and forethought'. The joint family bound together 'distant relatives not necessarily drawn to each other by any bond of mutual affection' and 'makes home-life (in the best sense of the word) impossible' (ibid.: 36).

At the same time, the Commission was forced to admit that although, as it put it (not wholly accurately), 'the gradual advance of the community towards patriarchical family-life has already gone far to make the Tarwad system unworkable in practice' (ibid.: 37), the legal reforms it was considering were 'not at present desired by a majority' (ibid.: 34). However, it continued: 'we also believe that the uninstructed majority will rapidly follow the lead of the enlightened classes, and that there need be no apprehensions that if the law be framed it will remain a dead letter' (idem.). Despite the Commision's conviction, though, the Malabar Marriage Act of 1896, providing for the legal registration of *sambandham* unions as marriages, did in fact remain a dead letter for a decade or so. In 1896-7,

133

36 unions were registered, in 1897-8 the total was 24, in 1898-9 it was 14 and between 1899 and 1903, 9 more unions were registered (Moore 1905: 90-91), a total of only 83 in seven years.

Although the Commission was, perhaps, rather ahead of Malabar Nayar public opinion, it was not long before reformist pressure led to the establishment of a similar Commission in Travancore. A bill similar to the Malabar Marriage Act had been introduced in Travancore in 1896, but it never reached the statute book. In 1899, an act permitting a man to leave half his self-acquired property to his wife and children – a provision also embodied in the Malabar Marriage Act – did come into force. But this was not enough, and a long campaign by Nayar leaders culminated in a meeting held in Trivandrum in 1907, with delegates from Cochin and Malabar, as well as Travancore. Krishnan Nair, a leading member of the community from Malabar, proclaimed that the Nayars' position was 'very deplorable' and 'fast deteriorating', and that the matrilineal joint-family system was the root cause (Jeffrey 1973: 287). Shortly afterwards, the Travancore government set up the Marumakkathayam Committee to investigate the problem.

The committee considered the legal situation as it then stood and made its recommendations for reform. Its tone is rather more even than that of its Malabar counterpart, but overall its arguments pursued a similar path. Its stress, however, differed slightly in that it particularly emphasised the Nayars' deteriorating economic situation. The Committee argued that the 'moral and material interests' of the Nayars were being subverted because, firstly, as all power and responsibility lay with the *karanavan*, the junior members of the joint family were prone to fecklessness or, if they were ambitious, to frustration; secondly, as the land was held jointly, no individual Nayar could obtain capital to start an enterprise and, even if he were to do so, the joint family and not his own wife and children would reap the benefit; and thirdly, because so many joint families were heavily in debt (or thought to be), an end to joint property-holding was required in order to discharge these debts. The Committee, although it concluded that it would be best if an individual were permitted to insist upon partition of his joint family, decided not to recommend this, but instead that partition could only be demanded by a section (*tavazhi*) of a joint family. The reason for this hesitation was its assessment of Nayar public opinion: 'individual partition is at present opposed to the sentiments of the community' (G.O.T. 1908: 69).

In 1913, the first Travancore Nayar Act was enacted; it recognised *sambandham* as a legal marriage and allowed the wife and children of a Nayar dying intestate one half of his self-acquired property. But this fell short of the Marumakkathayam Committee's recommendations and of the demands of the Nayar reform leaders. In 1914, the Nayar Service Society was founded in Changanacherry with, as an immediate aim, the forcing of more radical reform. The N.S.S., mainly because of its village base, grew rapidly. It was more militant than the older Nayar organisations, and before long it had eclipsed them all (Jeffrey 1973: 302). In 1925, the second Nayar Act came into force, allowing almost unrestricted partition of joint-family property. In 1933 and 1938, similar acts were put on the statute books in Malabar and Cochin respectively.[5]

Changes in the twentieth century

Legal changes did not, of course, always coincide with actual partitions of joint-family property 'on the ground'. In much of Travancore, as we have seen, *taravad* division was occurring on a wide scale even before the passing of the 1925 Act. Much land which was theoretically impartible and inalienable was being sold or mortgaged (Varghese 1970: 99–100). Many of these partitions, however, were almost certainly between *tavazhis,* not individuals. In Ramankara, as we saw earlier, individual partitions only became commonplace during the interregnum, although, lacking other evidence, it is difficult to assess the situation elsewhere in Travancore. A total of 32 903 *taravads* are said to have partitioned their property within five years of the 1925 Act. Only a few families applied for exemption from the Act's stipulations: 'proof positive of the eagerness with which the community has availed itself of even this permissive provision' (Census 1931, Travancore: I, 168–9).

In South Malabar and Cochin, on the other hand, property division generally occurred later than in Travancore. Gough (1961: 646) states that the 'great majority' of *taravads* 'divided their property between individuals or between groups of uterine siblings [*tavazhis*] soon after the acts were passed in the 1930's which permitted such division. In most *taravads* which had not divided their property, moreover, "partition suits" were pending in the courts'. Some *taravads,* though, mainly very wealthy ones, were still unpartitioned in the 1950s. Mencher (1962: 237) says that many of the larger *taravads* began to divide their property 'immediately after' the 1933 Act; after Independence, further legislation, especially land reform measures, greatly encouraged partition and 'by 1960, all of the large *taravads* in Malabar either had been partitioned or had cases pending in court'. In the Cochin *taravad* studied by Nakane, the first division between *tavazhis* was made in 1898 'and the final partition of the property by individual members was in 1944' (1962: 21).

The explanation for the later division of *taravads* in Central Kerala, as compared with Travancore, lies in developments during the nineteenth century, which have already been discussed. The different land policies pursued by the various governments meant that alienation of land was easier in Travancore than in Central Kerala; further, the rise of the Syrians in the northern part of Travancore meant that there were more potential purchasers of land in this region and greater pressure on the Nayars to partition. Developments in the twentieth century were simply a continuation of those which began in the late nineteenth century. A crucial aspect of the process as a whole is that it was the poorest, rather than the richest, *taravads* which broke up soonest and, overall, partition tended to damage

8. A Communist party demonstration on behalf of small farmers; a regular occurrence in 1971–72. Most of the demonstrators are Christians, although the leader is a Nayar.

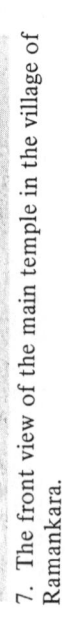

7. The front view of the main temple in the village of Ramankara.

The Disintegration of the Matrilineal Joint-family System

further the economic standing of the Nayar community. A 'downward spiral' effect came into play. The poorer the joint family, the greater the strain on its corporate solidarity as each *tavazhi,* or individual, tried to obtain its share of the joint property, in order to use the capital released in this way either for some more profitable venture or to liquidate its debts, or merely to escape the control of a *karanavan* who was favouring his own *tavazhi,* when faced with a situation of extreme stringency. For most Nayars, the only method of realising the value of a share of property was to sell or mortgage it to a more prosperous member of a lower-ranking community, who wished to acquire some land. The cumulative effect was thus another slide in the Nayar community's economic well-being. Varghese (1970: 101) discusses this spiral, in which the Travancore Nayars in particular were trapped, and the figures for land sales and purchases, broken down by community, which he quotes for the years 1926, 1930, 1935 and 1940, show that the Nayars were selling land throughout this period, mainly to the Christians (ibid.: 103).[6] However the Nayars' worsening plight was probably not confined to Travancore. According to the 1931 Cochin Census Commissioner, the effect of the 1920 Cochin Nayar Regulation had been as follows:

Many who were at least theoretically in affluent circumstances as members of well-to-do families, and who would never have become destitute but for the partition of their family properties, have thereby been reduced to the verge of poverty and misery ... On the whole it almost looks like a period of transition for the Nayars from the [matrilineal] to the [patrilineal] system, a period of uncertainty, gloom and general distress. (Census 1931, Cochin: I, 262)

In sum, then, partitioning *taravad* property was not the panacea the Nayars sought. On the contrary, it seems to have aggravated their problems. I shall return to some of the wider implications of this below.

Inheritance and household structure

The alterations in the inheritance system, which accompanied the partition of joint-family property, are not entirely clear. For Central Kerala, Gough (1952a: 81) refers to the development of 'a somewhat unstable form of bilateral inheritance, in which ancestral paddy-land and large joint-family houses still tend to be inherited matrilineally, and small new houses, cash and much garden land to be passed on from father to children'. Unni (1956: 55–6) states that, in South Malabar, 'property descended through the mother continues to be inherited matrilineally', whereas 'any property given by the father is divided only among his sons and daughters equally'. Unni does not describe this system in detail, but I think it likely that it is in fact very similar, if not identical, to that of the Ramankara Nayars. It is not clear whether Gough is describing a completely different system, or merely explaining it in terms of types of property, rather than of categories defined by kinship referents.

The Nayars Today

The partition of *taravad* property did not invariably coincide with the division into separate households. When *taravads* were partitioned between *tavazhis,* the division into separate residential units often occurred before the partition of property, as we have seen (cf. Nakane 1962: 18). The final stage of property division, that between individuals, implies of course the disappearance of property-groups, so that the congruence of the property-holding and residential groups is necessarily eliminated as well. We must now look at what types of residential grouping then appear. Gough (1952a: 81-2; 1961: 647) stresses the emergence of the nuclear family which, she says, by 1947 was 'rapidly becoming the effective unit of residence, economic cooperation, legal responsibility, and socialization' (idem.). This bold assertion does not, however, appear to be supported by the data available and Gough herself, in a recent paper (1975), has qualified her earlier remarks by referring to the 'rather slow' transition to nuclear households in Kerala.

Gough's paper is the most detailed account and analysis of changing household types in a Kerala village that has been published. It is also the only one presenting data collected at two different times, 1949 and 1964, enabling us to see clearly the direction of change. In addition to Gough's data, collected in a Cochin village only three miles from a large town of which it is now more or less a suburb, there is also some evidence gathered by Unni in two South Malabar villages in 1954-5, and some gathered by Mencher in another South Malabar village in 1959-60. The different periods at which information was collected and, perhaps more significantly, the different ways in which it has been presented and analysed, make direct comparisons between the various villages impossible. Nonetheless, some conclusions can be drawn.

Gough's article includes many tables, appertaining to other castes represented in the village as well as Nayars, intended to illustrate various facets of the process of change. Here, I shall only reproduce the data on Nayar household types and residence patterns. The former is summarised in table 19, a slightly simplified version of Gough's table (1975: chart IV). Her information on the residence of married Nayar men is summarised in table 20, a simplified version of Gough's table (1975: chart XI). Chart XI excludes men who partly live in the village but visit wives outside it; it includes men living entirely in the village and also those who partly live elsewhere but visit wives in the village.

Before commenting on tables 19 and 20, I shall look at Unni's and Mencher's data. Unni's information was collected in two South Malabar villages in 1954-5 (1956: 46-9). His figures on household types are difficult to interpret. Out of a total of 126 Nayar households in the two villages, 116 (92%) contain one *tavazhi,* 7 contain two *tavazhis,* 2 contain three *tavazhis* and 1 contains four *tavazhis.* Of these households, 67 include women with visiting husbands. The significance of Unni's data is problematic, for it is fairly clear that many of the single-*tavazhi* households are not really based on a group of matrilineal kin. Unni's figures relating to the residence of the husbands of the 165 married women in the two villages, presented in table 21, are easier to understand.

The Disintegration of the Matrilineal Joint-family System

Table 19. *Household types in a Cochin village, 1949 and 1964*

Types	1949 No.	%	1964 No.	%
Nuclear families	19	28	29	32
Sub-nuclear (individual or part of nuclear family)	1	1	16	18
Supplemented nuclear (nuclear + relative of H or W)	2	3	10	11
Joint family (usually matrilineal segment) incl. no married couples	9	13	8	9
Joint family incl. one married couple	23	33	12	13
Joint family incl. two/more married couples	15	22	16	18
All	69	100	91	101

Table 20. *Residence of married men in a Cochin village, 1949 and 1964*

Place of residence	1949 No.	%	1964 No.	%
Own natal home	4	5	11	12
Wife's home (natal or partitioned)	17	22	41	45
Own private home	10	13	16	18
Home owned jointly by H and W	9	12	7	8
Own natal home + wife's home (natal or partitioned), i.e. visiting husband	38	49	16	18
All	78	101	91	101

Finally, we may look at the evidence Mencher collected in a South Malabar village in 1959-60 (1962: 237-40). Her data refer to the households of members of matrilineal castes in two census tracts within the village, and the samples include others besides Nayars. There is a higher proportion of Nayars in census tract A than in tract B.

Two striking changes are revealed by tables 19 and 20. The first is the fall in the proportion of households which are joint – 68% in 1949 to 40% in 1964 – the concomitance, of course, of the rise in the proportion of nuclear families. (The actual percentage of 'pure' nuclear families has not grown greatly, but it seems legitimate to class the sub-nuclear and supplemented nuclear families under the same heading, for they are of the nuclear rather than the joint form.) The second change is the decline in the proportion of visiting husbands – from 49% in 1959 to 18% in 1964. In her paper, Gough tries to correlate her figures on changing household structures with a number of other variables: age-distribution of the population, population increase, stages in the developmental cycle of the household, house-

Table 21. *Husbands' residence in two South Malabar villages*

Residence of husband	No.	%
Visits wife regularly	84	51
Visits wife annually, or at long intervals	12	7
Virilocal (H head of *tavazhi*)	12	7
Neolocal (H and W living in town)	32	19
Uxorilocal: both partners' house in W's village	8	5
Uxorilocal: W's house (H manager)	10	6
Uxorilocal: W's house (H not manager)	7	4
All	165	99

Table 22. *Household types in a South Malabar village*

Types	Tract A (No.)	Tract A (%)	Tract B (No.)	Tract B (%)
Small *tavazhis* (3 generations or more)	37	42	15	29
2-generation matrilineal households	6	7	7	13
Nuclear: W's house	15	17	6	12
Nuclear: both partners' house	13	15	9	17
3-generation *tavazhi* + W and/or Ch of male	3	3	10	19
Others	15	17	5	10
All	89	101	52	100

hold income, household landownership and occupation of household members. Most correlations were insignificant. Only with occupation was there a strong correlation; the greater the reliance on personal wage- or salary-earning employment, as opposed to a reliance on the land – either as an owner-cultivator, tenant-farmer or landlord – the greater the tendency to live in nuclear households or in the simpler kinds of joint households. In the light of the overall trends in this region, which I looked at earlier, this correlation is not unexpected.

But perhaps the most striking fact of all, which is revealed by these tables, is the extent to which 'traditional' family forms have persisted. By 1964, the majority of households in Gough's Cochin village were of the nuclear type, but this had not been so in 1949, and in both Unni's and Mencher's villages, when the data were collected, only a minority of households were of the nuclear type. Similarly, the visiting husband custom continued to survive and it had still not died out in the Cochin village in 1964. This is not to say that there had been no change. Unni (1956: 52-3) states that the visiting husband custom, although still prevalent, had undergone modification. The visiting husband is, to translate a Malayalam phrase, a 'more wanted fellow' in his wife's house; he no longer comes to see her only at night, but may stay during part of the day as well. Sometimes he spends long periods at his wife's house, taking an active role in her household's affairs and, in some instances, he may even become the manager of her household. Mencher (1962: 241) confirms that many of Unni's remarks apply to her own data too.

Household types in these four Central Kerala villages contrast markedly with those in Ramankara where, as we saw, the nuclear family is now unequivocally the norm. Even allowing for the fact that my investigation was conducted much more recently, clear differences remain. My own evidence suggests that by 1949, and certainly by 1964, the *tavazhi* had ceased to be the predominant household type in Ramankara; nor did the visiting husband custom still survive. It is possible that in Central Kerala villages today, the distribution of household types is more like that in Ramankara than it used to be, but even if this is so, change in that region has obviously been less rapid than in Central Travancore. This conclusion is obviously in line with the evidence concerning the disintegration of the joint family as a property-holding unit, which I discussed in the previous section. From the evidence on the different regions, it is clear that although property groups and residential groups did not invariably break up in the same way, at the same time, the process of disintegration acted in both cases in parallel.

North Malabar

Information on the North Malabar Nayars is sparse, but a brief outline of the changes in their kinship and marriage system seems worthwhile. Like the Nayars to the south, their property group was, as I outlined above, a matrilineal joint family (*taravad*), headed by the eldest male member. But although the visiting husband custom did exist, women normally lived with their *sambandham* partners on the latter's estates. Thus the residential group typically comprised a set of matrilineal kinsmen, wives and unmarried children, plus separated or widowed kinswomen. Although the North Malabar Nayars had both the *tali*-rite and the *sambandham* institution, it is plain that their *sambandham* relationships approximated much more closely to the Indian norm of marriage, than did those of the Central Kerala Nayars. North Malabar *sambandham* unions joined one man and one woman, they were expected to be permanent (although divorce and widow remarriage were possible), and both partners had a series of rights over and obligations towards each other, including some of an economic nature (Gough 1961: 390-91, 396-9).

The difference between the marriage systems of North and Central Kerala means, of course, that the transformation of *sambandham* relationships, which was so critical in the central region, was not reproduced in the north. Moore (1905: 88) states that the nineteenth-century trend towards formalisation of the *sambandham* began in North Malabar; if he is correct, this

141

seems logical, given that in the north *sambandham* was already close to 'formal marriage'. However, I have no confirming evidence at all for Moore's assertion.

According to Gough, all Nayar *taravads* were landlords (*janmis*) over at least some land. Junior members of the joint family might sometimes lease land, for usufruct, from their own *taravads* and, occasionally, could even lease land from their wives' *taravads*, in which case any improvements made to it would become the separate property of the wife and her matrilineal descendants. Further, says Gough, some men managed to transfer part of their own *taravad's* land to their wives and children. The ability of husbands to transfer land to their wives, or to improve their wives' land, led to the establishment of *tavazhi-taravads*; that is, *tavazhis* which remained within the *taravad* and retained shares in the joint estate, but which also derived a separate income from the transferred or improved land. This land was managed either by the *karanavan* of the wife's *taravad* or, more commonly, by her eldest son. Sometimes, such *tavazhi-taravads* eventually separated from the original *taravad* to form a new one.

Property transfers to wives, and improvements to their land, became more frequent during the nineteenth century; indeed, *tavazhi-taravads* were rare among commoner Nayars until the second half of the century. More and more men also began to acquire uncultivated land which they bequeathed to their wives and children. Gough shows that the dynamic element underlying these changes was agricultural expansion. North Malabar, unlike most of the rest of Kerala (except for the highland regions), was lightly populated and contained much uncultivated land. The expansion of cash-cropping, together with demographic growth, led to a considerable increase in the area under cultivation. The British had granted ownership rights to landlords (*janmis*) in Malabar. Therefore, as most *taravads* had such rights, buying uncultivated land was probably quite simple. By this method, individuals came to own marketable property (Gough 1961: 390-93).

It is impossible to trace developments in North Malabar in detail. I do not know, for example, whether any sense of crisis developed among the Nayars in the region at the end of the nineteenth century. The Malabar Marriage Commission's characteristically acerbic comment that the North Malabar Nayars' kinship system was 'a travesty of [matriliny], and is in fact a deformed growth' (G.O.M. 1891: 33), cannot be taken as evidence of any 'grass-roots' discontent. It seems highly probable that the strain, if one can use the term, placed upon the northern Nayars' kinship and marriage system by nineteenth-century developments, must have been slighter than that imposed on the system of Nayars further south. This is because, firstly, the nature of affinal bonds had changed considerably less in North Kerala, and secondly, the northern Nayars were not subject to the various newly-emerging economic pressures affecting those to the south.

Some data on residence patterns in a North Kerala village, collected by

Table 23. *Household types in a North Malabar village*

Types	No.	%
'Traditional' matrilineal joint family	12	29
Nuclear families (some + relative of H or W)	20	48
Widows or divorced women + unmarried children	6	14
Matrilineal segment, H visits W	3	7
Man + unmarried children	1	2
All	42	100

Table 24. *Residence of married couples in a North Malabar village*

Residence	No.	%
W lives in matrilineal home of H ('traditional')	14	26
H visits W (some cases only temporary separation)	8	15
Neolocally: H's house	26	49
HF's home or WM's home	5	10
All	53	100

Gough in 1948 (1961: 393–4), are available. Of 42 Nayar houses in the village, 23 (55%) had been built by individual men, and given to their wives and children; the remainder had been constructed by a group of matrikin for the joint family. The distribution of household types among these 42 houses is presented in table 23. Figures for the residence of the 53 married couples in the village are given in table 24. Significant here, when compared with the figures for Central Kerala, is the high proportion of nuclear families and of neolocal residence, which was promoted by the development of cash-cropping and agricultural expansion; at this time, anyway, it appears that the shift from traditional forms had gone further in North than in Central Kerala.

Matriliny and joint families: some conclusions

For many decades, majority opinion among sociologists and anthropologists, historians and economists, held that there existed a universal tendency for matriliny to give way to patriliny or bilaterality, and for large joint families or extended kin groups to break down into nuclear families. In the nineteenth and early twentieth centuries, this view was embedded in an overall theory of evolution and progress. Later, consonant with the rise of the functionalist paradigm, it was asserted that there existed a functional 'fit' between, for example, nuclear families and modern, industrial, capitalist society on the one hand, and joint or extended families and traditional, agricultural, pre-capitalist society on the other. Recently, however, there has been a shift of opinion among scholars working in this area, although it is probably true that the older view is still current amongst non-specialists. There are several reasons for this change of opinion, but two are especially important. The first has to do with conceptual and definitional muddles which have beset so much writing on the subject. It has now been realised that terms like ' family ', ' household ', ' kin group ', etc. have often if not usually, been inadequately defined. For instance, analytically distinct aspects of the ' family ' - as a kinship group, as a residential group, as a property-owning group, as a consumption group, etc. - have not been separated. Needless to say, failures of this kind have vitiated much discussion of the subject. The second reason has to do with recent empirical research. Anthropologists and historians have demonstrated that nuclear families, and bilateral kinship systems, are and were common enough in pre-industrial and pre-capitalist societies, disproving the notion that they are confined to the modern West. Further, work in such disparate areas as Japan, India and West Africa has revealed that non-nuclear families and ' traditional ' kinship systems do not inevitably die as a result of modern economic development. Altogether, then, serious doubt has emerged about the older theories, which linked family and kin organisation to social structure, although it would be exaggerating to say that these theories have actually been refuted.

The literature on this subject is vast, and the range of topics which would have to be considered in the course of a full discussion is immense. Such a discussion is ruled out here. In the Indian context, attention has naturally been focussed on the disintegration - or otherwise - of joint families. Latest findings tend to suggest that disintegration is not apparent, or at least that no simple, unidirectional change is occurring. A sample of the alteration in opinion on this issue, may be gained by comparing Mandelbaum's views in his article on the joint family (1948) with those in his recent magnum opus (1970: 642-6). The Nayars have an extra interest for those concerned with this debate, for not only do they raise the issue of joint-family breakdown; they also, of course, supply evidence for the debate on the decline of matriliny. As we have seen, there has been a breakdown of the Nayars' matrilineal joint-family system over the last hundred and fifty years or so, and the question I want to look at in this final section is whether the Nayars do in fact, as they at first sight appear to do, provide support for the older theories of family and kinship change. One old lesson which has, perhaps, been relearnt recently in the subject under investigation, is that unanalysed concepts, allied to unidirectional, ' catch-all ' theories of change, must be rejected in favour of precisely-defined concepts, associated with careful scrutiny of evidence specific to the case in point. This lesson seems to me especially crucial when looking at the Nayar material.

I have already argued that there was a functional connection between the Nayars' military organisation and their matrilineal joint-family system,

The Disintegration of the Matrilineal Joint-family System

and that the demobilisation of the armies had an effect on this system, in that it promoted the strengthening of the *sambandham* bond. I have argued that this development was significant, and that it probably represented the first crack in the old system's structure. But the Nayar armies and their disbandment were unique historical 'events', and cannot be assessed as regular features of modern socio-economic development. This particular feature of the changing Nayar system therefore provides no evidence about the general relation between kinship systems and the wider society.

At the close of the eighteenth century and throughout the nineteenth, a series of fundamental economic changes occurred: the granting of ownership rights to various categories of landholders, the rise of cash-cropping and a capitalist agriculture, the expansion of employment opportunities, etc. Related to these developments, too, was increased demographic growth. An explanation of how these changes were linked to the disintegration of the matrilineal joint-family system has already been presented, and repetition is hardly desirable. Discussion of the wider implications can profitably start with a consideration of Gough's argument in 'The modern disintegration of matrilineal descent groups' (1961). As one would expect, she pays special attention to the case of the Nayars. Gough contends (1961: 640) that the 'root cause' of modern change in matrilineal kinship systems, including the Nayars', is incorporation of the respective societies into a unitary, capitalist market economy. Especially critical is the entry of land into the market, and this affects both matrilineal and patrilineal descent groups, for both of them 'lose their economic basis when land is constantly being bought and sold, individuals work chiefly for wages, production becomes vested in such groups as the factory or the plantation, and ownership is by individuals or by joint-stock companies' (ibid.: 648). (Cf. Gough 1975, where this argument emerges again in a more carefully qualified, but not radically different, form.)

This argument is, however, too simple. In both Central Kerala and Travancore, land entered the market. But it did so in significantly different ways and at different times. The British, as the reader will recall, conferred ownership rights on the Malabar landlords (*janmis*) in 1793, shortly after annexing the country. Although Cochin did not actually copy British policy, the situation there resembled Malabar more closely than Travancore. In the latter state, ownership rights were conferred on the state's tenants (*kanamdars*) in 1865. These divergent land policies were, as I have tried to make clear, immensely significant to the different ways in which northern and southern Kerala developed. But what is particularly pertinent to the present discussion is that ownership rights were conferred on a relatively small number of large landholders in Malabar (and effectively in Cochin), whereas they were granted to a relatively large number of smaller landholders in Travancore. Now it is clear enough, from all the evidence (e.g. Gough 1961: 645-6), that poorer joint families tended to break up faster than wealthier joint families. Giving joint families the opportunity to sell previously impartible, inalienable land clearly promotes such disintegration and, to that extent, I agree with Gough. But in this context, it obviously implies that Travancore land policy tended to lead to faster disintegration of more Nayar *taravads,* than did Malabar and Cochin policy. As we know, this was the case. But by themselves, differences in land policy are insufficient to explain the pattern of change. Land policies may have *promoted taravad* break-up, in the sense that they allowed it to occur when previously it could not, but they alone did not *cause* it. What is critical here is the presence in Travancore, or more accurately in Central and northern Travancore, of significant numbers of people belonging to a lower-ranking community – the Syrian Christians – who were growing more prosperous and wished to buy land. In Central Kerala, this situation did not exist. Further, there was in the latter region a significant proportion of Nayars – even though they may not have numbered many in total – acquiring property of their own.

Before continuing my own argument, I would like to query some aspects of Gough's approach. Merely to talk about the entry of land into the market obscures one of the most important questions: on whom were ownership rights conferred? For Kerala, the significance of this point can hardly be over-estimated, but Gough does not mention it. This patently illustrates the explanatory inadequacy of unidimensional theories such as she, and others, propose. One simple question isolates the issue: if the entry of land into the market was determinant, why did *taravads* in Malabar persist as joint-property holders for so much longer than those in Travancore, when land entered the market in Malabar seventy years before it did in Travancore?

But my own argument is as yet incomplete. To take the Travancore situation first, we have seen the importance of the Syrian Christians' role. All the evidence shows very clearly that one of the principal factors, leading to the break-up of Nayar joint families in this region, was the example of the Syrians, whose patrilineal nuclear-family system was thought to be directly promoting their material success. And the reason for this belief was precisely that ideas concerning the relation between family organisation and economic progress, of the type current among European scholars, had reached the Nayar reformist leaders, who were persuaded by them. The effect of economic development on the Nayar system was therefore indirect, and partly caused by the growing prosperity of another community, whose example was in turn mediated for the Nayars by a particular ideology. This ideology derived from a theory which, I am arguing here, was invalid. The theory contended, of course, that both matriliny and joint families were a bar to economic progress. Obviously, there is a sense in which such theories, to some extent at least, are self-fulfilling prophecies. If everyone, particularly people with matrilineal joint-family systems, thinks that these systems are doomed in the modern world, then that is likely to be their eventual fate.

In Central Kerala, as the reader will recall, the problem of self-acquired property had considerable importance – although the numbers of men involved may not have been so large. This is one of the aspects of economic change which Gough (ibid.: 647) claims as evidence to support her arguments, for disputes over the inheritance of self-acquired property were a major factor in breaking up the joint families. But, as I argued earlier, there is no direct causal chain here. Disputes occurred because the *sambandham* bond had become so much stronger during the nineteenth century; had this not been so, there is no reason to suppose that conflict would have emerged. In other words, the disputes, and their weakening effect on the joint-family system, cannot be attributed to economic development. Expanding employment opportunities were neither necessary nor sufficient causes of change in the kinship system (cf. Gough 1975).[7]

Close attention to regional differences, and to the particularities of the process of change, insofar as this is feasible given the data available, leads to the conclusion that no single determinant, such as increasingly complete incorporation into the capitalist economy, can be regarded as the cause of the process. On the one hand, unique factors like disbandment of the armies played a crucial role; on the other, economic development was not identical in all regions and, in any case, by itself it did not invariably bring about alterations in the family and kinship system. Any attempt to explain historical events, in terms of causes and effects, must necessarily place these events in the correct temporal order. It seems to me that this most obvious of truisms has, nevertheless, been frequently forgotten by anthropologists, who have all too often agglomerated all the various symptoms of change, under the apparent impression that they could be understood synchronically. Gough's analysis of Kerala matrilineal systems (1961: 641-9) suffers, in my opinion, from this failing – one of the reasons why the factors to which I have drawn attention are obscured in her argument.[8]

Defenders of the thesis that incorporation into the capitalist economy explains the process of change might, I suppose, save the appearances by arguing that even those changes unique to the Nayars, such as their demobilisation, stemmed directly from British annexation of Malabar, itself in turn caused by capitalist development in the metropolitan power. Such an argument has some validity but does not, in my view, explain anything very useful.

The Nayar data also point to the need to distinguish between the property-owning group and the residential group for, as we have seen, changes in the two did not always coincide. In any case, the property group no longer exists, as property is owned by individuals. In Ramankara today, the residential group (household) is normally a nuclear family, and the Central Kerala evidence indicates some movement in the same direction, although the predominance of the nuclear family, at least until recently, was far from being established everywhere. One of the commonest arguments, concerning the nuclear family's alleged functional adaptation to modern society, appeals to geographical mobility. It is proposed that the modern economy, capitalist or industrial, requires the free movement of those involved directly in the production process, mainly of course men. Nuclear families are potentially mobile units, whereas extended families, in which individual members may each hold different jobs and responsibilities tying them locally, are not. Gough (ibid.: 645) endorses this argument as applicable to previously poor joint families, which have now broken up, whose members have become labourers and thus need to move around to find employment. In fact, the mobility argument seems to me questionable even for Western capitalist economies. Although mobility may be demanded of the professional middle-class family, this is much less the case, at least nowadays, for the working-class family. The argument certainly does not appear to be generally applicable in India, where it is common throughout the entire country for individual men to migrate in search of employment, leaving their families behind in the villages. This pattern, according to Unni (1956: 50ff), was frequently found among Nayars with professional occupations in the towns, even in the 1950s. This suggests, therefore, that it is not a necessary condition, for a mobile labour force, that residential groups be nuclear families.

Among the Nayars, the nuclear family has emerged as one of the principal types of residential group cum economic unit, and is found widely, if not ubiquitously, throughout Kerala. This has occurred as a consequence of the steadily growing strength of the *sambandham* tie, in the end equivalent to a marital tie, and of the concomitant disintegration of the joint families. No special congruity between the nuclear family and the modern Kerala economy can be inferred from this historical evidence. In any case, many discussions on the supposed adaptation of nuclear families to modern societies tend to be vitiated by a failure to recognise that, in spite of their apparent similarities, nuclear families do not everywhere reveal the same structure and form, nor are they always linked identically to other kin groupings. Some recent writers, for example Goody, have pointed out that, overall, the historical trend has not been the breakdown of extended kin groupings into nuclear families, but rather, as he puts it (1972: 119): 'the disappearance of many functions of the wider ties of kinship, especially those centring on the kingroups such as clans, lineages and kindreds. These ties may continue ... but the functions radically alter with the proliferation of other institutional structures that take over many of their jobs.' The range of kinship ties contracts, no doubt with some exceptions, to the families of birth and marriage.

The process to which Goody refers has clearly occurred among the Nayars. Wider matrilineal groupings no longer have their previous importance. In part, this merely restates that joint families have collapsed, but it also refers to the fact that kin groupings wider than the joint family – the clan or lineage – have also lost much of their significance. Most of their ritual and legal functions have gone, and the range over which kin ties are recognised, for example by common pollution observance, has shrunk. On the other hand, the importance of wider kin connections has not diminished to the level typical in the modern West. To some extent at least, this appears to be a simple consequence of the fact that the Nayars still mainly live in an agrarian society. In such a society, geographical mobility is inevitably restricted by land inheritance; this means that kin are often bound to live in fairly close proximity to each other. Although propinquity does not cause kin ties to be maintained, it clearly promotes it. Gough (1975), in discussing the persistence of joint families in her Cochin village, correctly points too to the welfare functions of large families in a society like Kerala, where there is no 'welfare state'; a function of wider kin ties, as well as large families, which appears to be widespread in poorer communities. Another aspect of this is, perhaps, more interesting, and it relates to the internal structure of the nuclear family. Among the Nayars, like the vast majority of modern Indians, marriages are arranged by a couple's parents. Other close kin may also have a say. Further, much more than it does in the West, marriage institutes an affinal relationship, of more than marginal significance, between the respective families. Marriage is a sphere, in other words, where kinship links still retain an importance that they have lost in the West. This also means, of course, that the nature of marriage itself is different. The marital tie among the Nayars (and other Indians), partly because it does not follow on the free choice of the couple themselves - nor is it based, like most Western marriages ideally are, on any bond of romantic love - and partly because of the persistence of wider kin ties, does not carry the same implications that it does in the West. For instance, marriage does not have the same mutually supportive function for most Indian couples. In certain respects, therefore, the internal structure and form of the modern Nayar nuclear family are not identical to those of the modern Western one, from which we may conclude that the trend towards this pattern of family organisation is neither a simple process, nor one needing no further analysis.

A critical aspect of the entire process of change is ideological. A continuous weakening in the force of the Nayar matrilineal ideology has had its converse in an increasingly strong ideology stressing affinal and paternal ties. For instance, there has arisen a growing emphasis on the pre-marital virginity of women, sexual constancy in marriage, paternal authority over children, etc. But there has been no emergence of a powerful patrilineal ideology - over and above the concept of paternal authority within the family - like that in many other Indian communities. Nor has there come into being an ideology of marriage and the family, closely resembling that in the West, wherein an ideally exclusive love-relationship between husband and wife is regarded as central. Change in the ideology of male-female relations is evidently a critical part of the overall transformation. The autonomy of the Nayar woman vis-a-vis men has declined; their status and position has relatively worsened, although it remains, of course, considerably higher than that of the majority of Indian women. The future is subject to too many imponderables for prediction. The disparate effects of economic change, of further alteration in the caste system, of political developments, of educational advancement and, perhaps eventually, the rise of a feminist movement in India, all combine to render analysis of the possible course of future events hopelessly speculative. This course, though, is unlikely to interest only the Nayars themselves.

Postscript

Lovers of the exotic may well find cause for regret in the history of the Nayars. The 'nobles of Malabar' are no longer so, and their unique solution to the conundrums of sex and marriage has slid, some may feel, into dull conformity. Many readers of this book may consider that this is not progress, but a significant step backwards. On the other hand, it must be remembered that the nobility of the Nayars was contingent on the servility of most of the rest of Kerala's people. A better life for them had to mean a relative decline for the Nayars. Logan, prone, despite his acuity, to a characteristically British imperial attraction to colonised nobles, said of the Nayars (1887: iv): 'to the present day we find them spread throughout the length and breadth of the land, but no longer – I could almost say, alas! – "preventing the rights (of all classes) from being curtailed or suffered to fall into disuse."' But rights in Kerala were, as they still are though to a lesser extent, unequally distributed and what the Nayars were protecting was, as much as anything else, this distribution. Despite its connection with the military organisation, and with the draconian seclusion of Nambudiri women, the Nayar kinship and marriage system was not perhaps – to indulge in speculation for a moment – doomed to extinction, and regret for its passing may be entertained. But the disappearance of most other aspects of traditional Nayar life can be only very ambiguously mourned. On the other hand, the appalling poverty in which most modern Malayalis live is not a question which should induce any ambiguity. Most Nayars are scarcely better provided for than most of their compatriots; ultimately, if there is to be a solution to their problems, it will rest in the hands of all Malayalis and all Indians, including the Nayars.

Notes

1. 'The Nobles of Malabar': Foreign Images of the Nayars

1. The phrase 'the nobles of Malabar' is Gibbon's (*Decline and Fall,* ch. 47; 1898: V, 151). They were the object of an invidious comparison with the nobles of France by Burke, in his *Reflections on the Revolution in France* (1881: 159).

   A complete list of all foreign notices of Kĕrala, even if it excluded modern works, would certainly be very long. To the best of my knowledge, no such list exists, and the accounts referred to below do not purport to form one. I mention only those known to me which provide useful information on Kerala – particularly on the Nayars – or are, for some other reason, of special interest.

   All those mentioned in the following list wrote their accounts on the basis of personal experience, except for Chao Ju-kua, a Chinese customs official, who compiled his from information provided by sailors he met in the course of duty. I have grouped the travellers by century; in several cases, the precise dates of their sojourns in Kerala are unknown, and these are, in any case, not very important for our purposes. The dates in brackets refer to the published accounts listed in the bibliography.

   9th century: Sulaiman the merchant and Abu Zaid Hasan of Sirat (Renaudot 1717, 1733).
   13th century: Chao Ju-kua (Hirth 1896).
   14th century: Ibn Batuta (1829, 1929); Friar Jordanus (1863); Wang Ta-Yuan (Rockhill 1915).
   15th century: Abdu'r Razzak (Major 1857, I); Nicolo Conti (ibid., II); Fei Tsin (Rockhill 1915); Ma Huan (1970, Rockhill 1915).
   16th century: Duarte Barbosa (1921); Cesare Federici (1927); Hieronimo de Santa Stefano (Major 1857, IV); Jan Huyghen van Linschoten (1885); Ludovico da Varthema (1863); Zain al-Dīn al-Ma'bari (1883).
   17th century: Phillipus Baldaeus (1704); Giovanni Francesco Gemelli Careri (1704); Charles Dellon (1698, 1699); Roger Hawes (1625, 1905); Sir Thomas Herbert (1638); Albrecht Herport (1930); Jan Nieuhof (1704); François Pyrard de Laval (1887); Jacob Roggeveen (1764); Pietro della Valle (1892).
   18th century: Jonathan Duncan (1801); John Henry Grose (1772); Alexander Hamilton (1727, 1930); Fr. Paulino da San Bartolomeo (1800, 1808); Pierre Sonnerat (1782, 1788); Jacobus Canter Visscher (1862, see also Menon 1924–37).
   19th century: Francis Buchanan (1807); Sir Richard Burton (1851); Francis Day (1863); Heber Drury (1858, 1890); Abbé Dubois (1906); James Forbes (1813); Karl Graul (1854); William Logan (1887); Samuel Mateer (1871, 1883a).

Notes to pages 1-17

In addition to these, we have, for the sixteenth century, the writings of the three principal Portuguese historians: João de Barros, Herman Lopes de Castanheda and Gaspar Correa. Barros' *Asia* is not available in English or, except for a few (to us irrelevant) extracts (Castro e Almeida, n.d.), in French. There is an English translation of Castanheda's *History* (Castanheda 1811); extracts from Correa's *Lendas da India* have been translated into English (Correa 1869). Much of the most important information in these Portuguese accounts, and a discussion of it, is to be found in Lach (1968: 347–69). Lach (ibid.: 427–67) also discusses the important data available from Jesuit accounts, particularly through their letters. There is, too, the Jesuit historian Giovanni Maffei's *Historiarum Indicarum* (1588) of which an inaccurate French translation exists (1665). Another Jesuit account is by Francesco Barretto (1646).

By the close of the nineteenth century, the era of the traveller had come to an end. Logan's *Malabar* (1887) resembles less the accounts of most of those listed above and more a modern ethnography-cum-history-cum-geography. Modern Indian ethnography arose out of the pioneering work of the early Census Commissioners; the first systematic Indian census was taken in 1871. Since then, there has been little use for travellers' accounts of the country – now merely the reports of tourists.

2. A note on geographical names may be helpful. Europeans generally referred to the 'Malabar Coast' or, more briefly, 'Malabar'. 'Kerala' is the name of the mainly Malayalam-speaking state, which was formed in 1956, although it is a name which has long been used by Malayalis to refer to their own country. Before Indian Independence in 1947, what is now Kerala was divided into Malabar District, Cochin and Travancore. Confusion has often been engendered by writers using the name 'Malabar', but failing to make clear whether they are referring to the Malabar Coast, i.e. Kerala, as a whole, or merely to Malabar District.

3. The description of Nayar soldiers in Giovanni Botero's *Relations* (1608: 317-18; Johnson's translation), which has frequently been quoted, resembles Maffei's account so closely that I think it highly likely that Botero plagiarised Maffei; the latter's work appears to have been published a few years before the first edition of Botero's.

I should like to thank Jan Chapman for her help in translating Maffei's Latin.

2. Introduction to the Nayars in Central Travancore

1. I have avoided encumbering this historical sketch with an endless series of references. Detailed histories are to be found in the various gazetteers: Aiya (1906: I) and Pillai (1940: I) for Travancore; Logan (1887) for Malabar; Menon (1911) for Cochin. Less detailed, but bringing the picture closer to the present day, are the historical outlines in the modern Kerala District Gazetteers of Menon (1962-72). Three other useful sources are Panikkar (1960), Das Gupta (1967) and Kumar (1965). Varghese (1970) is an excellent account of land policy and its effects from 1850 to 1960. Jeffrey (1973) is a scholarly account of late nineteenth-century developments in Travancore.

2. The Kerala land tenure system is extremely complex and has been the subject of endless political and academic controversy; the translation of *janmi* and *kanamdar* is central to this controversy. The best account is Varghese's (1970). The reader interested in the subject may refer to Logan (1887: 605-25); Baden Powell (1892: 151-84); Aiya (1906: III, Ch. 18); Mayer (1952: 79-95); Kumar (1965) amongst other authorities.
3. This assertion is based on the figures contained in G.O.K. (1971: App. XV, XVI, XVII, XVIII). On the Nayars in nineteenth-century Travancore, Jeffrey (1973) is the main source.
4. On the N.S.S. and other communal interest groups in Kerala, see Nayar (1966); also Gough (1963) and Rudolph and Rudolph (1967: 71-6). There is an official history of the N.S.S. in Malayalam (N.S.S. 1972).
5. The question is analysed at length in my unpublished dissertation (1974: Ch. 3).
6. This, like other inadequacies in my data on Ramankara, partly arises out of the fact that I was also studying another, Syrian Christian village.
7. The Travancore Land Settlement was carried out between 1883 and 1911; see Aiyar (1913) and Varghese (1970: 85-91).
8. There is a slight error in table 4 in that the total area given is 73 acres less than the amount of cultivated land in the revenue unit (11258.08 acres); this may be due to printing errors in the report, my arithmetic or both.
9. Gazetted officers occupy the higher positions in the service, and their appointments are reported in the government gazette; non-gazetted officers occupy the lower positions.
10. The Kerala Land Reforms Act, 1963, which came into force in January 1970 – although a similar reform was first proposed by the Communist government of 1957 – fixes a ceiling (approximately 15 acres on average) on a household's landowning.
11. This is a very important topic, of great current social and political significance, too often neglected by anthropologists. As Béteille (1974: 187) has said, in reference to West Bengal (but it is true too of much of Kerala): 'events in the countryside seem to have overtaken the social anthropologist and made a little obsolescent the study of so many problems... to which he has devoted so much patience and care'. My justification for omitting an analysis is, firstly, limitations of space, and secondly, that I have not yet fully worked out my own data or theoretical perspective.
12. Distance pollution figures quoted here are taken from Census 1931, Cochin: I, 267-75. Different sources provide different figures; a summary of these may be found in Hutton (1961: 79-81).
13. Detailed ethnographies of all the Kerala castes, even if now rather dated, are to be found in such works as Iyer (1909, 1912) and, of course, in Thurston's massive compendium (1909).
14. The only modern ethnography of the Syrian Christians is my own (Fuller 1974; 1976). Otherwise, there is Ayyar (1926) which is useful but contains some important errors. The best history of the Syrians, containing much sociological information too, is by Brown (1956). My own attempts to make sense of the data on Malabar Muslims have not been very successful; see, e.g. Gough (1961: Ch. 9; 1963); D'Souza (1959); Logan (1887: 191-9).

15. 'Scheduled Castes' are equivalent to Harijan castes; they are given various privileges, guaranteed by the President of India, such as reduced education fees, job reservation in government employment, etc., with the intention of mitigating their economic backwardness. 'Scheduled Tribes' receive similar privileges.
16. Subdivision names have been standardised throughout in accordance with the spelling in Gundert's dictionary.

3. The Nayar Kinship System in Ramankara

1. My terms have been chosen to aid comparability with Gough's work. Her distinction between clan and lineage is, however, inappropriate in the Ramankara context. Gough does not define any segment as a sub-clan; I have adopted it because use of a term such as lineage might falsely imply some functional or structural difference between clan and sub-clan (cf. Gough 1961: 323–6).
2. My clan and sub-clan names are pseudonymous, but are similar in form to real clan names except that the latter are often very long. Clan names are quite unromantic: e.g. Vadakkil – 'in the north'; Puthenveedu – 'new house'. They are never based on the names of ancestresses.
3. The Vadakkil Puthenveedu property group appears to have had no adult male members in 1908, for in the Settlement Report this group's land is all held in the name of women.
4. Kolenda's (1968: 346–7) classification of household types is as follows ('single' means unmarried, separated, widowed or divorced throughout):
    1. *Nuclear*: couple with/without unmarried children;
    2. *Supplemented nuclear*: nuclear family plus one/more single relative(s) of parents, other than unmarried children;
    3. *Subnuclear*: fragment of former nuclear family, e.g. widow plus unmarried children;
    4. *Single person*;
    5. *Supplemented subnuclear*: members of formerly complete nuclear family plus other single relative(s) not members of original nuclear family, e.g. widow plus unmarried children plus her widowed mother-in-law;
    6. *Collateral joint family*: two/more married couples related by sibling bond (usually B-B) plus unmarried children;
    7. *Supplemented collateral joint family*: collateral joint family plus single relative(s), e.g. widowed mother of brothers;
    8. *Lineal joint family*: two couples with lineal link (usually parents – married S) plus unmarried children;
    9. *Supplemented lineal joint family*: lineal joint family plus single relative(s) not belonging to either of lineally-linked nuclear families, e.g. father's widowed brother;
    10. *Lineal-collateral joint family*: three/more married couples linked lineally and collaterally, e.g. parents plus two/more married sons, plus unmarried children;
    11. *Supplemented lineal-collateral joint family*: lineal-collateral joint family plus single relative(s) not belonging to any of lineally-linked nuclear families;
    12. *Other types*.

5. The system under discussion is coherently formulated and operated; the 'somewhat unstable form of bilateral inheritance' where ancestral houses and paddy land are mostly inherited matrilineally, but garden land and cash are mostly inherited patrilineally, which existed in Central Kerala (Gough 1952a: 81), is not found here. (See also chapter 6).
6. In 1975, the Kerala Hindu Act was put on the statute book. Unfortunately, I have not seen the text of this Act. However, I understand that under the provisions of the new Act all land is treated identically. So a woman's land, however she obtained it, is now divided equally between her children only; her daughters' children no longer receive any share.
7. This parsimonious explanation by informants is disputed by Tambiah (1973: 105-7). Note too the contrast with Sinhalese systems combining bilateral inheritance with dowry.
8. This Nayar norm is strictly comparable with the Syrian Christian norm that brothers should inherit precisely equal shares. A case in the Syrian village I studied, in which brothers had inherited unequally, was widely, if privately, commented upon and was generally regarded as scandalous. I would defend myself against the charge of naïveté by contending that had such a scandal occurred in Ramankara, I would have come to know about it as I did in the Syrian village. Norms of equality such as these have important theoretical implications; Parry (1974: 112-14 and passim) draws attention to the *ideological,* and not solely empirical, stress on equality in many Indian inheritance systems and points to the need to modify the model of 'homo hierarchicus'.
9. There is some evidence, mostly circumstantial, that during the Great Depression, which struck Travancore in 1930 and lasted for nearly a decade, the competition for land was sharpened as it was the only reasonably secure form of wealth; this may have hastened the change from *taravad* to individual property.

4. The Nayar Marriage System in Ramankara

1. *Murappennu* and *muraccherukkan* are reference terms only; they are not used in address. The term *murappennu* (but not apparently *muraccherukkan*) is used by Nayars in some parts of Central Kerala (Mencher & Goldberg 1967: 99), but the preferential marriage rule described here is not found there.
2. The distinction between the two systems of kin categorisation has an implication which is worth pointing out: given that in India, a man must be older than his wife, and given that there are likely to be women older than himself included in a single category of female classificatory cross-cousins, any rule stating that ego should marry a cross-cousin fails to specify precisely the category of preferred wives. Further, because in a cross-cousin system, all members of one sibling group refer to all the members, of the same sex, in another sibling group in the cross category by a single term, the system is not truly egocentric (cf. Beck 1972: 215), as is the 'right man' and 'right woman' categorisation.
3. The Malayalam *paramparyyam* is almost certainly the same word as the Sinhalese *parampara* or *parapura* and appears to mean the same (Obeyesekere

1967: 13; Yalman 1962: 553; 1967: 142). The logical confusions to which a similar notion of ancestry appears to lead among the Kandyan Sinhalese (ibid.: 140–42) is absent among the Nayars. I would attribute this to the coherent ideology of unilineal descent held by the Nayars; the absence of such a coherent ideology among the Kandyans makes the unilineal transmission of status an inconsistent notion.

4. A chart of all these marriages is included in my dissertation (Fuller 1974); it has not been feasible to reproduce it in this book. The numbering of the charts in my dissertation is not the same as that in this book.
5. One section of the Vadakkil clan migrated to a village called Manimala.
6. The complete accuracy of the figures in table 15 cannot be guaranteed as they do not appear in the Report itself, but were calculated by me from the 3000-odd individual entries, one for each survey number. However, the figures are certainly broadly correct and provide concrete evidence of the close correlation between genealogical knowledge and wealth. These figures were calculated after leaving the field; the correlation I have noted was not predetermined by my questioning only members of the wealthiest clans.
7. Chart 5 includes G26, said by some informants to have been a sister of Aiyappan Kunnam (G21) who died young and by others to have belonged to another branch of the subclan, perhaps that headed by his half-brother. I was unable to resolve this problem.
8. I would like to draw attention to an inherent methodological difficulty in the above analysis. As the 'right man'/'right woman' rule is preferential, not prescriptive, we would expect it to generate a 'statistical', not a 'mechanical' marriage model (cf. Lévi-Strauss 1970: xxxv). The economic factor, of course, can only lead to the generation of a statistical model. Our interregnum marriage pattern is therefore the resultant of two statistically-defined variables. But a genuine statistical analysis is impossible; firstly because adequate economic data are unavailable and, secondly, because genealogical data are intrinsically biased, for the poor and insignificant are usually forgotten by informants and omitted from genealogies.
9. Clearly, there is no Dravidian-type marriage alliance among the Ramankara (or Central Travancore) Nayars today and, as one might expect (Dumont 1957a: 29), they do not place much stress on gift exchange between affines. At marriage, the groom gives the *tali*, a sari (*mantrakoti*) and a gold chain to his bride; she presents him with a gold ring. There are no other gifts exchanged between members of the two families. On the fourth day after marriage, the bride's parents visit the groom's parents, and the groom presents his bride's mother with a special cloth (*kacca*). When the wife becomes pregnant, she returns to her parents' home, two or three months before the baby is due. On this occasion, food is given by the wife's parents to the husband's parents. If the wife is already living with her parents, then the food is not given. Twenty-eight days after birth, the baby is given a waist-chain (*irupattettu*) by either its father's or mother's parents. Three months after birth, the mother's parents donate ornaments, including a gold chain, to the baby. They also present food to the father's parents, and a wardrobe (almirah) to their daughter and her husband. The latter gives a gold ring to his mother-in-law. These various gifts must be exchanged for the birth of

the first child. They are sometimes exchanged for the second child too, but rarely for subsequent children. When a man dies, the special funeral cloth (also known as *kacca*) placed on his body is donated by an affine, usually his wife's brother. The husband's sister's husband is the affine normally responsible for giving this cloth when a woman dies. No other gifts are exchanged at the funeral, or at the annual death ceremonies (*sraddham*). In comparison with other Indian communities, this list of exchanges between affines is not long, nor are the gifts exchanged with the frequency or regularity found elsewhere (cf. Tambiah 1973: 95–105). Just as there is no stress on affinity or alliance, nor of course is there any stress on unilineal corporate descent today, as there was, by contrast, under the matrilineal joint-family system.

5. The 'Traditional' Nayar Marriage System

1. Barbosa (1921: 42) makes it plain that defloration did *not* necessarily occur at the Nayar *tali*-rite; the defloration to which he refers occurred *after* the rite (cf. Gough 1955: 53). The suggestion that girls lost their virginity in royal and chiefly *tali*-rites, especially in the Zamorin's family, is more plausible; Gough (idem.) quotes evidence for this and Barbosa (1921: 11–12) specifically mentions it in describing royal *tali*-rites. As a further footnote to chapter 1, I may mention that the alleged custom of defloration generated some curious fantasies in the minds of European visitors; for instance, Roggeveen: 'This was formerly a very considerable Advantage to such Foreigners as were settled here, the Malabars making Choice of them, rather than their own Countrymen [to take a girl's virginity]; and on such occasions they made very large Presents, which sometimes amounted to 5 or 600 Florins.' (1764: 297) But, regrets Roggeveen, the Brahmans have now become 'so very religious' that they always perform their duty!
2. Ramankara Nayars sometimes employ Harijan girls as kitchen servants, whereas they will not take on Harijan women in this role. They explain this practice by saying that the girls are not polluting, because they do not menstruate.
3. There were exceptions to this in the case of very poor families, whose daughters' *talis* were tied at a small ceremony held at the side of a proper *tali*-rite, at the house of a richer relative or friend, or in front of a temple, a Brahman's house or a chief's residence. The tier was not infrequently the girl's mother or aunt (Census 1901, Cochin: 159; Census 1901, Travancore: 329; G.O.M. 1891: 19; Innes 1908: 175; Iyer 1912: 27). In such instances there can, of course, be no question of affinal relations being generated in the *tali*-rite, as discussed later in this chapter. After some indecisiveness on this question, I have now concluded that these poor families should be regarded as exceptional cases, forced to deviate from the norm by economic circumstances. They are therefore not evidence to set against the arguments proposed in the rest of this chapter.
4. Dumont's view that the Dravidian kinship terminology is 'an expression of marriage' was mainly set out in two early papers (1953; 1957a). It has been attacked many times; most recently and pertinently by Scheffler (1971) who has observed that Dravidian terminologies are

found in many societies in Oceania which lack a marriage system like that of the South Indians. Carter (1974: 41) seems to agree with Scheffler, but goes rather further (I think unjustifiably) in saying that Dravidian kinship systems, as opposed to terminologies, do not imply a positive rule of cross-cousin marriage. Dumont (1964: 78) earlier drew attention to the importance of the distinction between kinship systems and kinship terminologies.

5. The 'principal' and 'subsidiary marriages' of a man are equivalent, but not identical, to the 'primary' and 'secondary marriages' of a woman (Dumont 1970a: 114).

6. My criticism of Dumont here is at a very simple level. A more sophisticated discussion would have to take into account the distinction between the structure and function of affinal relations. In speaking of the weakness of affinity, I am operating primarily at the functional level, whereas Dumont claims to be at the structural level, although in fact he tends to use evidence concerning the functions of affinity in order to argue about the structure of affinal relations (e.g. the functions of affines at funerals, etc.). This is a highly technical argument which I do not think I can pursue even in a footnote, and in any case I am not certain of my own position on the issue.

Carter (1974: 49–50) also sees the *enangan* relation as basically similar to affinal relations elsewhere, but I do not find his analysis of the Nayars either clear or illuminating. He asks why there are not terms for 'kin types which in other South Indian systems would be classed as affines' and why *enangans* perform the duties elsewhere undertaken by affines; this problem seems false because it presupposes affinity in the first place. He then answers his own question by extension of his paradigm which is, though, based on the premise that the Nayars are all hypergamous. The answer is ipso facto unsatisfactory for commoner Nayars. But in my view, he has the cart before the horse; the first task is to study the Nayars sui generis, rather than to try to force them into some all-Indian paradigm.

Yalman (1967: 365–72) also has a paradigm of Dravidian kinship which he wishes to apply to the Nayars. As part of this endeavour, he attempts to prove that the Central Kerala Nayars had a cross-cousin marriage system; the fact that they had no cross-cousin terms (Gough 1952a: 82; 1961: 380–83) is dismissed as an 'intriguing lacuna'. Parts of his discussion I find more or less impossible to follow, and other parts seem misleading. I also think that he misinterprets Gough's data; for example, he quotes from her section on commoner Nayars (1961: 323–72) when trying to make a point about aristocratic Nayars (cf. ibid.: 372–80), and he tries to use data on *tali*-tiers as evidence about hypergamous *sambandham* unions. For a fuller understanding of the points at issue, the reader is invited to compare Yalman's analysis (and Karve's highly inaccurate account (1953) of the Nayars on which he draws) closely with that by Gough (1961), which he so strongly attacks.

7. The drawbacks of the term 'hypergamy' have been discussed by Dumont (1964: 86–90), who points to the differences between the hypergamy of North Indian communities and that of the Nayars. As I feel that the introduction of a new term for the Nayar situation may cause further

Notes to pages 115–133

confusion, I follow conventional usage. Jonathan Parry has suggested to me that in fact the differences between hypergamy in North and South India have been exaggerated and the analytical distinction between them overdrawn.

8. A more detailed description and analysis will be found in Fuller (1975).
9. I have come across one report (Census 1901, Cochin: 162) which states that Nambudiris only took Nayar women as *sambandham* partners if they were from aristocratic families, which would imply that there was a danger to a Nambudiri's purity in consorting with low-status women. But this report is contradicted by most other sources.
10. It is normally the case in South India that a primary marriage is isogamous. Among aristocratic Nayars, by contrast, 'the status difference appears in the primary marriage. The hierarchy of statuses invades the kinship domain, it enters into ritual affinity' (Dumont 1961: 23); a situation which, although exceptional, is 'very Indian'. This assertion is, of course, purely descriptive. Dumont's argument about an exchange of Nambudiri status for Nayar power, when a Nambudiri tied a Nayar girl's *tali* (ibid.: 27), has been dealt with by Mencher and Goldberg (1967: 104–5). They point out that this hypothesis rests on inaccurate ethnography and that any such exchange was located in the *sambandham* relationship, although their own argument has its problems, which need not be considered here. Dumont's claim that it looks as if the kings and chiefs, through the hypergamous system, sacrificed their sons' claims to the throne in exchange for a gain in status (1961: 29), is more speculative than factual.

6. *The Disintegration of the Matrilineal Joint-Family System*

1. Occasional exceptions to each of the statements in this paragraph probably still exist. In December 1975, I visited Joan Mencher in a village in Palghat District, where she was conducting research. In this village, I went to an old *taravad* house occupied by members of a branch of the former Palghat royal family (strictly of Samantan, not Nayar, status). Under the one roof of this house, seventy-five people still lived together, although each component conjugal family formed a separate economic unit.
2. Nayar (1952: 26–8) relates an amusing tale of a succession dispute which occurred in his own joint family. In an argument about their relative ages between two rivals to the *karanavan*-ship, the younger forged his horoscope and took the case to court; he lost.
3. This shows that the dissemination of Western ideas, documented for British India by Stokes (1959), occurred in the Native States too.
4. Joan Mencher has told me that in her view, which is based on extensive knowledge of Central Kerala, favouritism by despotic *karanavans* was perceived as probably the worst problem in this region. She points out that the development of a cash economy made favouritism easier in that, within the *taravad*, it would have been much simpler to make an inequitable division of cash, than of land. Another interesting point she makes is that a very large number of Nayars entered the legal profession, and thus acquired the wherewithal to bring their own family disputes to court. That they wanted to do this was partly due to the

close ties which grew up between many Nayar professionals and British officials; from the latter, these Nayars imbibed Western ideas about justice and the family, which they then tried to put into practice.
5. Travancore Nayar Act, 2 of 1100 M.E./1925; Madras Marumakkattayam Act, 22 of 1933; Cochin Nayar Act, 29 of 1113 M.E./1938. Acts covering the other matrilineal communities (and the Nambudiri Brahmans) were also passed. They were, with amendments in some cases, still in force until very recently (see Derrett 1963: 349–62 for their provisions). The Kerala Hindu Act, 1975, has, I understand, brought about considerable changes (see above, ch. 3, n. 6).
6. Varghese's reprinting of Tampi's table (1941: 27) contains errors. His '1935: buyers' column does not add up to 100; 'Other Hindus' should read 9.7 not 6.2, and 'Backward Hindus' should read 2.5, not zero. The '1940: buyers' column, in both Tampi's original report and Varghese's table, totals 89.9. This is most plausibly explained by a printing error: the Nayar figure should read 37.7, not 27.7. It is worth adding that it does not seem that all categories of Christians were buying land. An analysis of Tampi's data (in table XI) for Changanacherry taluk (in which Ramankara lies) shows that it was non-agriculturalists who were buying most of the land, not agriculturalists. This is, I think, an important qualification to Varghese's analysis.
7. Bailey (1957: 92) argues, in his study of an Oriya village, that expanding non-agricultural employment opportunities caused the partition of joint families. Epstein (1962: 178), in her study of two Mysore villages, contends that the development of a cash economy, in what was previously a subsistence economy, necessarily leads to the break-up of joint families. Both these writers are, in my opinion, mistaken; certainly their theories do not hold for the Nayars. Recent work on the joint family in India would suggest they do not hold in India as a whole either.
8. Unnithan, in a recent article (1974), makes a number of scathing references to Gough and Nakane, and insists on the necessity of looking at family change in its full economic and political context. Unfortunately, he fails to adhere to his own prescriptions and does little more than jumble together different features of Kerala's recent history. His paper is superficial and, in places, highly tendentious.

Glossary

The Malayalam alphabet is transliterated as follows: a, ā, i, ī, u, ū, r̥, e, ē, o, ō, ai, au, am, ah, (u' = 'half-u'), k, kh, g, gh, ṅ, c, ch, j, jh, ñ, ṭ, ṭh, ḍ, ḍh, ṇ, t, th, d, dh, n, p, ph, b, bh, m, y, r, l, v, ś, ṣ, s, h, ṛ, ḷ, zh, (ṛ + ṛ = ṭṭ, n + ṛ = nḍ).

anṭubali – feast marking the end of death pollution.
dewan – prime minister of a Native State.
enangan (strictly iṇaṅṅan) – 'linked lineage' among the Nayars; see especially chapter 5.
illam – Nambudiri Brahman joint family.
irupatteṭṭú – lit. 'twenty-eight'; silver waist-chain given to baby 28 days after its birth.
jajmāni – traditional internal economic system of Indian village.
janmi – holder of *janmom* land; landlord.
janmom – 'absolute ownership'; type of tenure in which no rent or tax is paid.
jīvanāmśam – lit. 'life-share'; right over land, or income from it, held until death.
kacca – cloth presented by affine at funeral and by man to wife's mother after marriage.
kalyāṇam – marriage, ceremony.
kāṇam – land held from *janmi* or state, on which tax or rent is paid.
kāṇamdār – holder of *kanam* land; tenant.
kara – village.
kāraṇavan – head of *taravad*.
karayōgam – village caste council (of Nayars); local branch of Nayar Service Society.
kūliparambu – lit. 'wage-place'; place where wages for low-caste labourers were left by high-caste landowner.
lingam – phallic emblem of Siva.
macchampikkār – in Travancore, family with hereditary duty to provide *tali*-tiers to other Nayar families in village.
macchunan – male cross-cousin term.
macchunicchi – female cross-cousin term.
mahārājā – lit. 'great king'; title taken by kings of Cochin and Travancore.
makkattāyam – lit. 'son-share'; patrilineal descent system.
maṇavāḷan – *tali*-tier.
mantrakōti – sari presented by groom to bride at wedding.
mantram – religious formula or chant.
marumakkattāyam – lit. 'sister's son-share'; matrilineal descent system.
mēlādāyam – type of *jivanamsam* in which income from trees is collected.
muṛaccheṛukkan – 'right man'; preferred husband among Ramankara Nayars; see chapter 4.

161

Glossary

muṟappeṇṇu – 'right woman'; preferred wife among Ramankara Nayars; see chapter 4.
oṭṭi – type of tenure in which land is mortgaged to holder.
pantal – temporary loggia in which *tali*-rite is held.
pāramparyyam – 'ancestry' of descent groups; see chapter 4.
pratilōma – hypogamous marriage.
rājā – king.
sambandham – sexual union of Nayar man and woman; see chapter 5.
sarppakāvu – serpent grove.
smarttivicāram – trial of Nambudiri woman accused of illicit sexual relations.
srāddham – annual death ceremony.
strīdhanam – lit. 'woman's wealth'; dowry.
tāli – emblem tied around Nayar girl's neck at *tali*-rite; emblem indicating a woman's married status.
tālikeṭṭukalyāṇam – lit. '*tali*-tying ceremony'; *tali*-rite undergone by Nayar girls before puberty; see chapter 5.
taravād (strictly taṟavāṭú) – Nayar matrilineal joint family.
tāvazhi – segment of *taravad*.
tīṇṭal jāti – caste which pollutes at a distance.
tirantukuḷi – ceremony marking Nayar girl's first menstrual flow.
vibhāgam – subdivision or subcaste among Nayars.
vivāham – marriage; word mainly used by Brahmans.
Zamorin (from sāmūtiri) – king of Calicut.

References

Aiya, V. Nagam   1906   *The Travancore State Manual,* 3 vols. Trivandrum, Govt Press.
Aiyappan, A.   1932   Nayar Polyandry. *Man,* 32: 78–9.
— 1944   *Iravas and Culture Change.* Bull. of the Madras Govt Museum, N.S., General Section, vol. 5, no. 1. Madras, Govt Press.
— 1965   *Social Revolution in a Kerala Village.* Bombay, Asia Publ. House.
Aiyar, S. Padmanabha   1913   *Revenue Settlement of Travancore 1883–1911: Final Report.* Trivandrum, Govt Press.
Ayyar, L. K. Anantakrishna (see also Iyer)   1926   *Anthropology of the Syrian Christians.* Ernakulam, Govt Press.
Baden-Powell, B. H.   1892   *The Land Systems of British India,* vol. 3. Oxford, Clarendon Press.
Bailey, F. G.   1957   *Caste and the Economic Frontier.* Manchester, Univ. Press.
Baldaeus, Philippus   1704   *A Description of the most celebrated East-India Coasts of Malabar and Coromandel as also of the Isle of Ceylon.* In *A Collection of Voyages and Travels,* vol. 3. London, Printed for Awnsham and John Churchill. (First publ., Amsterdam, 1672.)
Barbosa, Duarte   1921   *The Book of Duarte Barbosa: An account of the countries bordering on the Indian Ocean and their inhabitants,* vol. 2 (ed. M. L. Dames). London, Hakluyt Society. (Written c. 1518; original Portuguese edition, Lisbon, 1812.)
Barretto, Francesco   1646   *Relation des missions de la Province de Malabar de la Comp. de Jesus.* Tournay. (First publ., Rome, 1645.)
Beck, Brenda E. F.   1972   *Peasant Society in Konku: A study of right and left subcastes in South India.* Vancouver, Univ. of British Columbia Press.
Béteille, André   1974   *Studies in Agrarian Social Structure.* Delhi, O.U.P.
Botero, Giovanni   1608   *Relations of the most famous kingdoms and commonweales through the world.* London. (First publ., Ferrara, 1592.)
Brown, L. W.   1956   *The Indian Christians of St Thomas.* Cambridge, Univ. Press.
Buchanan, Francis   1807   *A Journey from Madras through the countries of Mysore, Canara, and Malabar,* vol. 2. London, Black, Parry and Kingsbury.
Burke, Edmund   1881   *Reflections on the Revolution in France.* In *Select Works,* vol. 2 (ed. E. J. Payne). Oxford, Clarendon Press. (First publ., London, 1790).
Burton, Richard F.   1851   *Goa, and the Blue Mountains.* London, Richard Bentley.

References

Camoens, Luis de   1940   *The Lusiad* (trans. Richard Fanshawe, ed. Jeremiah D. M. Ford). Cambridge, Mass., Harvard Univ. Press. (First publ., Lisbon, 1572; English trans., London, 1665.)

Carter, A. T.   1974   A Comparative analysis of systems of kinship and marriage in South Asia. *Proceedings of the R.A.I., 1973:* 29–54.

Castanheda, Herman Lopes de   1811   History of the Discovery and Conquest of India by the Portuguese. In *A General History and Collection of Voyages and Travels,* vol. 2, pt. 2 (ed. Robert Kerr). Edinburgh, Wm. Blackwood. (First publ., Coimbra, 1551.)

Castro e Almeida, Virginia de (ed.) n.d. *Chroniques de João de Barros, Damião de Goes, Gaspar Correa, Garcia de Resende: La decouverte de l'Inde par Vasco da Gama.* Brussels, L. Desmet-Verteneuil (1939).

Censuses
- 1875   Report on the Census of Native Cochin. Madras, 1877.
- 1875   Report on the Census of Travancore. Trivandrum, 1876.
- 1881   Imperial Census: Operations and Results in the Presidency of Madras, vol. IV – Final Census Tables. Madras, 1883.
- 1891   Report on the Census of Cochin, pt. I. Cochin, 1893.
- 1891   Census of India, Madras, vol. XIII – Report; vol. XIV – Tables; vol. XV – Tables. Madras, 1893.
- 1901   Census of India, vol. XX, Cochin, pt. I. Ernakulam, 1903.
- 1901   Census of India, vol. XXVI, Travancore, pt. I. Trivandrum, 1903.
- 1911   Census of India, vol. I, India, pt. I. Calcutta, 1913.
- 1911   Census of India, vol. XXIII, Travancore, pt. I. Trivandrum, 1912.
- 1921   Census of India, vol. XIII, Madras, pts. I, II. Madras, 1922.
- 1921   Census of India, vol. XXV, Travancore, pt. I. Trivandrum, 1922.
- 1931   Census of India, vol. XXI, Cochin, pts. I, II. Ernakulam, 1933.
- 1931   Census of India, vol. XIV, Madras, pts. I, II. Madras, 1932.
- 1931   Census of India, vol. XXVIII, Travancore, pts. I, II. Trivandrum, 1932.
- 1941   Census of India, vol. XIX, Cochin, pt. II. Ernakulam, 1944.
- 1941   Census of India, vol. XXV, Travancore, pt. I. Trivandrum, 1942.
- 1961   Census of India, vol. VII, Kerala, pt. IA(i). New Delhi, 1965.
- 1971a   Census of India, Series I – India. Paper 1 of 1972 – Final Population. New Delhi, 1972.
- 1971b   Census of India, Series 9 – Kerala, pt. II-A. General Population Figures. New Delhi, 1972.

Chettur, K. N.   1901   The Nambudri-Brahmins of Kerala. *Calcutta Review,* 113: 121–36.

Correa, Gaspar   1869   *The Three Voyages of Vasco da Gama and his Viceroyalty, from* Lendas da India, *of Gaspar Correa* (trans. and ed. E. J. Stanley). London, Hakluyt Society. (Written c. 1556; first publ., Lisbon, 1858–64.)

Das Gupta, Ashin   1967   *Malabar in Asian Trade 1740–1800.* Cambridge, Univ. Press.

Day, Francis   1863   *The Land of the Permauls, or Cochin, its Past and its Present.* Madras, Adelphi Press.

Dellon, Charles   1698   *A Voyage to the East Indies.* London.
  1699   *Nouvelle Relation d'un voyage fait aux Indes Orientales.* Amsterdam. (First publ., Paris, 1685.)

References

Derrett, J. Duncan M. 1967 *Introduction to Modern Hindu Law.* Bombay, O.U.P.
Diderot, D. 1880 *Encyclopédie,* vol. 22, pt. II. Berne, Les Societes Typographiques. (First publ., Paris, 1751-65.)
Drury, Heber 1858 Notes of an excursion along the Travancore Backwater. *Madras J. of Literature and Science,* N.S., 3: 203-19.
 1890 *Reminiscences of Life and Sport in Southern India.* London, W. H. Allen.
D'Souza, Victor S. 1959 Social Organisation and Marriage Customs of the Moplahs on the Southwest Coast of India. *Anthropos,* 54: 487-516.
Dube, S. C. 1953 Token pre-puberty marriage in Middle India. *Man,* 53: 18-19.
Dubois, Abbé J. A. 1906 *Hindu Manners, Customs and Ceremonies* (trans. and ed. H. K. Beauchamp). Oxford, Clarendon Press. (First publ., London, 1816; Paris, 1825.)
Dumont, Louis 1953 The Dravidian kinship terminology as an expression of marriage. *Man,* 53: 34-9.
 1957a *Hierarchy and Marriage Alliance in South Indian Kinship.* Occasional Papers of the R.A.I., no. 12. London.
 1957b *Une Sous-caste de l'Inde du Sud: Organisation sociale et religion des Pramalai Kallar.* Paris, Mouton.
 1961 Les mariages Nayar comme faits indiens. *L.'Homme,* 1: 11-36.
 1964 Marriage in India: the present state of the question. Postscript to part I; II: Marriage and status; Nayar and Newar. *Contributions to Indian Sociology,* 7: 77-98.
 1970 *Homo Hierarchicus: The caste system and its implications.* London, Weidenfeld and Nicolson.
Duncan, Jonathan 1801 Historical Remarks on the Coast of Malabar, with some description of the manners of its inhabitants. *Asiatick Researches,* 5: 1-36.
Epstein, T. Scarlett 1962 *Economic Development and Social Change in South India.* Manchester, Univ. Press.
Fawcett, F. 1901 *Nayars of Malabar.* Madras Govt Museum Bull., vol. 3, no. 3. Madras, Govt Press.
Federici, Cesare 1927 The Voyage of Master Caesar Frederick into the East India, and beyonde the Indus. In *The Principal Navigations, Voyages, Traffiques and Discoveries of the English Nation,* vol. 3 (ed. Richard Hakluyt). London, Dent (repr.). (First publ., Venice, 1587.)
Forbes, James 1813 *Oriental Memoirs,* vol. 1. London, White, Cochrane and Co.
Foster, William (ed.) 1925 *The English Factories in India, 1665-1667.* Oxford, Clarendon Press.
Fuller, C. J. 1974 *Nayars and Christians in Travancore.* Unpubl. Ph.D. dissertation, Univ. of Cambridge.
 1975 The Internal Structure of the Nayar caste. *J. of Anthrop. Research,* 31, no. 4.
 1976 Kerala Christians and the Caste System. *Man,* N.S., 11: 53-70.
G.O.K. (Government of Kerala) 1966 *Census 1961, Kerala State: District Handbook, 6, Kottayam.* Trivandrum, Govt Press.
 1971 *Report of the Backward Classes Reservation Commission, Kerala 1970,* vol. 2. Trivandrum, Govt Press.

References

1972   *Statistics for Planning, serial no. 1 - Agriculture.* (State Planning Board & Bureau of Economics and Statistics). Trivandrum, Govt Press.

G.O.M. (Government of Madras)   1891   *Report of the Malabar Marriage Commission.* Madras, Govt Press.

G.O.T. (Government of Travancore)   1869   *Report of the Administration of Travancore for the year 1044 M.E./1868-9.* Trivandrum, Govt Press.

1908   *Report of the Marumakkathayam Committee, Travancore.* Trivandrum, Govt Press.

Gemelli Careri, G. F.   1704   *A Voyage around the World.* In *A Collection of Voyages and Travels*, vol. 4. London, Printed for Awnsham and John Churchill. (First publ., Naples, 1699-1700.)

George, T. J. S.   1964   *Krishna Menon: A Biography.* London, Jonathan Cape.

Gibbon, Edward   1898   *The History of the Decline and Fall of the Roman Empire* (ed. J. B. Bury). London, Methuen. (First publ., London, 1776-88.)

Gonda, J.   1970   *Visnuism and Sivaism: A Comparison.* London, Athlone Press.

Goody, Jack   1972   The evolution of the family. In *Household and Family in Past Time* (ed. Peter Laslett and Richard Wall), pp. 103-24. Cambridge, Univ. Press.

Gough, E. Kathleen   1952a   Changing kinship usages in the setting of political and economic change among the Nayars of Malabar. *J.R.A.I.,* 82: 71-87.

1952b   Incest prohibitions and the rules of exogamy in three matrilineal groups of the Malabar Coast. *Internat. Archs. of Ethnog.,* 46: 81-105.

1955   Female initiation rites on the Malabar Coast. *J.R.A.I.,* 85: 45-80.

1959a   The Nayars and the definition of marriage. *J.R.A.I.,* 89: 23-34.

1959b   Cults of the dead among the Nayars. In *Traditional India: Structure and Change* (ed. Milton Singer), pp. 240-72. Philadelphia, American Folklore Society.

1961   Nayar: Central Kerala; Nayar: North Kerala; Tiyyar: North Kerala; Mappilla: North Kerala; The modern disintegration of matrilineal descent groups. In *Matrilineal Kinship* (ed. D. M. Schneider and E. K. Gough), pp. 298-442, 631-52. Berkeley, Univ. of California Press.

1963   Indian nationalism and ethnic freedom. In *The Concept of Freedom in Anthropology* (ed. David Bidney), pp. 170-207. The Hague, Mouton.

1965   A note on Nayar marriage. *Man,* 65: 8-11.

1970   Palakkara: Social and religious change in Central Kerala. In *Continuity and Change in India's Villages* (ed. K. Ishwaran), pp. 129-64. New York, Columbia Univ. Press.

1975   Changing Households in Kerala. In *Explorations in the Family and other Essays* (ed. Dhirendra Narain), pp. 218-67. Bombay, Thacker and Co.

Graul, Karl   1854   *Reise nach Ostindien über Palästina und Egypten von Juli 1849 bis April 1853,* vol. 3. Leipzig, Dörssling und Franke.

Grose, John Henry   1772   *A Voyage to the East Indies,* vol. 1. London. (First publ., London, 1757.)

References

Gundert, Hermann   1972   *Malayalam-English Dictionary.* Kottayam, Vidyarthi Mithram Press. (First publ., Mangalore, 1872.)
Hamilton, Alexander   1727   *A New Account of the East Indies,* vol. 1. Edinburgh. (Republ., London, Argonaut Press, 1930.)
Harper, Edward B.   1959   Two systems of economic exchange in village India. *Amer. Anthrop.,* 61: 760–78.
Hawes, Roger   1625   *Memorialls taken out of the Journall of Roger Hawes, touching the proceedings of the Factorie at Cranganur under the Great Samorine.* In *Hakluytus Posthumus, or Purchas His Pilgrimes,* pt. I, bk. 5 (ed. Samuel Purchas). London. (Republ., vol. 4: 495–502; Glasgow, James Maclehose and Sons, 1905.)
Herbert, Sir Thomas   1638   *Some Yeares Travels into divers parts of Asia and Afrique.* London. (First publ., London, 1634.)
Herport, Albrecht   1930   *Reise nach Java, Formosa, vorder-Indien und Ceylon, 1659-1688.* In *Reiseschreiben von Deutschen Beamten und Kriegsleuten im dienst der Niederländischen West- und Ost-Indischen Kompagnien, 1602-1797,* vol. 5 (ed. S. P. L'Honoré Naber). The Hague, Martinus Nijhoff. (First publ., Berne, 1699.)
Hirth, F. (ed.)   1896   Chao Ju-kua, a new source of mediaeval geography: Chao Ju-kua's ethnography [parts]. *J. Roy. Asiatic Soc.,* N.S., 28: 57–82, 477–508.
Hutton, J. H.   1961   *Caste in India: its nature, function and origin.* Bombay, O.U.P. (3rd ed.).
Ibn Batuta   1829   *The Travels of Ibn Batuta* (trans. Samuel Lee). London, Oriental Translation Committee.
    1929   *Travels in Asia and Africa 1325-1354* (trans. H. A. R. Gibb). London, Routledge.
Innes, C. A.   1908   *Madras District Gazetteers: Malabar and Anjengo,* vol. 1 (ed. F. B. Evans). Madras, Govt Press.
Iyer, L. K. Anantha Krishna (see also Ayyar)   1909   *The Cochin Tribes and Castes,* vol. 1. Madras, Higginbotham and Co.
    1912   Idem, vol. 2.
Janaki, V. A.   1953   Geographical basis for the distribution and pattern of rural settlement in Kerala. *J. of the M.S. Univ. of Baroda,* 2: 41–54.
Jeffrey, Robin   1973   *The Decline of Nayar Dominance: Society and Politics in Travancore, 1847-1908.* D.Phil. dissertation, Univ. of Sussex; publ. (same title) London, Chatto and Windus for Sussex Univ. Press, 1976.
Jordanus, Friar   1863   *Mirabilia Descripta: The Wonders of the East* (trans. and ed. Henry Yule). London, Hakluyt Society. (Written in 14th cent., first publ., Paris, 1839.)
Karve, Irawati   1953   *Kinship Organisation in India.* Poona, Deccan College.
Klausen, Arne M.   1968   *Kerala Fishermen and the Indo-Norwegian Project.* London, Allen and Unwin.
Kolenda, Pauline Mahar   1968   Region, caste and family structure: A comparative study of the Indian 'Joint' family. In *Structure and Change in Indian Society* (ed. Milton Singer and Bernard S. Cohn), pp. 339–96. Chicago, Aldine.
Kramrisch, Stella   1959   Traditions of the Indian craftsmen. In

References

 Traditional India: Structure and Change (ed. Milton Singer), pp. 18–24. Philadelphia, American Folklore Society.
Krishnan, T. V. 1972 *Kerala's First Communist: Life of 'Sakhavu' Krishna Pillai.* New Delhi, Communist Party of India.
Kumar, Dharma 1965 *Land and Caste in South India: Agricultural Labour in the Madras Presidency during the nineteenth century.* Cambridge, Univ. Press.
Lach, Donald F. 1968 *India in the eyes of Europe: The Sixteenth Century.* Chicago, Univ. Press. (Being vol. 1, pt. 3, ch. 6 of *Asia in the Making of Europe.* Chicago, Univ. Press, 1965.)
Leach, E. R. 1961a *Rethinking Anthropology.* London, Athlone Press.
 1961b *Pul Eliya: A village in Ceylon.* Cambridge, Univ. Press.
Lévi-Strauss, Claude 1970 *The Elementary Structures of Kinship.* London, Eyre and Spottiswoode. (Rev. ed.)
Linschoten, Jan Huyghen van 1885 *The Voyage of John Huyghen van Linschoten to the East Indies,* vol. 1 (ed. A. C. Burnell). London, Hakluyt Society. (First publ., Amsterdam, 1596.)
Logan, William 1887 *Malabar,* vol. 1. Madras, Govt Press.
Maffei, Giovanni 1588 *Historiarum Indicarum Libri XVI.* Florence.
 1665 *L'Histoire des Indes Orientales et Occidentales.* Paris.
Ma Huan 1970 *Ying-Yai Sheng-Lan, 'The Overall Survey of the Ocean's Shores' (1433)* (trans. and ed. J. V. G. Mills). Cambridge, Univ. Press (for Hakluyt Society).
Major, R. H. (ed.) 1857 *India in the Fifteenth Century.* London, Hakluyt Society.
Mandelbaum, David G. 1948 The family in India. *Southwest. J. of Anthropology,* 4: 123–39.
 1970 *Society in India,* 2 vols. Berkeley, Univ. of California Press.
Mateer, Samuel 1871 *The Land of Charity: a descriptive account of Travancore and its people.* London, John Snow.
 1883a *Native Life in Travancore.* London, W. H. Allen.
 1883b Nepotism in Travancore. *J.A.I.,* 12: 288–306.
Mayer, Adrian C. 1952 *Land and Society in Malabar.* Bombay, O.U.P.
 1960 *Caste and Kinship in Central India: A Village and its region.* London, Routledge and Kegan Paul.
Mencher, Joan P. 1962 Changing familial roles among South Malabar Nayars. *Southwest. J. of Anthropology,* 18: 230–45.
 1965 The Nayars of South Malabar. In *Comparative Family Systems* (ed. M. F. Nimkoff), pp. 163–91. Boston, Houghton Mifflin.
 1966a Kerala and Madras: A comparative study of ecology and social structure. *Ethnology,* 5: 135–71.
 1966b Namboodiri Brahmans: An analysis of a traditional elite in Kerala. *J. of Asian and African Studies,* 1: 183–96.
Mencher, Joan P. and Helen Goldberg 1967 Kinship and Marriage regulations amongst the Namboodiri Brahmans of Kerala. *Man,* N.S., 2: 87–106.
Menon, A. Sreedhara 1962 *Kerala District Gazetteers: Kozhikode.* Trivandrum, Govt Press.
 1962 Idem: *Trichur.*
 1962 Idem: *Trivandrum.*

References

1964   Idem: *Quilon.*
1965   Idem: *Ernakulam.*
1972   Idem: *Cannanore.*
Menon, C. Achyuta   1911   *The Cochin State Manual.* Ernakulam, Govt Press.
Menon, K. P. Padmanabha   1924   *History of Kerala,* vol. 1. Ernakulam, Govt Press.
   1929   Idem, vol. 2.
   1933   Idem, vol. 3.
   1937   Idem, vol. 4.
Menon, O. Chandu   1965   *Indulekha: A novel from Malabar* (trans. W. Dumergue). Calicut, Mathrubhumi Publ. Co. (English trans. first publ., Madras, 1890.)
Miller, E. J.   1954   Caste and territory in Malabar. *Amer. Anthrop.,* 56: 410-20.
Montaigne, Michel de   1928   *Essayes* (trans. John Florio). London, Dent. (First publ., Bordeaux, 1580.)
Montesquieu, Charles de Secondat, Baron   1952   *The Spirit of the Laws* (trans. Thomas Nugent). Chicago, Encyclopaedia Britannica. (First publ., Paris, 1748.)
Moore, Lewis   1905   *Malabar Law and Custom.* Madras, Higginbotham and Co. (3rd ed.).
N.S.S.   1972   Nāyar sarvvīs sosaiṯṯi caritram. (*History of Nayar Service Society,* in Malayalam). Changanacherry, N.S.S.
Nakane, Chie   1962   The Nayar family in a disintegrating matrilineal system. *Internat. J. of Compar. Sociol.,* 3: 19-28.
Nayar, Unni   1952   *My Malabar.* Bombay, Hind Katabs.
Nayar, V. K. S.   1966   Communal interest groups in Kerala. In *South Asian Politics and Religion* (ed. Donald E. Smith), pp. 176-90. Princeton, Univ. Press.
Nieuhof, Jan   1704   *Voyages and Travels into Brasil, and the East Indies.* In *A Collection of Voyages and Travels,* vol. 2. London, Printed for Awnsham and John Churchill. (First publ., Amsterdam, 1682.)
Obeyesekere, Gananath   1967   *Land Tenure in village Ceylon: A Sociological and historical study.* Cambridge, Univ. Press.
O'Malley, L. S. S.   1932   *Indian Caste Customs.* Cambridge, Univ. Press.
Panikkar, K. M.   1918   Some aspects of Nayar life. *J.R.A.I.,* 48: 254-93.
   1960   *A History of Kerala, 1498-1801.* Annamalainagar, Annamalai University.
Parry, Jonathan   1974   Egalitarian values in a hierarchical society. *South Asian Review,* 7: 95-121.
Paulino da San Bartolomeo, Father   1800   *A Voyage to the East Indies.* London. (First publ., Rome, 1796; English translation of German translation.)
   1808   *Voyage aux Indes Orientales.* Paris. (French translation of original.)
Pillai, Elamkulam P. N. Kunjan   1970   *Studies in Kerala History.* Trivandrum, The Author.
Pillai, T. K. Velu   1940   *The Travancore State Manual,* 4 vols. Trivandrum, Govt Press.

References

Pocock, David F. 1957 Inclusion and Exclusion: a process in the caste system of Gujerat. *Southwest. J. of Anthropology,* 13: 19-31.
    1972 *Kanbi and Patidar: A study of the Patidar community of Gujarat.* Oxford, Clarendon Press.
Pyrard de Laval, François 1887 *The Voyage of Francois Pyrard de Laval* (trans. and ed. Albert Gray), vol. 1. London, Hakluyt Society. (First publ., Paris, 1611.)
Renaudot, Eusebius (trans.) 1717 *Anciennes relations des Indes et de la Chine de deux voyageurs Mahometans, qui y allerent dans le neuvieme siecle.* Paris.
    1733 *Ancient accounts of India and China by two Mohammedan travellers who went to those parts in the 9th century* (translated from French). London.
Rockhill, W. W. 1915 Notes on the relations and trade of China with the Eastern Archipelago and the Coast of the Indian Ocean during the fourteenth century, [parts]. *T'oung Pao,* 16: 61-84, 435-67.
Roggeveen, Jacob 1764 *An Account of Commodore Roggewein's Expedition.* In *Navigantium atque Itenerantium Bibliotheca, or A Complete Collection of Voyages and Travels,* vol. 1 (ed. John Harris). London. (Written c. 1722.)
Rudolph, Lloyd I. and Susanne H. Rudolph 1967 *The Modernity of Tradition: Political development in India.* Chicago, Univ. Press.
Scheffler, Harold 1971 Dravidian-Iroquois: The Melanesian evidence. In *Anthropology in Oceania* (ed. L. R. Hiatt and C. Jayawardena), pp. 231-54. Sydney, Angus and Robertson.
Sonnerat, Pierre 1782 *Voyage aux Indes Orientales et a la Chine,* vol. 1. Paris.
    1788 *A Voyage to the East Indies and China.* Calcutta.
Srinivas, M. N. 1952 *Religion and Society among the Coorgs of South India.* Oxford, Clarendon Press.
    1955 The social system of a Mysore village. In *Village India* (ed. McKim Marriott), pp. 1-35. Chicago, Univ. Press (reprint).
    1965 *Social Change in modern India.* Berkeley, Univ. of California Press.
Stevenson, H. N. C. 1954 Status evaluation in the Hindu caste system. *J.R.A.I.,* 84: 45-65.
Stokes, Eric 1959 *The English Utilitarians and India.* Oxford, Clarendon Press.
Tambiah, S. J. 1973 Dowry and bridewealth and the property rights of women in South Asia. In *Bridewealth and Dowry* (by Jack Goody and S. J. Tambiah), pp. 59-169. Cambridge, Univ. Press.
Tampi, A. Narayanan 1941 *Enquiry into the Sub-division and Fragmentation of Agricultural Holdings.* Trivandrum, Govt Press.
Thurston, Edgar 1909 *Caste and Tribes of Southern India,* 7 vols. Madras, Govt Press.
Turlach, Manfred 1970 *Kerala: Politisch-soziale Struktur und Entwicklung eines Indischen Bundeslandes.* Wiesbaden, Otto Harassowitz.
Unni, K. Raman 1956 Visiting husbands in Malabar. *J. of the M.S. Univ. of Baroda,* 5: 37-56.
    1958 Polyandry in Malabar. *Sociological Bull.,* 7: 62-79, 123-33.

References

Unnithan, T. K. N.   1974   Contemporary Nayar family in Kerala. In *The Family in India: A Regional view* (ed. George Kurian), pp. 191–203. The Hague, Mouton.
Valle, Pietro della   1892   *The Travels of Pietro della Valle in India*, vol. 2 (ed. Edward Grey). London, Hakluyt Society. (First publ., Rome, 1650.)
Varghese, T. C.   1970   *Agrarian Change and Economic Consequences: Land tenures in Kerala, 1850–1960*. Calcutta, Allied Publs.
Varthema, Ludovico di   1863   *The Travels of Ludovico di Varthema, A.D. 1503–8* (ed. J. W. Jones). London, Hakluyt Society. (First publ., Rome, 1510.)
Visscher, Jacobus Canter   1862   *Letters from Malabar* (trans. and ed. Heber Drury). Madras, Adelphi Press. (First publ., Leeuwarden, 1743.)
Yalman, Nur   1962   The structure of the Sinhalese kindred: A re-examination of the Dravidian terminology. *Amer. Anthrop.*, 64: 548–75.
   1963   On the purity of women in the castes of Ceylon and Malabar. *J.R.A.I.*, 93: 25–58.
   1967   *Under the Bo Tree: Studies in caste, kinship and marriage in the interior of Ceylon*. Berkeley, Univ. of California Press.
Yule, Henry (trans. and ed.)   1915   *Cathay and the Way thither, being a collection of medieval notices of China*, vol. 1: preliminary essay (rev. ed., Henri Cordier). London, Hakluyt Society.
Zain al-Dīn al-Ma'bari   1833   *Sheikh Zeen-ud-deen: Tohfut-ul-mujahideen; An historical work in the Arabic Language (1579)* (trans. M. J. Rowlandson). London, Oriental Translation Committee.

Index

British (incl. English), 2, 8, 14, 18, 19, 21, 124, 142, 145, 147, 160

Calicut, 1–2, 17; Zamorin of, 2, 9, 14, 15, 116, 117, 157
caste, 10–11, 109; behaviour and belief, 47–8; change in, 14, 21, 44, 46–7; and class, 33, 45, 153; councils (Nayar), 13–14, 60; in Central Travancore and Ramankara, 43–8; in Kerala, 11–14, 20, 33–8, 43; and landownership in Ramankara, 28–32; populations in Kerala, 36–8
Castes (major ones only): Ambalavasis, 13, 29, 34, 37, 103; Brahmans, 10, 12, 13, 19, 20, 29, 34, 36–8, 42, 43, 45, 103, 108, 115, 117, 157; Harijans, 10, 20, 32, 35, 37–8, 44, 47, 50, 154, 157; Izhavas (incl. Tiyyans), 12, 13, 20, 28–30, 34–5, 36–8, 43, 46, 129; Kshatriyas, 34, 37, 42, 43, 115–19; Nambudiri Brahmans, 2, 3, 11, 13, 14, 34, 36–8, 48, 74, 75, 85, 109, 111, 116–23, 125, 128, 133, 150, 159, 160; Parayas (Sambavars), 12, 28–30, 34–8; Pulayas (incl. Cherumans), 11, 12, 14, 29–30, 34–8, 43, 50; Samantans, 34, 37, 42, 43, 115–17, 119, 159; Tamil Brahmans, 11, 18, 21, 34, 37, 116, 130, 131; Veluthedathu Nayars, 34, 37, 42; Vilakkittala Nayars, 29–30, 34, 37, 42
Christians, 22, 36, 38, 130; New, 28–30, 36, 37; Syrian, 20, 28–30, 32, 36, 37, 43, 54, 79, 91, 128–32, 137, 146, 153, 155
clan, Nayar, 53–4, 154; in Ramankara, 55–6, 71, 154
Cochin, 1–2, 9, 17–22, 25, 131–3, 145–6, 152; royal family of, 9, 13, 116, 118
Cochin Nayar Act, 1938, 160
Cochin Nayar Regulation, 1920, 137

Communists, 18, 22, 45, 153
Congress Party, 21–2
Cranganore, 18; chiefly family of, 116

Dutch, 2, 8

education, 31–2, 130
enangan, 75, 102, 110–14, 117, 119, 120, 158

French, 7

Gandhi, Mahatma, 21, 27, 46–7

Haider Ali, 4, 18–19
household: classification of, 154; modern Nayar in Kerala, 137–43, 147–9; modern Nayar in Ramankara, 63–5, 67–8, 70–1, 94, 141, 147

inheritance, Nayar, 5, 123, 137, 155; in Ramankara, 65–72, 94

joint family: Nambudiri, 2, 3, 38; Nayar, *see under taravad*

karanavan, 54–8, 71, 76, 82, 85–6, 107, 108, 126, 128, 130, 132–4, 137, 142, 159; role of, 58–60, 62–3; succession to, 60, 159
Kerala, 2, 8–9, 17, 22–5, 126, 152, 153; foreign notices of, 1, 151–2; population of, 23–5, 126; villages in, 25, 27
Kerala Hindu Act, 1975, 72, 155, 160

labourers in Ramankara, 32–3, 43–4
land: Nayar loss of, 28, 129–31, 135, 137, 160; policy and reforms, 18–21, 32, 33, 128–9, 132, 135, 137, 142, 145–6, 153
landowners in Ramankara, 32–3
landownership and caste, *see under* caste

172

macchampikkar, 75, 111–12
Madras Marumakkattayam Act, 1933, 135, 160
Mahdeva Rao, Sir T., 25, 127
Malabar, 2, 17–22, 25, 131–3, 142, 145–6, 152
Malabar Marriage Act, 1896, 133
Malabar Marriage Commission, 126, 132, 133, 142
marriage
  Nambudiri, 2–3
  traditional Nayar, 2–6, 73; and affinity, 105–6, 110–15, 119–20, 157–9; and cross-cousins, 113, 157–8; hypergamy in, 3, 115–20, 158, 159; in relation to military role, 5, 121–5, 144–5; in relation to Nambudiris, 3, 74–5, 109, 115–16, 118–21, 125, 128, 133, 159; origin of, 121–2
  Nayar in Ramankara: and caste endogamy, 50, 60, 74, 78, 89, 94; and clan, 77–80, 85, 89, 155–6; and cross-cousins, 77–8, 83, 155; and economic factors, 75–6, 79–80, 82, 86–9, 90–5; in interregnum, 80–9; in new order, 89–94, 156–7; in old order, 75–80; and *muraccherukkan/murappennu* rule, 73, 76–8, 85, 89, 94, 155, 156; and residence, 56, 62–5, 90–3; rules of, 74; and status factors, 76, 77, 79–80, 82, 85–6, 88–9, 94; and village endogamy/exogamy, 73, 78, 82–3, 89–93
Martanda Varma, 17–18, 21, 51, 60
matrilineal system, traditional Nayar, 2–6, 51–5, 121–3; change in, 20–1, 127–8, 130, 133, 142, 144–9, 160
Menon, V. K. Krishna, 22
military role of Nayars, 6–9, 18, 123–6, 144–5, 147; in relation to marriage, *see under* marriage, traditional Nayar
Muslim League, 22
Muslims, 11, 15, 19–21, 29, 36–8, 153
Mysoreans, 2, 4, 18–19

names, Nayar, 53–4, 71
Nayar Service Society, 21, 22, 42, 60, 75, 134–5, 153
Nayars, character of, 15–16

Palghat, 2, 17; royal family of, 159
pollution, 12–14, 50; birth, death and menstrual, 48–50, 53, 71, 106, 111–12, 157; 'distance', 11, 12, 35, 43–4, 153
Portuguese, 1, 2, 8, 15
property, self-acquired, 60–1, 126–8, 131–4, 142, 146–7

Rama Varma, 18
Ramankara, description of, 23–33

sambandham, 3, 73, 99–100, 105–10, 112, 114–15, 118, 120, 123, 141, 159; and modern marriage, 74, 124–6, 128, 133–4, 141, 147, 148; partners and status, 42, 109–11, 115–20, 158
subdivisions, Nayar, 38–43, 55, 74, 112, 115–18, 154

tali, 3, 101, 104, 156; -rite, 3, 73, 99–107, 118, 120, 123–5, 141, 157–9; -tiers and status, 42, 75, 110–20, 157–9
taravad, 2, 51–3, 75, 100–2, 106–9, 123, 130, 131, 159; in North Malabar, 100, 141–2; in South Travancore, 100; partition of, 58, 125–8, 130, 132–3, 135, 137, 138, 146–9, 159–60; and subdivisions, 42, 115, 117
  in Ramankara, 53, 63, 65, 70–1, 75–6, 82; in interregnum, 61–3; in old order, 56–61; partition of, 56–8, 61–3, 135; and property, 53, 55, 60–1, 63, 86–7
tavazhi, 125, 126, 128, 131–5, 137, 138, 142; in Ramankara, 53, 58, 62, 65, 71, 141
Tippu Sultan, 4, 19
tirantukuli, 101, 125
Travancore, 2, 9, 17–22, 25, 128–9, 135, 137, 145–6, 152, 155; royal family of, 116–17
Travancore Marumakkathayam Committee, 134
Travancore Nayar Act, 1913, 134
Travancore Nayar Act, 1925, 47, 51, 135, 160

Vaikom, temple satyagraha, 21, 45–7

Walluvanad, 2, 17; royal family of, 116
women, position of Nayar, 5–6, 55, 72, 149